PEARSON

my World

Social Studies ®

The Growth of Our Country

PEARSON

Boston, Massachusetts
Chandler, Arizona
Glenview, Illinois
New York, New York

ISBN-13: 978-0-328-63930-4
ISBN-10: 0-328-63930-3

17   18

Program Consulting Authors

The Colonial Williamsburg Foundation
Williamsburg, Virginia

Dr. Linda Bennett
Associate Professor, Department of Learning, Teaching, & Curriculum
College of Education
University of Missouri
Columbia, MO

Dr. Jim Cummins
Professor of Curriculum, Teaching, and Learning
Ontario Institute for Studies in Education
University of Toronto
Toronto, Ontario

Dr. James B. Kracht
Byrne Chair for Student Success
Executive Associate Dean
College of Education and Human Development
Texas A&M University
College Station, Texas

Dr. Alfred Tatum
Associate Professor, Director of the UIC Reading Clinic
Literacy, Language, and Culture Program
University of Illinois at Chicago
Chicago, IL

Dr. William E. White
Vice President for Productions, Publications and Learning Ventures
The Colonial Williamsburg Foundation
Williamsburg, VA

Consultants and Reviewers

PROGRAM CONSULTANT

Dr. Grant Wiggins
Coauthor, *Understanding by Design*

ACADEMIC REVIEWERS

Bob Sandman
Adjunct Assistant Professor of Business and Economics
Wilmington College–Cincinnati Branches
Blue Ash, OH

Jeanette Menendez
Reading Coach
Doral Academy Elementary
Miami, FL

Kathy T. Glass
Author, *Lesson Design for Differentiated Instruction*
President, Glass Educational Consulting
Woodside, CA

Roberta Logan
African Studies Specialist
Retired, Boston Public Schools/ Mission Hill School
Boston, MA

PROGRAM TEACHER REVIEWERS

Glenda Alford-Atkins
Eglin Elementary School
Eglin AFB, FL

Andrea Baerwald
Boise, ID

Ernest Andrew Brewer
Assistant Professor
Florida Atlantic University
Jupiter, FL

Riley D. Browning
Gilbert Middle School
Gilbert, WV

Charity L. Carr
Stroudsburg Area School District
Stroudsburg, PA

Jane M. Davis
Marion County Public Schools
Ocala, FL

Stacy Ann Figueroa, M.B.A.
Wyndham Lakes Elementary
Orlando, FL

LaBrenica Harris
John Herbert Phillips Academy
Birmingham, AL

Marianne Mack
Union Ridge Elementary
Ridgefield, WA

Emily L. Manigault
Richland School District #2
Columbia, SC

Marybeth A. McGuire
Warwick School Department
Warwick, RI

Laura Pahr
Holmes Elementary
Chicago, IL

Jennifer Palmer
Shady Hills Elementary
Spring Hill, FL

Diana E. Rizo
Miami-Dade County Public Schools/Miami Dade College
Miami, FL

Kyle Roach
Amherst Elementary, Knox County Schools
Knoxville, TN

Eretta Rose
MacMillan Elementary School
Montgomery, AL

Nancy Thornblad
Millard Public Schools
Omaha, NE

Jennifer Transue
Siegfried Elementary
Northampton, PA

Megan Zavernik
Howard-Suamico School District
Green Bay, WI

Dennise G. Zobel
Pittsford Schools–Allen Creek
Rochester, NY

Social Studies Handbook

Civil War and Reconstruction

THE BIG **What is worth fighting for?**

A Confederate soldier's hat, shoes, and gloves

Expanding West and Overseas

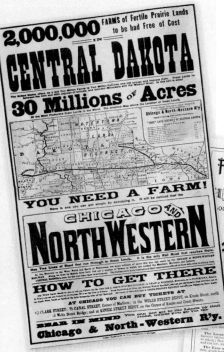

Nineteenth-century railroad posters urged people to settle the West.

Industry and Immigration

What are the costs and benefits of growth?

Early electric light

Struggle for Reform

THE BIG When does change become necessary?

Jim Crow laws denied African Americans their civil rights.

Good Times and Hardships

THE BIG
? How do people respond to good times and bad?

1920s fashion illustration of a flapper

America Changes

When does change become necessary?

Elvis Presley performs rock and roll.

Reading Skills

Main Idea is the most important idea about a topic.

Details support the main idea.

Americans Today

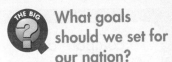

What goals should we set for our nation?

Wind turbines produce electricity.

Compare and Contrast

To compare and contrast is to look for similarities and differences in things.

Draw Conclusions

When we draw conclusions, we make decisions or form opinions about what we read.

Classify and Categorize

When we classify and categorize, we look at how things are related based on their characteristics.

RECYCLING

GLASS

PAPER

Cause and Effect

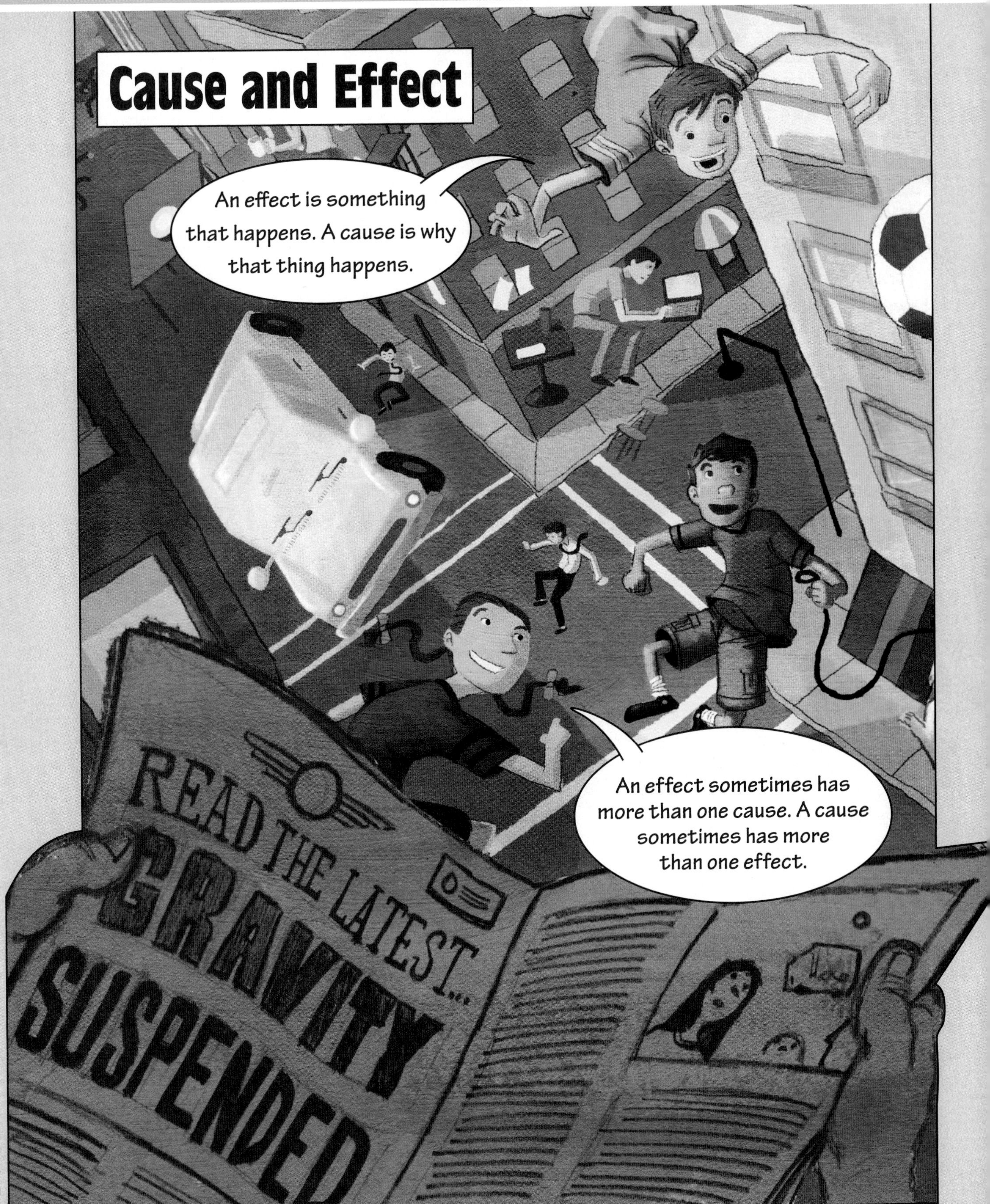

Reading Skills

Generalize

To generalize is to make a broad statement or rule that applies to many examples.

You can go faster on a bike than on skates!

Fact and Opinion

I'm taller than you!

But I'm funnier than you.

A fact is something that can be proved true or false. An opinion can't be proved.

Reading Skills

Sequence

Sequence refers to the order of events. We use sequence when we list the steps in a process.

21st Century Learning Online Tutor

You can go online to myworldsocialstudies.com to practice the skills listed below. These are skills that will be important to you throughout your life. After you complete each skill tutorial online, check it off here in your worktext.

Target Reading Skills

- [ ] Main Idea and Details
- [ ] Cause and Effect
- [ ] Classify and Categorize
- [ ] Fact and Opinion
- [ ] Draw Conclusions
- [ ] Generalize
- [ ] Compare and Contrast
- [ ] Sequence
- [ ] Summarize

Collaboration and Creativity Skills

- [ ] Solve Problems
- [ ] Work in Cooperative Teams
- [ ] Resolve Conflict
- [ ] Generate New Ideas

Graph Skills

- [ ] Interpret Graphs
- [ ] Create Charts
- [ ] Interpret Timelines

Map Skills

- [ ] Use Longitude and Latitude
- [ ] Interpret Physical Maps
- [ ] Interpret Economic Data on Maps
- [ ] Interpret Cultural Data on Maps

Critical Thinking Skills

- [ ] Compare Viewpoints
- [ ] Use Primary and Secondary Sources
- [ ] Identify Bias
- [ ] Make Decisions
- [ ] Predict Consequences

Media and Technology Skills

- [ ] Conduct Research
- [ ] Use the Internet Safely
- [ ] Analyze Images
- [ ] Evaluate Media Content
- [ ] Deliver an Effective Presentation

Keys to Good Writing

The Writing Process

Prewrite
- Choose a topic, gather details about it, and plan how to use them.

Draft
- Write down all your ideas, and don't worry about making it perfect.

Share
- Share your writing with others.

Edit
- Check your spelling, capitalization, punctuation and grammar.
- Make a final copy.

Revise
- Review your writing, looking for the traits of good writing.
- Change parts that are confusing or incomplete.

The Writing Traits

Good writers look at six qualities of their writing
to make it the best writing possible.

Ideas	Share a clear message with specific ideas and details.
Organization	Have a beginning, middle, and end that are easy to follow.
Voice	Use a natural tone in your writing.
Word Choice	Choose strong nouns and verbs and colorful adjectives.
Sentence Flow	Vary your sentence structures and beginnings to create writing that is easy to read.
Conventions	Follow the rules of spelling, capitalization, punctuation, and grammar.

Geography is the study of Earth. This study can be divided into five themes that help you understand why Earth has such a wide variety of places. Each theme reveals something different about a place, as the example of the Everglades shows.

Where can the Everglades be found?

The Everglades are located in southern Florida.

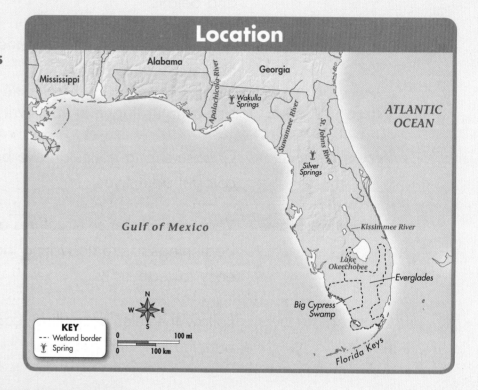

Location

Mississippi

Alabama

Georgia

Apalachicola River

Wakulla Springs

Suwannee River

St. Johns River

ATLANTIC OCEAN

Silver Springs

Gulf of Mexico

Kissimmee River

Lake Okeechobee

Everglades

Big Cypress Swamp

Florida Keys

N W E S

KEY
- - - Wetland border
Y Spring

0   100 mi
0   100 km

Place

How is this area different from others?

The place is wetlands where a plant called sawgrass grows. There are dry islands called hammocks that are covered with trees.

Human/Environmental Interaction

How have people changed the place?

Highways have made the Everglades a place visitors can explore more easily.

Movement

How has movement changed the region?

Population growth and tourists have led to increased use of the area.

Region

What is special about the region that includes the Everglades?

There are vast areas where many endangered species live.

Special-Purpose Maps

A special-purpose map gives information related to a certain theme. For example, a **population-density map**, like the one of California on this page, shows the average number of people who live in an area. You could use it to compare how many people live in the coast as opposed to inland.

There are many other kinds of special-purpose maps. A **satellite map** shows a picture of the land and cities from space. An immigration map could show which states have the highest rates of immigration. A zip-code map shows the zip codes of each area of a state or country. Weather maps are used to track storms. Knowing the path of a storm helps people be prepared.

Special-purpose maps contain a lot of information. You can use the information to compare different places or to gather details about one place. You could draw a special-purpose map of your neighborhood. It might show your home, your friends' homes, your school, and your favorite places to visit.

14. What special information does this map show?

....

....

....

15. Which city has a greater population density, Hanford or San Jose?

....

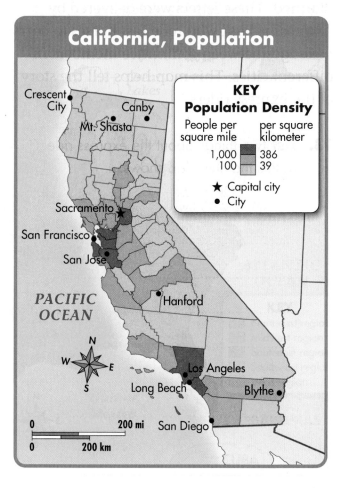

California, Population

Crescent City
Canby
Mt. Shasta
Sacramento ★
San Francisco
San Jose
PACIFIC OCEAN
Hanford
Los Angeles
Long Beach
Blythe
San Diego

N W E S

0   200 mi
0   200 km

KEY
Population Density

People per square mile		per square kilometer
1,000		386
100		39

★ Capital city
● City

Current-Events Maps

Some special-purpose maps deal with current events. They help people decide what laws to make or how to work for change. They can also show the outcome of an election. The map below shows the results of the 2010 senatorial elections.

Vocabulary

population-density map

satellite map

2010 Senatorial Election Results

KEY
- Democratic
- Republican
- Republican gain
- No election

*New York elected 2 senators

16. On a separate sheet of paper, **make** a bar graph to show how many states elected Republican senators and how many states elected Democratic senators.

Got it?

17. **Look** at the current events map above. On a separate sheet of paper, describe election results for your region.

18. How is the special-purpose map on the previous page different from a physical map of California?

Vocabulary

consumer

demand

supply

Supply and Demand

Economics is the study of the production, distribution, and consumption, or use, of goods and services. Economists are experts who study those processes. They analyze the changing habits of **consumers,** or people who buy goods and services. They also analyze the shifting relationship between supply and demand.

In economics, **demand** means consumers' desire to buy a particular thing or service. For example, if the students at a school start admiring a fancy new brand of sneakers, they might create a high demand for them. The level of demand for a product is related to its price. Therefore, if some of the students at school can't afford the new sneakers, those students won't be part of the quantity of sneakers demanded.

The more people who want an item, the greater the demand.

The term **supply** means the amount of goods or services that are available. For example, suppose that a store owner receives a big shipment of the fancy new sneakers. She has a large supply. She might worry that she won't be able to sell all those shoes. So she lowers the price. Suddenly, the quantity demanded goes up. Those kids at school who couldn't afford the shoes before are now added to the quantity of sneakers demanded. They have the ability to pay for the shoes because the price went down.

1. Suppose there are 100 students who want to buy sneakers. The store, however, only has 50 pairs. Should the store owner raise or lower the price of the sneakers?

   ....

2. Suppose a store has 100 pairs of sneakers, but only 50 students want to buy them. Should the store owner raise or lower the price of the sneakers?

   ....

3. Based on your answers to the questions above, **circle** the correct answer.

   When demand goes up, prices go up/down.

   When supply goes up, prices go up/down.

   When demand goes down, prices go up/down.

   When supply goes down, prices go up/down.

The Marketplace

The United States has a **free market economy.** In this economic system private people, not the government, own the factories, businesses, and stores that make, sell, and distribute goods or services. In a free market, businesses can make most decisions about what to produce and what prices to charge. Individuals choose what to buy in the marketplace. In a free market, these types of decisions are made all the time by millions of people. A free market works by meeting the needs and wants of private parties.

Competition is the struggle among producers for the money consumers spend. In a free market, competition usually makes prices lower. High demand for goods means businesses need to hire more workers. When people work, they have money to buy goods. This increases demand and causes businesses to increase supply. More people working is good for a free market economy.

4. **Circle** the marketplace that would be the right place for you to offer your babysitting services.

Buyers and sellers exchange goods and services in a marketplace.

Scarcity and Opportunity Cost

We want many things and, in general, more and more of those things. Yet, we can't always have everything that we want because of scarcity. **Scarcity** means that there is a limit to what we can have. We must make choices, for example, about how and where we spend our money.

All choices have a cost. If a student chooses to spend his allowance on a book, he might not be able to go to the movies with friends. The trip to the movies is the **opportunity cost.** It is the thing you have to give up to get the thing you want.

Vocabulary

free market economy

competition

scarcity

opportunity cost

5. In each row, **circle** the option you would choose. **Write** the option you would not choose, or the opportunity cost, in the third column.

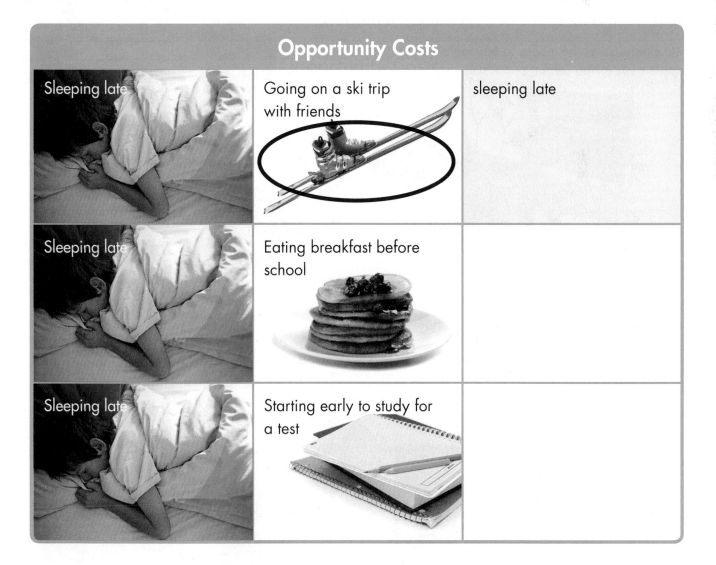

Opportunity Costs		
Sleeping late	Going on a ski trip with friends	sleeping late
Sleeping late	Eating breakfast before school	
Sleeping late	Starting early to study for a test	

Banks

Many people put their money into a bank to keep it safe or to earn interest. This is called having a **bank account.** You might think that a bank saves each dollar you give it in a special, hidden place. That is partly true. But banks also lend their customers' money to businesses and individuals. They promise to pay the bank back according to a schedule and for a small fee called **interest.** In exchange for using your money, the bank pays you some of the interest.

Sometimes banks offer a credit card to their customers. A **credit card** is a card that allows its holder to use it for small loans. The cardholder may buy things with the card, based on the promise to pay the bank back. If you are late paying back the money on your credit card, the bank will charge you interest.

How Banks Work

Kevin deposits money in his bank account.

The bank uses the money deposited by Kevin and other customers to loan Mr. Daniels money.

Mr. Daniels uses the money to buy more apple trees for his farm.

Mr. Daniels sells the apples from his new trees.

6. **Write** a checkmark next to the image that shows the bank lending money.

7. **Circle** the image that shows the bank paying interest.

Mr. Daniels pays the bank back the money he borrowed with interest.

The bank pays Kevin interest for using his money.

The Economy Today

Every day we make economic decisions that affect the economy. We decide what to buy based on what we can afford. We consider what we have to give up in order to get what we want. The government also influences the economy. It helps people who lose their jobs or homes. It helps very poor people find food and shelter. It makes rules about how banks should lend money to businesses. It enforces legal contracts, and it provides currency, or money, for the country to use.

One of the most important economic decisions that our government makes is called a **trade agreement.** The United States has trade agreements with individual countries. It is part of a multi-nation trade agreement with countries such as China and India. These agreements makes it easy for businesses to **import** (bring in) or **export** (send out) goods to and from these countries. As a result, goods made in those places are cheaper to buy in America than goods made in other countries that do not have favorable trade agreements. Both China and India have become economic superpowers partly because of their trade agreements with the United States.

Vocabulary

bank account
interest
credit card
trade agreement
import
export

U.S. Trade Partners

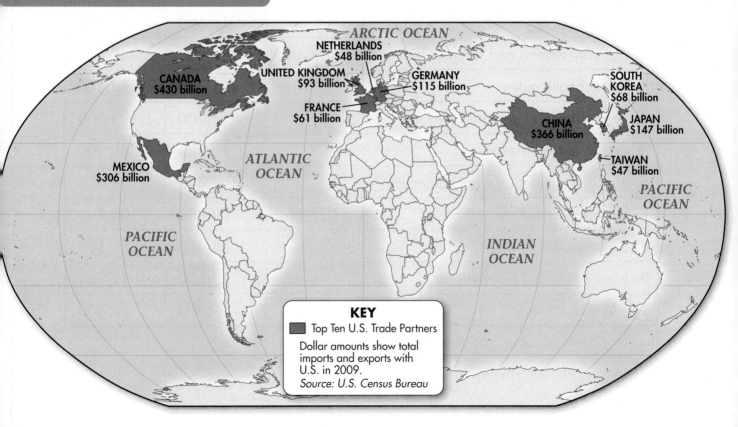

NETHERLANDS
$48 billion

CANADA
$430 billion

UNITED KINGDOM
$93 billion

GERMANY
$115 billion

SOUTH KOREA
$68 billion

FRANCE
$61 billion

CHINA
$366 billion

JAPAN
$147 billion

MEXICO
$306 billion

TAIWAN
$47 billion

KEY
Top Ten U.S. Trade Partners
Dollar amounts show total imports and exports with U.S. in 2009.
Source: U.S. Census Bureau

Jobs

Some economic conditions make it cheaper for companies to hire workers in countries such as China and India to **manufacture**, or make, goods. As a result, many manufacturing jobs are moving to those and other Asian countries. Many American businesses used to make manufactured goods like automobiles and clothing. Now more businesses offer services instead. Service jobs include nursing, teaching, and sales. However, some services, such as technology help, are now also performed overseas.

8. Name three additional service jobs not listed in the chart.

....

....

....

Most of the 10 fastest-growing jobs are jobs in which people offer a service to other people.

10 Fastest-Growing U.S. Jobs		
Occupation	Number of People Employed	
	2008	2018
1. Biomedical engineers	16,100	27,600
2. Network-systems and data-communications analysts	292,000	447,800
3. Home health aides	921,700	1,382,600
4. Personal and home-care aides	817,200	1,193,000
5. Financial examiners	27,000	38,100
6. Medical scientists, except epidemiologists	109,400	153,600
7. Physician assistants	74,800	103,900
8. Skin-care specialists	38,800	53,500
9. Biochemists and biophysicists	23,200	31,900
10. Athletic trainers	16,400	22,400

Source: Bureau of Labor Statistics, United States Department of Labor

Technology and Specialization

Businesses make decisions that help them earn more money or lower their costs. Some businesses become more competitive by improving their technology. Others become more competitive by specializing in one product or having their workers specialize in one job. To **specialize** is to concentrate in one particular area.

Vocabulary

manufacture

specialize

These workers are trained to do a specialized job. The business runs smoothly when people know their jobs well.

9. What are some specialized jobs needed to make a movie?

....

....

10. **Circle** a worker using technology to make movies more exciting.

Got it?

11. **Name** at least three factors that influence the price of goods.

....

....

....

Vocabulary

representative
  democracy

constitution

separation of powers

checks and balances

article

amendment

What Is Government?

Government is a system for running a community, state, or country. The government of the United States is a **representative democracy.** That means we elect people to act as our representatives, or people who express our ideas and opinions, in the government. They run the government for us.

We expect a lot from our government. For example, we expect all people to be treated equally, no matter what their race, religion, or gender is. We believe that people deserve to make free choices about what they believe and how they live. As a nation, we agree to follow the lead of a majority, or the largest number of people, as long as the rights of the minority, or the smallest number of people, are respected.

The U.S. Constitution

A **constitution** is a written plan for government. The United States Constitution was written more than 200 years ago by a group of leaders now known as the Founding Fathers. The Constitution set up the plan for our government by creating three branches to govern the nation: the executive, legislative, and judicial branches. The executive branch includes the President of the United States and the officials who work with him or her. The legislative branch, also known as Congress, is made up of members of the Senate and the House of Representatives. The judicial branch includes the Supreme Court, which is made up of nine justices. They insure that the nation's laws are interpreted according to the Constitution. Other courts in the judicial branch help settle conflicts.

The Constitution also established a separation of powers. The **separation of powers** means that each of the three branches of our government has its own responsibilities and powers. Also, each branch can check, or limit, the powers of the others. This plan is called a system of **checks and balances.** It is designed to make sure that the powers of the three branches of government are balanced, or equal.

Three Branches of Government

Branch	Duties	Checks
Executive	• Makes sure laws are carried out • Commands the armed forces	• Can veto, or reject, laws passed by Congress • Appoints judges
Legislative	• Makes laws • Establishes taxes	• Can reject vetoes • Can refuse to confirm judges appointed by the President
Judicial	• Interprets laws • Decides if laws follow the Constitution	• Can overturn President's actions if these actions go against the Constitution • Can stop laws that go against the Constitution

1. Who is the head of the executive branch?

....

2. How does the judicial branch check the other branches?

....

....

The Bill of Rights

The Constitution is divided into laws called **articles.** One of the most important parts of the Constitution is its plan for making changes to those laws. A change to an article in the Constitution is called an **amendment.** Just after the Constitution was ratified, or approved, its authors added ten very important amendments. They are called the Bill of Rights.

To write the Constitution, the Founders relied on English law and its concept of **individual rights,** or freedoms protected by law. The rights protected in the U.S. Bill of Rights are based, in part, on those granted to English citizens under the Magna Carta of 1215 and the English Bill of Rights of 1689. The U.S. Bill of Rights protects free speech, freedom of religion, and other important rights.

To amend the Constitution, two-thirds of the members of both houses of Congress must vote for the proposed change. Or, two-thirds of state legislatures may call for a constitutional convention. Three-fourths of the states must approve the amendment before it becomes law. Since the Bill of Rights was added, the Constitution has been amended 17 times. In 1870, an amendment extended voting rights to all men, regardless of race. In 1920, an amendment gave voting rights to women.

The U.S. Constitution also divides power between the national and state governments. This system is called **federalism** and it is another factor limiting the power of the federal government. The national government may print money, declare war, or make treaties with other nations. States may not, but they may establish local governments and conduct elections. Local governments run many of the other services we use every day.

Federalism: National, State, and Local Government

Federal	State	Local
• military forces • interstate highways • national parks • provides some financial assistance to schools	• state police • state highways • state parks • sets school standards and provides financial assistance	• police force and fire fighters • neighborhood roads • town recreation areas • makes day-to-day decisions for schools, including how to spend money from state and federal government

3. **Circle** the government duty that you think is the most important. On a separate sheet of paper, **write** a paragraph explaining your choice.

Popular Sovereignty

The Constitution includes other important ideas about how the government works and how its powers are limited. One key concept is the rule of law. The **rule of law** means that the law applies equally to all people, no matter how powerful or wealthy they are. Everyone, including the President, must obey the laws of the land. Another important idea is popular sovereignty. **Popular sovereignty** means that the citizens of a country have a right to choose what kind of government they have.

Vocabulary

individual rights
federalism
rule of law
popular sovereignty

Voting is an important right. It gives citizens a right to choose their representatives in government.

4. Draw a line between each term and its definition.

separation of powers	The idea that the government exists because the people of a country want it to exist and agree to follow its rules
federalism	The idea that the law applies equally to all people no matter how powerful or wealthy people are
popular sovereignty	Freedoms protected by law
checks and balances	The system of government in which powers are divided between cities, states, and the nation as a whole
rule of law	The system that separates the jobs and powers of government among three branches
individual rights	The system that gives each branch as much power as the others and allows each branch to limit the power of the others

Government in Action

The state and national governments have big responsibilities. They operate schools, keep the nation and cities safe, and protect parks for everyone to enjoy. Americans pay money every year to the state and national governments to help pay for the services they receive. This money is called **taxes.**

Sometimes, the government makes laws that protect people from hurting animals, the environment, or one another. For example, there is a law that people riding in a car must wear a seat belt. Many cities and states require residents to recycle glass bottles, metal cans, and plastic containers. City, state, and national governments all have laws that protect the environment. These laws protect what is called the common good. The **common good** means what is good for everyone.

Government Workers

Postal Worker

Teacher

Firefighter

5. **Circle** the picture if you have ever used the services of this government job.

6. **Name** the job of two or more government workers you saw today.

....

....

Politics

Of course, not everyone agrees with how the government does its job. Some people join groups in order to share their ideas about government. Many voters join a political party to try to influence government decisions. A **political party** is a group of people who have the same beliefs about how government should be run.

Each political party nominates a **candidate**, a person who runs for a particular office, or job. The members of the party try to convince others to vote for their candidate. Then, on election day, voters decide which candidates they want to lead the government.

Of course, after an election, the losing political party is disappointed because its candidate has not been elected. However, elections in the United States are peaceful. Although voters may feel strongly that the common good would be better served if their candidates had won, they accept the decision of the majority. This is a key principle of a stable democracy.

Vocabulary

tax
common good
political party
candidate

Barack Obama was the first African American to run for President on a major party ticket. He was elected to office in 2008.

Being a Good Citizen

Democracy, even more than other forms of government, depends on good citizenship. The government can best serve the people of a country when they stay involved. There are a number of important ways to be a good **citizen.**

This group of volunteers in Miami, Florida, is painting a mural to decorate a local elementary school.

7. **Circle** the actions on the chart that you can do now as a good citizen.

Ways to Be a Good Citizen	
Obeying the Law	Good citizens respect the rights of others by obeying the law.
Voting	Citizens cast their ballots to tell who they want to serve as government leaders. Voters must be at least 18 years old.
Paying Taxes	Every citizen benefits from the services of the city, state, and federal government. These services are paid for by people who pay taxes on the money they earn.
Volunteering to Do Community Service	Volunteering to help one's town and helping one's neighbors are great ways to be a good citizen.
Petitioning Government Leaders	Good citizens make their voices heard by writing letters and letting their elected officials know what they think.

How We Participate in Government

Vocabulary

citizen

Good citizens do more than exercise their most basic rights and responsibilities. To improve our government and society, they stay informed about issues by reading or watching the news. Many citizens volunteer or join organizations that work on issues they care about. Others run for political office. Still others write letters to the newspaper to share their views on a subject.

Communicating with your elected representatives is an important way to participate in government. You can find the name and address of your elected representatives by calling the offices of your town, or searching the Internet. Most elected officials are glad to receive letters or e-mails, and they try to write back to explain how they think about your issue.

8. **Make** a list of three things you would like to do to participate in government.

....

....

....

....

....

Got it?

9. **Name** three rights that are held by citizens of the United States.

....

....

10. **Explain** why it is important to be a good citizen in a democracy.

....

....

Civil War and Reconstruction

What is worth fighting for?

Describe a time when you wanted to stand up for another person. Then **write** to explain how and why you handled the situation in the way that you did.

....

....

....

....

....

This memorial in Boston honors an African American regiment from Massachusetts that fought bravely during the Civil War.

Gettysburg National Battlefield
Fighting for a Cause

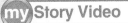
my Story Video

Eleven-year-old Trent is a history buff. He especially likes studying wars and battles. He is excited to be visiting Gettysburg National Battlefield in Pennsylvania, the site of one of the most important battles of the Civil War.

Trent enters the visitor's center, where he views the collection of guns, ammunition, and other artifacts of the battle. He studies the uniforms on display. "They look hot," says Trent, "especially since this battle took place during the summer."

Trent next visits the Gettysburg Cyclorama. Painted in the 1880s, this 360-degree painting shows how the battle unfolded. For three days in July 1863, the Union Army held off the Confederate soldiers led by Robert E. Lee. "It looks like they fought on farm land," says Trent. "I didn't realize normal people and their homes were impacted by the fighting."

Trent is eager to see the battlefield for himself. "Hi Trent, are you ready for our tour?" asks Renae, a Battlefield Guide. "I sure am!" says Trent. The two of them head out to the battlefield.

Trent is happy to be visiting the site of the battle of Gettysburg.

303

Trent studies a Union soldier's uniform.

This statue is a memorial to the mascot of soldiers from Pennsylvania. She died with the soldiers who fought at Oak Ridge.

11TH PENNSYLVANIA INFANTRY.

Renae shows Trent the statue of a citizen soldier. This man was named John Burns. He was a 70-year-old and lived in Gettysburg. Although he was too old to join the army, he fought alongside the Union forces.

It's easy for Trent to see why this man would fight. "He needed to protect his home!" Trent explains. "I'd like to think I would have done the same thing."

This statue looks over the field where fighting broke out on the first day of battle. Lee's troops fought bravely, but the Southerners were tired from their long march. By the next day, the Union soldiers had taken up strong positions and were able to hold off the advancing Southerners.

There are markers, statues, and monuments scattered across the huge battlefield. Trent spots a statue with a little dog. "Whoa. Dogs on the battlefield?" Trent asks.

"Soldiers often brought their dogs with them when they joined the army," says Renae. "They were away from home for months and sometimes years, and their dogs helped keep them from getting homesick."

Next Trent and Renae visit a place called the Devil's Den, where soldiers hid among rocks and caves. Trent gets to sit in a spot from which a Confederate sharpshooter fired. "The shooter was really protected here, and could probably see for miles," Trent marvels.

John Burns was 70 years old, but he wanted to defend Gettysburg. He grabbed a gun and joined the fight.

MY THANKS ARE SPECIALLY DUE TO A CITIZEN OF GETTYSBURG NAMED JOHN BURNS WHO ALTHOUGH OVER SEVENTY YEARS OF AGE SHOULDERED HIS MUSKET AND OFFERED HIS SERVICES TO COLONEL WISTER ONE HUNDRED AND FIFTIETH PENNSYLVANIA VOLUNTEERS COLONEL WISTER ADVISED HIM TO FIGHT IN THE

These rocks, called the Devil's Den, offered protection to Confederate shooters.

Thousands of grave markers identify those who died at Gettysburg.

Renae tells Trent about the battle of Little Round Top. The Confederates attacked this hill and nearly broke the Union lines. Union soldiers charged down the hill against the attacking Confederates. "Why did they follow their leader down a hill against hundreds of armed soldiers?" Trent asks. "Well," Renae explains, "their leader, Joshua Chamberlain, was well liked and bravely fought alongside them."

Their next stop is the place where the battle ended on July 3. Trent is amazed at the rows of cannons. Renae explains that both Union and Confederate forces fired hundreds of cannons. But the Confederate soldiers could not defeat the Union army. Eventually, General Lee retreated.

Trent ends his visit to Gettysburg with a trip to Soldiers' National Cemetery. He walks among the grave markers and wonders about the thousands of men who lost their lives. He stops before a small stone plaque and reads the inscription: "Four score and seven years ago our fathers brought forth on this continent a new nation conceived in liberty, and dedicated to the proposition that all men are created equal."

As Trent reads the Gettysburg Address, the famous speech delivered by President Lincoln, he begins to understand what some of the soldiers at Gettysburg may have been fighting for. "It was for our freedom," he decides. "All of our freedom. I'd say that is something worth fighting for!"

Think About It Based on this story, why do you think both sides in the battle fought so fiercely? As you read the chapter ahead, think about the things people were willing to fight for.

Struggles Over Slavery

Envision It!

Different geography created different economies in the North and the South.

*"Yes, we'll rally round the flag, boys, we'll rally once again,
    Shouting the battle cry of Freedom."*

The words above are from the song "The Battle Cry of Freedom," written by George F. Root in 1862.

The song "The Battle Cry of Freedom" was popular during the U.S. Civil War. Both sides were fighting for freedom but disagreed about what *freedom* meant. Their fight was the bloodiest in U.S. history. What divided our nation so deeply? Read on to find out.

The North and South Grow Apart

The North and South had developed quite differently due to differences in geography. Much of the South is low and level with rich soil. The climate is warm and sunny for much of the year. Big farms called **plantations** developed. In the 1800s, most Southerners lived on plantations or in small towns. Many of the farmworkers were enslaved people. Although only about one third of the farmers owned slaves, the Southern economy depended upon their work.

The United States, 1860

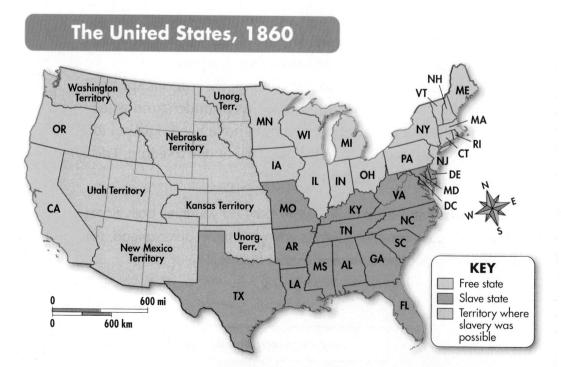

KEY
- Free state
- Slave state
- Territory where slavery was possible

0   600 mi
0   600 km

Washington Territory, OR, CA, Utah Territory, Nebraska Territory, Kansas Territory, New Mexico Territory, Unorg. Terr., MN, WI, IA, MO, AR, Unorg. Terr., TX, LA, MS, AL, MI, IL, IN, OH, KY, TN, GA, FL, SC, NC, VA, PA, NY, DC, MD, DE, NJ, CT, RI, MA, ME, NH, VT

Vocabulary

plantation
Union
states' rights
compromise

Underground Railroad
abolitionist
secession
Confederacy

Put an *S* on the picture that represents the South and an *N* on the picture that represents the North.

The geography of the Northeast is very different from that of the South. The Northeast has hills, mountains, and lakes. The climate is cold and snowy in the winter. In places, the ground is rocky, so farming is not easy. Northeast resources include coal for making steel. In the 1800s, many Northerners worked in factories. More and more people crowded into large towns and cities. Most big cities had good harbors, so shipping raw materials to factories and finished goods from factories was easy.

The South did not have as many ports as the North. However, the southern port of New Orleans was important to both the South and North. People far inland could ship goods down the Mississippi River to New Orleans and then around the world.

These differences in geography led to differences in economies and ways of life. The North had many workers, and so did not rely on enslaved people. These and other issues led to conflict.

1. ◉ **Generalize Write** a generalization based on the data in this graph.

....

....

....

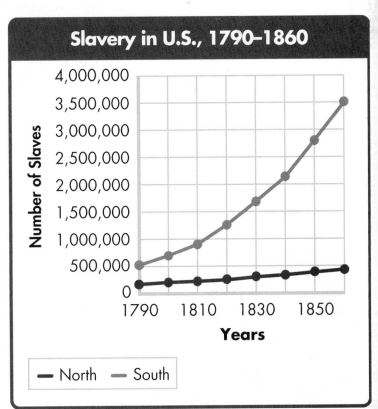

Source: University of Virginia Library

2. Write to explain the main ideas of each law below.

Missouri Compromise
- Missouri would be a slave state.
- ....
  ....
- ....
  ....
  ....

Compromise of 1850
- California would be admitted as a free state.
- ....
  ....
  ....

Daniel Webster was a Northern Congressman who pushed for the Compromise of 1850.

Tough Compromises

At the end of the American Revolution, the United States had obtained from Britain the large region we now call the Midwest. Known then as the Northwest Territory, it more than doubled the size of the country.

Congress passed a law called the Northwest Ordinance of 1787. It outlined how new states could be formed as the country grew. Once admitted to the **Union,** as the United States was often called, a new state would have the same rights as other states.

Slavery was prohibited in this territory. This sparked arguments. Many wanted the same number of slave states, where slavery was allowed, and free states, where it was illegal. They feared that if there were more representatives in Congress for either side, it might threaten **states' rights**, the rights of states to make their own local laws.

In 1819, Missouri asked to join the Union as a slave state. That would upset the balance in Congress. A compromise was worked out. A **compromise** is when each side gives in a little to reach an agreement. A law known as the Missouri Compromise was passed in 1820.

According to the Missouri Compromise, Missouri could be a slave state and Maine would join the Union as a free state. Also, not all states formed from the Northwest Territory would be free. Instead, an imaginary line, called the Mason-Dixon line, was used. States north of the line would be free states. States south of the line could allow slavery if they wished.

More New States

In 1845 the Republic of Texas was annexed (united or joined) to the United States. Part of the republic became the state of Texas. The rest of the territory was to be divided into four new states. Texas was admitted to the Union as a slave state. Of the other four new states, those north of the line set by the Missouri Compromise would be free. But those south of the line could vote on whether to allow slavery.

Tensions flared again in 1849 when California applied to join the Union as a free state. The country made another tough bargain called the Compromise of 1850. To satisfy the North, California was admitted as a free state. To satisfy the South, the North agreed to the Fugitive Slave Law.

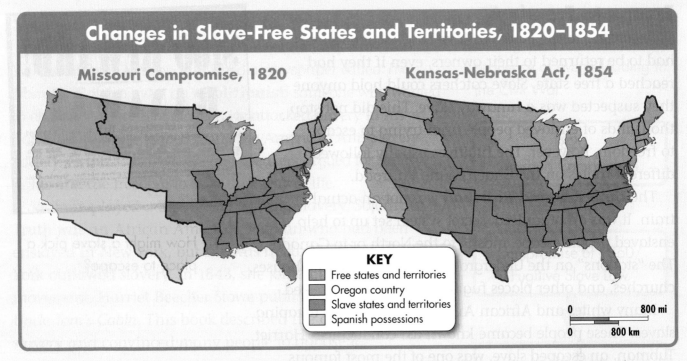

Changes in Slave-Free States and Territories, 1820–1854

Missouri Compromise, 1820

Kansas-Nebraska Act, 1854

KEY
Free states and territories
Oregon country
Slave states and territories
Spanish possessions

0   800 mi
0   800 km

A fugitive is someone who escapes and runs away. The Fugitive Slave Law said that escaped slaves must be returned to their owners, even if they had reached a free state. Daniel Webster and other members of Congress from the North hoped that this law would keep the country united.

In 1854 Nebraska was split into the Nebraska Territory and Kansas Territory. Under the Kansas-Nebraska Act, the people of each territory could vote to decide if they would allow slavery.

3. Look at the maps. **Write** how the Kansas-Nebraska Act affected the spread of slavery.

....

....

....

....

....

....

"Bleeding Kansas"

A majority vote would decide whether Kansas would be free or allow slavery. Northerners opposed to slavery rushed to Kansas to vote. Southerners also rushed to Kansas to vote for slavery.

When the votes were counted, the pro-slavery side had won. The Kansas Territory would allow slavery.

Northerners demanded that the vote be thrown out. Southerners argued that the vote should stand. Most people who lived in Kansas wanted peace, but leaders on both sides stirred up trouble. People clashed all over the Kansas Territory. By 1856, this violence had earned the territory the sad name "Bleeding Kansas."

In "Bleeding Kansas," anti-slavery forces prepared to attack supporters of slavery.

309

The War Begins

Envision It!

Union soldier

The U.S. Civil War split the nation and often split communities and families, as well.

Most leaders of the Confederacy expected the secession to be peaceful. They believed deciding to secede was one of a state's rights. They didn't think their actions would lead to a long, bloody war. They were very wrong.

The First Shots

A Union force controlled Fort Sumter in South Carolina. It was in a Confederate state, so Confederate President Jefferson Davis thought the Union force should surrender the fort. He sent South Carolina's governor to ask the Union soldiers to leave the fort, but they refused.

On April 8, 1861, the governor learned that Lincoln was sending a ship to resupply the fort. Jefferson Davis sent soldiers to help the governor.

On April 11, the Confederates again asked the Union soldiers to leave. Again, they refused. At 4:30 A.M. on April 12, Confederate forces began to fire on the fort. The next day, with no supplies left, the Union force surrendered the fort to the Confederates. No one had been killed, but the Civil War had begun.

Confederate forces fired on Fort Sumter on April 12, 1861. This event touched off the Civil War.

Confederate soldier

UNLOCK THE BIG ？

I will know the strategies and key battles in the first years of the Civil War.

Write what you think each soldier might say to the other about why they are fighting.

Vocabulary

enlist
blockade

The Civil War Begins

Lincoln responded to the attack on Fort Sumter by raising an army. Virginia, Arkansas, Tennessee, and North Carolina joined the Confederacy. The Confederacy now had 11 states; the Union consisted of 23. Men on both sides eagerly enlisted. To **enlist** is to join the military. After all, it was an important cause. The North wanted to preserve the unity of the United States as a whole. The North also didn't want to lose access to the Mississippi River. The South was fighting for states' rights and a way of life.

The First Battle of Bull Run

At first, it seemed that the war *would* be over soon— and the Confederates would win. Lincoln sent 35,000 troops against the Confederate capital, Richmond, Virginia. On July 21, 1861, they met Confederate troops at a stream called Bull Run. The Union soldiers did well at first. But the Confederates stood their ground, inspired by a general named Thomas Jackson. "There stands Jackson like a stone wall," declared another Confederate general. This earned the general the nickname "Stonewall" Jackson. When Southern reinforcements arrived, the overwhelmed Union soldiers fled.

1. ◉ **Sequence Put** the events on these pages in the correct sequence.

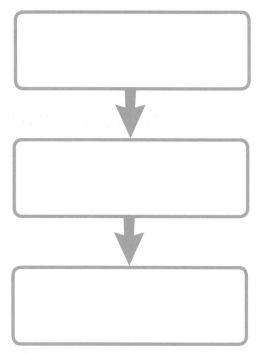

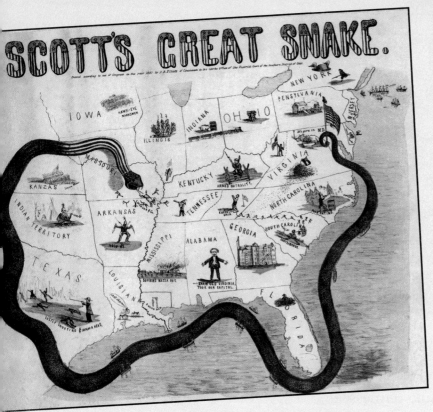

SCOTT'S GREAT SNAKE.

General Scott's plan was to wrap around the South and "squeeze" it, like a giant snake.

Lincoln Versus Davis

Abraham Lincoln, the President of the Union, and Jefferson Davis, the President of the Confederacy, were both skilled leaders. Both were born in Kentucky, but Davis had moved to Mississippi and Lincoln had moved to Illinois. Lincoln trained as a lawyer. Davis, a West Point graduate, became an army officer. Both served in Washington, D.C.

Lincoln and Davis faced different challenges as the war began. The South had fewer resources than the North, but it had better military leaders and stronger reasons to fight.

The two men were different in their war time strategies, too. Lincoln sought advice from General Winfield Scott, a Mexican War veteran.

2. ◎ **Compare and Contrast Complete** this chart to compare the Union and the Confederacy.

The Union and the Confederacy		
	United States of America	**Confederate States of America**
President		
Strategy		
Strengths	• Produced 90% of the country's weapons, cloth, shoes, and iron • Produced most of the country's food • Had more railroads and roads • Had more people	• Had more experienced hunters and soldiers • Had a history of producing great military leaders • Believed they were fighting for freedom • Were fighting for—and on—their own land
Challenges	• Didn't have many war veterans • Didn't have as many talented military leaders	• Lacked big manufacturing centers • Had fewer railroads

Scott planned a three-part strategy. First, the Union would form a naval blockade of the coasts. A **blockade** is a barrier of troops or ships to keep people and supplies from moving in and out of an area. Under a blockade, the South would not be able to ship cotton to European countries and wouldn't have money to pay for the war.

Second, Scott planned to take control of the Mississippi River. This would cut the Confederacy in half. Third, Scott planned to attack the Confederacy from the east and west. He called his strategy the Anaconda Plan because it would squeeze the Confederacy like an anaconda, a huge snake.

Davis had his own strategy. First, he planned to defend Confederate land until the North gave up. Southerners believed that Union troops would quit fighting because they weren't defending their own land. Second, Davis believed the British would help because they needed Southern cotton. Davis was wrong. Britain offered no help to either side.

New Tools of War

Wars often result in the invention of new tools and technologies. During the Civil War, guns were improved. The new guns could shoot farther and more accurately. Both Union and Confederate soldiers used early versions of the hand grenade. The Confederacy built a submarine, a ship that could travel under water.

The Confederates created another new weapon: the ironclad. It was a ship covered, or clad, in iron, so cannonballs simply bounced off it. To make the ironclad, the Confederates covered an old Union ship, the *Merrimack*, with iron plates. They named it the *Virginia*. The *Virginia* successfully sank several Union ships. The Union built its own ironclad, the *Monitor*, which fought the *Virginia*. Since both ships were ironclads, they were unable to cause serious damage to each other.

3. **Write** a newspaper headline for the battle of the *Monitor* and the *Virginia*.

....

....

....

....

General Robert E. Lee was respected by people on both sides, even during the war.

Brilliant Confederate Generals

While the Union had far greater resources than the Confederacy, the South had brilliant generals, especially Thomas "Stonewall" Jackson and Robert E. Lee. These generals often outsmarted Union forces many times larger than their own.

In 1862, Union General George McClellan hoped to capture the Confederate capital of Richmond, Virginia. McClellan planned to sail his troops to a place on the coast of Virginia, to avoid the Confederate army in northern Virginia. At first, it seemed as though McClellan's plan would work. However, Stonewall Jackson was fighting so successfully in Virginia's Shenandoah Valley that extra Union troops had to be sent there. There was no help for McClellan. Robert E. Lee then badly defeated McClellan's forces at Richmond. Some people feared that the Confederates would now move on Washington, D.C.

With each Confederate success, there was more pressure on Lincoln. Northerners had expected a swift, easy victory. It was beginning to look like the war might be long, and people began to question Lincoln's decision to fight.

4. The painting below is of the Battle of Antietam. **Write** a newspaper headline to go with this painting.

....

....

The Battle of Antietam

The Union needed a victory. It got one on September 17, 1862, at the Battle of Antietam (an TEET um). This battle was the single bloodiest day in the war. In the end, about 23,000 men lay dead or wounded, evenly divided between North and South. This horrific battle led Lincoln to make a decision that would change the war and the country.

Got it?

5. ⊙ **Main Idea and Details Fill in** this chart to show the purpose, or main idea, of the Anaconda Plan. Then fill in details to show how the plan would work.

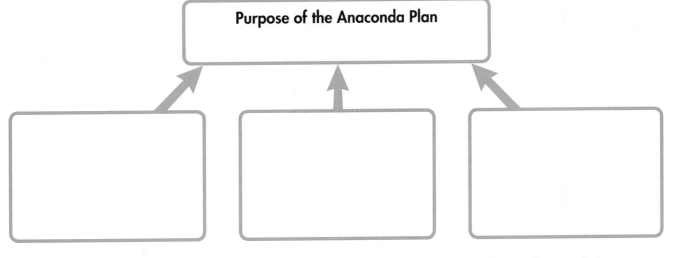

Purpose of the Anaconda Plan

6. **Write** a short dialogue between Lincoln and Davis about why they are willing to fight.

....

....

....

....

....

◼ **Stop!** I need help with ....

❚❚ **Wait!** I have a question about ....

▶ **Go!** Now I know ....

Lesson 3

Life During the Civil War

Mathew Brady used the new technology of photography to record the people and events of the Civil War.

The U.S. Civil War didn't start as a war to end slavery. President Lincoln just wanted to keep the country together. By 1862, however, Lincoln's thinking had changed. He said, "Slavery must die that the nation might live."

The Emancipation Proclamation

Some of Lincoln's advisors said ending slavery would divide the North and unite the South. They were right. But Lincoln was determined. On January 1, 1863, he issued a **proclamation**, or official announcement. It called for the **emancipation**, or setting free, of slaves. Lincoln's Emancipation Proclamation freed slaves in states at war with the Union.

The proclamation did not end slavery in the border states, slave states that stayed loyal to the Union. These were Delaware, Kentucky, Maryland, Missouri, and West Virginia. It freed slaves in the Confederacy, but only those areas controlled by the Union benefited. As a result, most African Americans remained enslaved. Many would not learn of emancipation until much later.

When the Civil War ended, General Gordon Granger was sent to the state of Texas. On June 19, 1865, he read to the people of Galveston, "The people of Texas are informed that . . . all slaves are free." African Americans in Texas celebrated this day as their day of freedom. The tradition of celebrating on this day spread quickly to other states. This day is now known as **Juneteenth**.

1. Write the feelings shown in this painting of African Americans learning they were free.

....

....

322

UNLOCK THE BIG ?Q I will know the importance of the Emancipation Proclamation and the roles of different groups in the Civil War.

Vocabulary

proclamation

emancipation

Juneteenth

A Diverse Army

Although the Emancipation Proclamation did not end all slavery, it did change the war. African American abolitionist Frederick Douglass supported Lincoln and encouraged other African Americans to help the Union. Large numbers of them responded by joining the Union Army.

By the end of the war, about 179,000 African American men had served as soldiers in the Union army. African Americans helped the war effort in other ways, too. They served as carpenters, cooks, guards, workers, nurses, scouts, spies, and doctors. African American women served as nurses, spies, and scouts. Harriet Tubman became the most famous African American scout.

Many recent immigrants also enlisted. Many German, Irish, British, and Canadian soldiers joined in the fight. They hoped to prove their loyalty to their new country.

About 20,000 Native Americans served in either the Confederate or Union armies. Some Native American nations, such as the Cherokee, were divided. General Ely S. Parker, a Seneca, wrote the surrender document that General Robert E. Lee signed at the end of the war. Parker later told how, during the surrender, Lee said to him, "I am glad to see a real American here." Parker replied to the general, "We are all Americans."

2. About what percentage of the Union Army was made up of immigrants?

Union Army

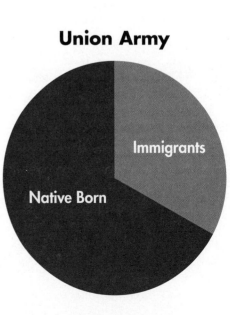

Immigrants

Native Born

A Soldier's Life

The average age of a Civil War soldier was 25. However, boys as young as 12 went into battle as drummer boys. For young soldiers and old, life on the Civil War battlefields was dirty, dangerous, and difficult.

Battles were horrible, but long, boring waits between battles were hard, too. Most battles were in the South, where summers were very hot. Soldiers almost always traveled on foot and might march up to 25 miles a day. The supplies in their backpacks weighed as much as 50 pounds. Marching proved even more difficult for Confederate soldiers. The Union blockade kept supplies from reaching the Southerners, so soldiers could not replace worn out shoes. They often marched and fought in bare feet.

Food was a problem, too. It was rarely fresh. The armies supplied beef and pork. Both were preserved so they did not spoil. Fresh pork had been salted to become "salt pork." Beef was pickled, or preserved in water and spices. In addition, the troops had beans and biscuits. These biscuits were tough flour-and-water biscuits called "hardtack." To survive, troops raided local farms to steal fresh fruits and vegetables.

3. Soldiers were away from home for long periods during the war. What does this photo tell you about how families solved this?

....

....

A Confederate soldier's hat, shoes, and gloves

Sick and Wounded

In the mid-1800s, the idea that germs caused disease was a new and untested theory. Most doctors hadn't heard of it. Many doctors never washed their hands or medical instruments.

A wounded soldier who made it to a hospital might be put in a bed in which someone just died of fever—without the sheets being changed. Infections were common and disease spread quickly. There were few medicines and no antibiotics. Twice as many soldiers died of disease as died of gunshot wounds.

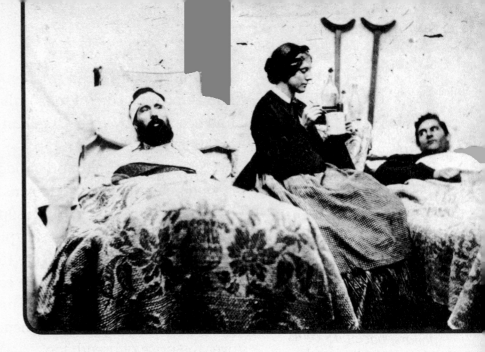

Civil War nurse caring for the wounded at a field hospital

Caring for the Soldiers

At this time, there were almost no nursing schools in the United States. Most nurses learned as they worked, and most were volunteers. One nurse described a field hospital this way: ". . . just across the lawn there are some of the worst cases & the sight & sounds we have to encounter daily are most distressing. I am mightily afraid we shall have some sort of infectious fever here for it is impossible to keep the place clean & there is a bad smell everywhere."

Clara Barton was the most famous of the volunteer nurses. She went out to where the soldiers were. Barton said her place was "anywhere between the bullet and the battlefield." At the battle of Antietam, as the cannons boomed, she held the operating table steady for the surgeon. She became known as "the Angel of the Battlefield." After the war, in 1881, she founded the American Red Cross.

Hundreds of women helped on both sides. Juliet Opie Hopkins from Alabama cared for Confederate soldiers. In 1861 she sold all her property and gave the money to the Confederacy to establish hospitals. She organized medical services in Richmond, Virginia, and then for the whole state of Alabama. Hopkins was shot twice while rescuing wounded men on the battlefield.

4. **Write** two things you might do to help nurse soldiers.

....

....

....

....

On the Home Front

Not all women could work on the battlefield. Most stayed home and took care of the families. They filled the jobs that had been held by men. They ran stores and planted crops. In addition, they worried.

Women in the South often had to move their families and belongings, as homes and towns were destroyed. They also had to deal with shortages of supplies caused by the North's blockade. Prices increased sharply. The average Southern family's monthly food bill rose from $6.65 just before the war to $68 by 1863. Almost no one could afford food. In April of that year, hundreds of women in Richmond, Virginia, rioted to protest the rise in prices. Women in other Southern cities rioted over the price of bread, too.

When they could, women hid their livestock as the armies came through. Hungry soldiers would kill and eat all the chickens and pigs. Of course, the army would take any other food they could find, too. Often, after an army had passed through, the civilians were left starving. This was the case when the Union army marched through the South.

Women also hid possessions from the enemy soldiers. These included items that had been in their families for generations.

In a letter dated August 23, 1862, a Virginia woman complained to her sister about hard times and high prices:

"Times are very hard here every thing is scarce and high . . . corn is selling for ten dollars, bacon 45 cents per pound . . . . We cannot get a yard of calico for less than one dollar."

5. **List** three things you would take with you if you had to escape before an enemy army came.

....

....

....

A Southern family flees the approaching Union army.

People in the North read about the war. Many sent husbands or sons to fight. In the South, families struggled with the direct effects of the war's destruction.

Women in Wartime

Women on both sides contributed to the war effort. In addition to being nurses on the battlefield or keeping farms and family businesses running, they sewed clothing and made bandages. They sold personal possessions to raise money and sent food to the armies.

Some women traveled with their soldier husbands and sons, cooking for them, nursing them, and helping them. A few women even became soldiers. Frances Clalin, for example, disguised herself as a man so that she could fight in the Union army.

Sojourner Truth, an African American and former slave, had worked for abolition before the war and would work for women's rights after the war. During the war, she gathered supplies for African American regiments. A popular speaker, she often told stories of her life as an enslaved person.

Some women became spies. Women had clever ways to carry secret documents, such as maps and messages. Documents and even weapons could be hidden under the large hoop skirts they wore.

Belle Boyd, nicknamed "La Belle Rebelle," was one of the most famous female Confederate spies. Union soldiers arrested her six times, but she kept spying for the Confederates. After one arrest, Boyd communicated to a Confederate by hiding messages inside rubber balls and throwing them between the bars of her cell windows!

I have borne thirteen children, and seen most all sold off to slavery, and when I cried out with my mother's grief, none but Jesus heard me!
—Sojourner Truth

Sojourner Truth told of her own life as she worked to end slavery.

Bringing the War Home

New technology changed the way the war was fought, but it also changed the way people at home experienced the war. People still got news from the battlefield through the "old" technology of soldiers' letters and newspapers.

For the first time, people back home also got to see something of what these soldiers were living through. A new technology, photography, made this possible. The Civil War was the first war to be "taken home" in images. Mathew Brady thought it was important to photograph the war.

People still learn from Brady's photographs showing the details of war. He took pictures of soldiers posing, resting, and cooking. Brady and other photographers also took photos of field hospitals, weapons, and dead bodies on the battlefield. Their photos appeared in newspapers and special exhibits.

6. Write how you think seeing photographs of the war might have changed people's feelings about war.

....

....

....

....

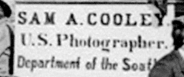

Civil War photographers and their camera and portable darkroom

Camera technology was not well developed at the time. Cameras were large and heavy. All the preparation and developing had to be done in the dark, so the photographers used a "darkroom" wagon. Photographs at that time were taken on specially treated glass plates. The glass plates had to be handled carefully as the wagon bumped through the countryside and across battlefields. Some people claim that as a result of all the letters home and all the photographs, civilians knew more about the Civil War than about any war before.

Mathew Brady spent his own money, buying equipment and hiring assistants, to capture the war in photographs.

Got it?

7. ◉ **Sequence** Put these events in the correct sequence: Emancipation Proclamation, Juneteeth holiday created, First Battle of Bull Run, Clara Barton starts the Red Cross, Battle of Antietam.

....

....

....

....

8. ❓ **Write** a letter from the point of view of a Confederate soldier telling his family about his experiences.

my Story Ideas

....

....

....

....

....

⬛ **Stop!** I need help with ....

⏸ **Wait!** I have a question about ....

▶ **Go!** Now I know ....

The War Ends

Envision It!

By April 1865, the Confederate capital, Richmond, Virginia, lay in ruins.

President Lincoln regularly met with Union officers at their military camps.

People were eager to see the Civil War end, and both sides became more aggressive. All major battles had been in the South, but in July 1863, for the first time, Lee led his forces north of the Mason-Dixon line. This line had come to represent the division between free and slave states. The Confederates marched toward Gettysburg, Pennsylvania.

Union Victory at Gettysburg

The Battle of Gettysburg was one of the most important battles of the war. It lasted three brutal days and was a turning point in the war.

General George Meade led the Union troops. On July 1, 1863, after a successful Confederate attack, Union soldiers retreated. However, the weary Confederates were unable to follow and gain the victory.

On July 2, fresh Union troops arrived. The Confederates attacked again, but this time the Union troops held their ground. The fighting was fierce.

On July 3, the Confederate forces fired more than 150 cannons. Northern cannons roared back. Commanded by General George Pickett, thousands of Confederate troops attacked. But "Pickett's Charge," as it was called, was a disaster. By the time it ended, more than 5,000 Confederate soldiers lay dead or wounded. The Union had won.

The Battle of Gettysburg was a key victory for the Union, but the victory came at a steep cost. More than 23,000 Union soldiers and 28,000 Confederate soldiers were dead or wounded.

UNLOCK THE BIG ?

I will know the people, battles, and events that led to the end of the Civil War.

Vocabulary

siege

total war

assassinate

Write, in the space above, what you think the picture suggests about the outcome of the war.

Union Victory at Vicksburg

The Confederates held a strong position at Vicksburg, Mississippi. They had turned back all previous Union attacks. But controlling Vicksburg meant controlling the Mississippi River, so the Union wanted to take Vicksburg.

Union General Ulysses S. Grant attacked Vicksburg from two directions at once, but the Confederates successfully defended Vicksburg. Grant attacked again and again, from the east and then, crossing the river, from the south. But direct attack continued to fail. So Grant laid siege.

A **siege** is a military blockade designed to make a city surrender. The siege lasted 48 days. People in Vicksburg dug caves into the hillside to escape fire from Union cannons. Confederate soldiers and civilians faced starvation. Vicksburg surrendered on July 4, 1863. The tide had finally turned in favor of the Union.

1. ◉ **Summarize Write** a sentence summarizing what the map shows about Civil War battles.

....

....

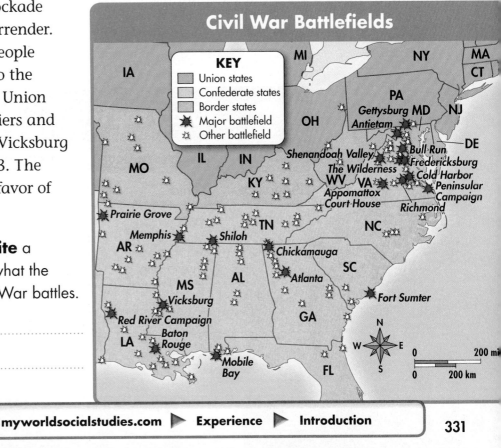

Civil War Battlefields

KEY
- Union states
- Confederate states
- Border states
- ✸ Major battlefield
- ✦ Other battlefield

IA, MI, NY, MA, CT, PA, Gettysburg, MD, NJ, OH, Antietam, DE, Shenandoah Valley, Bull Run, Fredericksburg, The Wilderness, Cold Harbor, WV, VA, Peninsular Campaign, Appomattox Court House, Richmond, MO, IL, IN, KY, Prairie Grove, TN, NC, Memphis, Shiloh, AR, Chickamauga, SC, MS, AL, Atlanta, Vicksburg, Fort Sumter, Red River Campaign, GA, Baton Rouge, LA, Mobile Bay, FL

N W E S

0   200 mi
0   200 km

Grant Versus Lee

President Lincoln once said of Ulysses S. Grant, "I can't spare this man. He fights." Grant proved to be the fighter the Union needed. In March of 1864, Lincoln promoted Grant and gave him control over the entire Union army. Grant was famous for his aggressive fighting style and for being relentless. He would just keep sending in more men until the other side ran out of food or ammunition.

Robert E. Lee, the chief commander of the Confederate troops, faced a terrible decision when the Civil War broke out. Lee loved the United States and was an officer in the U.S. Army. His father had fought alongside George Washington. However, he felt tied to Virginia. He resigned from the Union army and sided with the South.

As a general, Lee was famous for his brilliant military tactics. He was skilled, smart, and daring on the battlefield. He was also known as a gentleman. He was a soldier with refined manners. He used strategy rather than brute force. He inspired his troops, because they respected him so much.

Grant and Lee were alike in many ways. Both had received their military training at the U.S. Military Academy at West Point. Both had served in the Mexican-American War. Both were brilliant military leaders. After the war, both worked to reunite the nation.

2. **Write** how Lee and Grant were similar.

....

....

....

....

....

....

Grant and Lee

	Ulysses S. Grant	Robert E. Lee
Birthplace	Ohio	Virginia
Education	U.S. Military Academy at West Point	U.S. Military Academy at West Point
Prior Military Service	Mexican-American War	Mexican-American War
Military Rank	General	General
Side	North	South

Sherman in Georgia

Union General William Tecumseh Sherman played a major role in ending the war. Sherman's idea was that war should be as horrible as possible, so the enemy would stop fighting. He didn't just attack military targets; he worked to destroy the South economically, so it could no longer support an army. Sherman's approach came to be known as **total war.**

Leading 100,000 Union troops, Sherman began his invasion of Georgia in May 1864. He headed first for Atlanta. Confederate troops tried to stop Sherman's advance but were driven back by the huge number of Union soldiers.

Sherman began a siege of the city of Atlanta. By September 2, Sherman's forces controlled the city. They destroyed Atlanta's railroad center to disrupt the South's transportation system.

Sherman ordered everyone to leave and then burned much of the city. Union soldiers also took all the food and supplies they could find. Atlanta could no longer offer help to the Confederate army.

From Atlanta, Sherman headed for Savannah on the coast. With 62,000 soldiers, he cut a path of destruction across Georgia. This campaign came to be called "Sherman's March to the Sea." Union troops destroyed everything that might help the South keep fighting. Sherman gave his soldiers only bread to force them to raid villages for food.

Confederate soldiers continued to follow and fight Sherman's forces. They couldn't win, but they reduced the amount of damage done by the Union forces.

On December 21, 1864, Savannah fell without a fight. Union soldiers had caused $100 million worth of damage in their march across Georgia. They then turned north, marching into South Carolina, causing even more destruction in the state where the war began.

Sherman's forces tore up railroad tracks and burned towns as they marched across the South.

3. **Circle** the part of Sherman's route known as his March to the Sea.

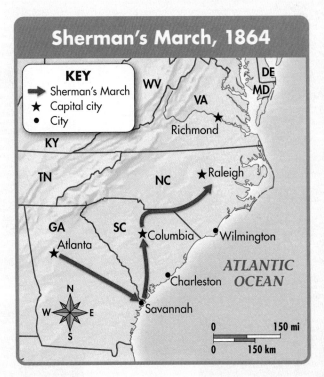

Sherman's path after Atlanta

333

The Road to Appomattox

Union forces were closing in on Lee's army in Virginia. On April 2, 1865, General Lee sent a message to Jefferson Davis that the Confederates should leave Richmond, Virginia. The next day, Union troops entered the city. The Union had captured the capital of the Confederacy! When President Lincoln arrived to tour Richmond, the city's former slaves cheered him.

Exhausted and starving, Lee's army of 55,000 men tried to escape west. Grant's force of about 113,000 soldiers trapped them. Grant met Lee in one last battle near the village of Appomattox Court House, Virginia, and once again defeated the weary Confederates. The end had come. The Civil War was over.

On April 9, 1865, General Grant and General Lee met at a farmhouse at Appomattox to discuss the terms of surrender. Among the many Union officers who witnessed the surrender was Ely S. Parker. A Seneca lawyer and Union officer, he had helped write up the terms of surrender.

4. **Label** Generals Lee and Grant in the painting.

Grant and Lee sign the terms of surrender at Appomattox Court House. Ely S. Parker is on the left, next to the fireplace.

Costs of the Civil War (in millions of 1860 Dollars)

	South	North	Total
Government expenditures	1,032	2,302	3,334
Physical destruction	1,487	0	1,487
Costs of the war			

5. Add up the costs of the war.

Grant wanted the healing of the nation to start right away. He didn't take Confederate soldiers prisoner. Instead, he allowed Lee's soldiers to go free. In addition, the Union allowed the Southerners to keep their personal weapons and any horses they had. Grant also offered to give Lee's men food from Union supplies. Lee accepted. As Lee returned to his men, the Union soldiers cheered and fired their rifles, to celebrate their victory over the South. Grant silenced them, saying, "The war is over; the rebels are our countrymen again."

The Cost of the Civil War

The Civil War was the most destructive war in our history. The human costs were very high. About 620,000 people died. Families were torn apart, as some members sided with the Union and others with the Confederacy. The governments of both sides spent billions to fight the war.

Other economic costs were shattering as well. Towns, farms, and industries in the South were ruined. Factories in the North that had relied on Southern cotton were in trouble. However, the economy of the South suffered far greater losses, particularly because the enslaved people on whom the economy depended were now freed.

There are many ways to think about the price that was paid. But no matter how the costs are estimated, the Civil War had a tremendous human and economic cost.

In spite of the destruction, Lincoln still hoped for the healing of the nation. After news of the Confederate surrender reached Washington, D.C., Lincoln appeared before a crowd and asked a band to play "Dixie," one of the battle songs of the Confederacy. "I have always thought 'Dixie' one of the best tunes I ever heard," he told the crowd.

Civil War Currency

"We here highly resolve that these dead shall not have died in vain, that this nation under God shall have a new birth of freedom, and that government of the people, by the people, for the people shall not perish from the earth."

—Abraham Lincoln, from the "Gettysburg Address"

6. Underline the words in this excerpt that describe democracy.

A reward was offered for the capture of Lincoln's assassin, John Wilkes Booth.

The Gettysburg Address

Abraham Lincoln left us a beautiful summary of why so many had to die in this terrible war. He wrote it a year and a half before the war ended.

In 1863, thousands of Americans had been killed at Gettysburg, so the battlefield was made into a national cemetery to honor them. On November 19, 1863, about 15,000 people gathered for the ceremony to establish the cemetery. At this event, President Lincoln gave what has become one of America's most famous speeches.

Lincoln's speech, now known as the Gettysburg Address, began with the words "Four score and seven years ago our fathers brought forth upon this continent a new nation." (A score is 20.) Lincoln was reminding people that it had been 87 years since the Declaration of Independence. The fight was about preserving the nation and about self government.

In the Address, Lincoln also praised the soldiers who had given their lives to keep the dream of America alive. It reminded Americans that there was still more work to be done, but also why the work was important.

A Terrible Loss for the Nation

Friday evening, April 14, 1865, President Lincoln and his wife, Mary, attended a play at Ford's Theater. During the play, the audience was surprised to hear a gunshot. This was followed by Mary Lincoln's screams. President Lincoln had been shot!

The bullet had entered the back of the president's head, and he was unconscious. He died a few hours later, on the morning of April 15.

Lincoln was **assassinated**, or murdered for political reasons, by John Wilkes Booth, a 26-year-old actor who supported the Confederacy. Booth escaped from the theater. But federal troops found him later in a Virginia barn. He refused to surrender. The soldiers shot and killed him. Booth had not worked alone, and Lincoln was not the only target. The whole group of plotters was captured, tried, and hanged.

A funeral train took Lincoln's body to his hometown of Springfield, Illinois, to be buried. People paid their respects along the route as the train traveled from Washington to Springfield. It was a tragic loss for the nation. But, before he died, Lincoln had achieved his goal. He had saved the Union.

Statue of Lincoln in the Lincoln Memorial, Washington, D.C.

Got it?

7. ◉ **Main Idea and Details Fill in** the missing details that support the main idea.

Main Idea
The war turned in the Union's favor.

| Detail | Detail | Detail |

8. ❓ **Explain** how not punishing the South relates to the Union's reason for fighting.

my Story Ideas

....

....

⬛ **Stop!** I need help with ....

⏸ **Wait!** I have a question about ....

▶ **Go!** Now I know ....

Lesson 5

Reconstruction

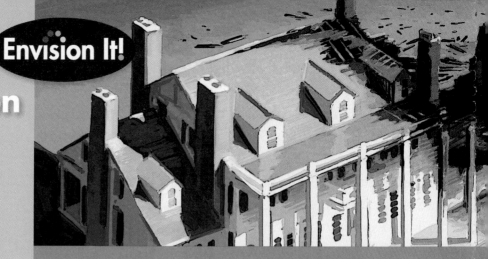

After the Civil War, the South was in ruins. Several plans were created to help repair and rebuild the region.

After President Lincoln's assassination, Vice President Andrew Johnson became President. Johnson wanted to carry out Lincoln's plan for **Reconstruction**, the rebuilding and healing of the country. However, Johnson lacked Lincoln's skill at dealing with people. He and Congress fought fiercely.

Lincoln and Johnson wanted to pardon Southerners who swore loyalty to the United States and promised to obey the country's laws. They would also welcome states back into the Union if they outlawed slavery and asked to be let back in. Congress thought these plans were too gentle and felt that the South should be punished for having seceded. However, Congress did want to help newly freed African Americans, called freedmen.

Like much of the South, Richmond, Virginia, had been destroyed during the Civil War.

Congress and Reconstruction

The Republicans who controlled Congress didn't trust Johnson. He was a Southerner and had been a Democrat before becoming Lincoln's vice president. Members of Congress began developing a new plan of Reconstruction. They passed the Civil Rights Act of 1866 to grant freedmen full legal equality. Congress then passed several Reconstruction Acts between 1867 and 1868.

Vocabulary

Reconstruction	segregation
amendment	black codes
impeachment	sharecropping
carpetbaggers	

List in the empty box things that would need to be reconstructed after the war.

The Acts divided the former Confederate states into military districts. The President sent federal troops to the South to keep order and enforce emancipation of slaves. The Acts required Southern states to write new state constitutions giving African American men the right to vote. The Acts prevented former Confederate leaders from voting or holding elected office. Congress also passed three new amendments to the Constitution. An **amendment** is a change or addition. You will read about these amendments later in this lesson.

Johnson opposed many of Congress's actions. He argued that the Reconstruction Acts were against the law because they had been passed without the Southern states being represented in Congress. He said passing laws with half the country unrepresented was unconstitutional. Johnson used his veto power to try to stop Congress. However, Congress was able to override Johnson's vetoes. Congress continued to make its own plans.

Angry about Johnson's attempts to block their laws, the Republicans in Congress tried to impeach Johnson. **Impeachment** is the bringing of charges of wrongdoing against an elected official by the House of Representatives. If an impeached President is found guilty in a Senate trial, he can be removed from office. In May 1868 the Senate found Johnson not guilty. However, Johnson's ability to lead the nation had been seriously weakened.

1. **Write** who supported the idea in each part of the Venn diagram.

Wanted to give pardons | Wanted to reunite country | Wanted the South punished

Rebuilding the South

Reconstruction had many successes. The Freedmen's Bureau had been created by President Lincoln to help freed slaves and refugees of the war. Congress strengthened the Bureau to help the 4 million recently freed slaves.

The Freedmen's Bureau built schools and hospitals. It hired African American and white teachers from the South and North. New leaders raised taxes to help rebuild roads and railroads, and to establish a free education system. Many industries were expanded, to provide more jobs.

For the first time, African Americans became elected officials. In Mississippi, two African Americans were elected to the U.S. Senate. In 1870, Hiram R. Revels won the Senate seat that Jefferson Davis once held. In 1874, Blanche K. Bruce was elected to the Senate. Twenty other African Americans were elected to the House of Representatives.

Some Southerners resented the new state governments that had been forced on them. Others disliked the Northerners who moved South to start businesses. Because they often carried their possessions in cloth suitcases called carpetbags, these newcomers were called "**carpetbaggers.**" Some carpetbaggers came to help, but many came to take advantage of the South's ruined condition. Southerners who supported Reconstruction were given the insulting nickname "scalawags."

People also disliked the new taxes. Many Southerners had a hard time paying these taxes because they were trying to rebuild their farms and homes.

Reconstruction also had some failures; segregation was one of these. **Segregation** is the separation of people, usually by race. Schools, hospitals, theaters, railroad cars, even whole towns were segregated.

Right after the war, some Southern states passed **black codes.** These laws denied African American men the right to vote. It kept them from owning guns or taking certain types of jobs. The Civil Rights Act was designed to protect African Americans from these codes.

Schools were opened to help African Americans learn new skills.

2. Write why education is important for freedom.

....

....

....

....

....

....

New Amendments

Ending slavery was one of the first steps in Reconstruction—and the most important. The Emancipation Proclamation had not ended all slavery. The Republicans in Congress now wanted slavery to be illegal everywhere in the United States.

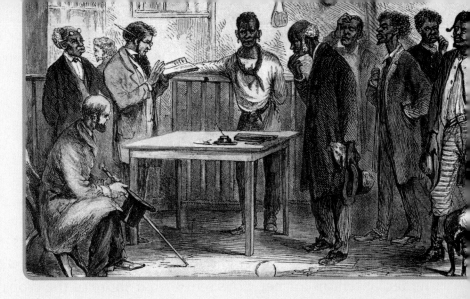

African American men voting

Congress passed the Thirteenth Amendment on January 31, 1865. It abolished slavery. The Fourteenth Amendment was approved in July 1868. It guaranteed equality under the law for all citizens—and it gave Congress the power to enforce this guarantee. It also ruled that important Confederate leaders could not be elected to political office.

The Fifteenth Amendment, passed by Congress in 1869 and approved by the states in February 1870, gave all male citizens the right to vote without regard to race. It was a big step forward for formerly enslaved African Americans.

Before being allowed back into the Union, former Confederate states had to accept all three amendments. Eventually, all did. By July 15, 1870, all the former Confederate states had been allowed back into the Union.

3. **◉ Summarize** what each of the three new amendments did.

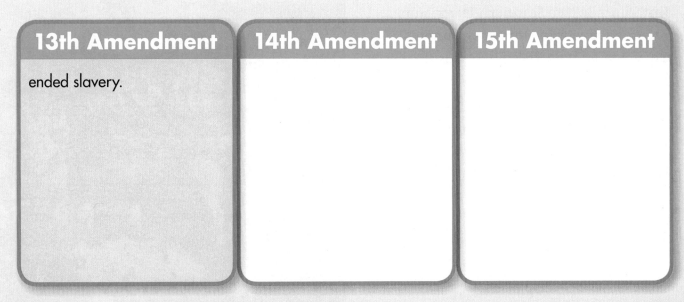

13th Amendment	14th Amendment	15th Amendment
ended slavery.		

After Reconstruction

After Reconstruction, the South remained the poorest section of the country. Rebuilding was slow. Poverty was widespread. African Americans lost much of the political power they had gained during Reconstruction. Northern whites began to lose interest in the problems of the South.

Many African Americans and poor whites in the South became trapped in a system called sharecropping. **Sharecropping** is a system in which someone who owns land lets someone else "rent" the land to farm it. The renter, or tenant farmer, pays rent with a share of the crops he or she raises. The renter then uses the rest of the crops to feed the family or sell for income.

In the South, sharecropping was run in a way that often kept people in debt. Landowners would charge high interest on money tenant farmers borrowed for seeds and tools. It was often impossible to pay off the debt. It was rare for sharecroppers to save enough to buy their own land.

Negative Reaction

During Reconstruction, some white Southerners objected to rights for African Americans. A few formed a group called the Ku Klux Klan. This group used terror to restore white control. They burned African American schools and homes. They attacked African Americans who tried to vote. Congress passed laws against the group and its activities. However, the Klan continued its activity for years.

In 1877, the federal government withdrew the last federal troops from the South. White Southern Democrats regained power in state governments. They passed new laws known as Jim Crow laws that reinforced segregation.

Other laws kept African Americans from voting. Some states charged a poll tax, or payment, to vote. Many African Americans couldn't afford the poll tax.

Many formerly enslaved people now worked as sharecroppers.

4. **Write** what a sharecropper might say about sharecropping.

....

....

....

....

....

Some states required African Americans to take a reading test before they could vote. Under slavery, many had not been allowed to learn to read or write, and so they failed the test.

A "grandfather clause" was added to some state constitutions. It said that men could vote only if their father or grandfather had voted before 1867. This "grandfather clause" kept most African Americans from voting, because they had not gained the right to vote until 1870. It would be a long time before most African Americans enjoyed the civil rights they should have as citizens.

Got it?

5. **Sequence Place** these events in the correct sequence on the timeline: 13th, 14th, and 15th Amendments, Civil Rights Act, first Reconstruction Act.

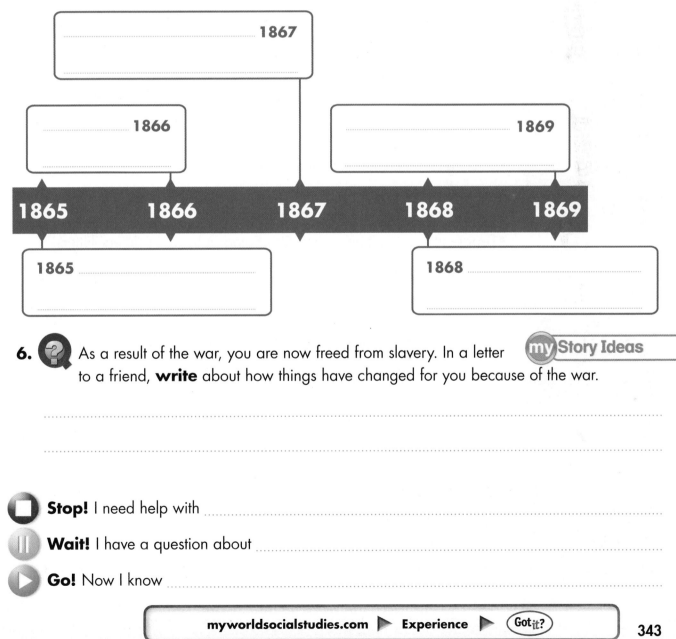

.... **1867**

.... **1866**

.... **1869**

| 1865 | 1866 | 1867 | 1868 | 1869 |

1865 ....

1868 ....

6. As a result of the war, you are now freed from slavery. In a letter to a friend, **write** about how things have changed for you because of the war.

my Story Ideas

....

....

Stop! I need help with ....

Wait! I have a question about ....

Go! Now I know ....

Study Guide

Lesson 1

Struggles Over Slavery

- The North and South disagreed sharply over the spread of slavery.
- The Underground Railroad helped enslaved people to escape from the South.
- Lincoln was elected President and Southern states seceded.

Lesson 2

The War Begins

- The Civil War began when the South attacked Fort Sumter.
- New tools and weapons were used in the Civil War.
- Battles at Antietam and elsewhere showed that the war would be bloodier and last longer than people expected.

Lesson 3

Life During the Civil War

- Lincoln issued the Emancipation Proclamation on January 1, 1863.
- African Americans, Native Americans, immigrants, and women contributed to the war in many ways.
- People at home got news through photographs and soldiers' letters.

Lesson 4

The War Ends

- Union victories at Gettysburg and Vicksburg were turning points.
- The costs of war grew with total war in the South.
- On April 9, 1865, Lee surrendered, and five days later Lincoln was assassinated.

Lesson 5

Reconstruction

- National leaders made different plans for Reconstruction.
- Congress passed laws to support newly freed African Americans.
- New Southern "Jim Crow" laws denied African Americans many rights.

Lesson 1

Struggles Over Slavery

1. How did the economies of the North and the South differ?

....

....

....

2. Write a sentence explaining the following:

a. Why people were concerned about new states coming into the Union

....

....

....

b. How the Missouri Compromise addressed this concern

....

....

3. What was the Underground Railroad?

....

....

4. What event led to Southern states seceding?

....

....

Lesson 2

The War Begins

5. How did the Civil War start?

....

....

6. What was the goal of the Anaconda Plan?

....

7. ◉ **Sequence** Use the numbers 1, 2, 3 to arrange the following events in time order.

_____ The First Battle of Bull Run

_____ The Battle of Antietam

_____ Southern states secede

Lesson 3

Life During the Civil War

8. Circle the letters that show what the Emancipation Proclamation did.

A. freed slaves in the Confederate states

B. ended slavery in the entire country

C. allowed slavery in the border states

D. ended the Civil War

9. What happened as a result of the Northern blockade of Southern ports?

....

....

....

Lesson 4

The War Ends

10. Give two reasons why the Battle of Gettysburg was important.

....

....

....

11. Sherman's approach to fighting became known as total war. What is total war?

....

....

....

....

12. **Complete** this Venn diagram to compare and contrast Lee and Grant.

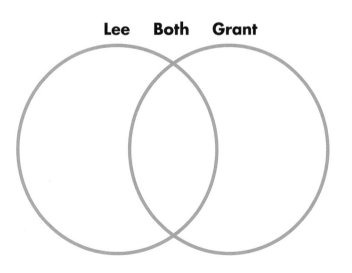

Lee   **Both**   **Grant**

Lesson 5

Reconstruction

13. **List** three effects of Reconstruction on the South.

a. ....

....

b. ....

....

c. ....

14. ? **What is worth fighting for?**

Use the question below to think more about the chapter's Essential Question.

What reason did each side have for going to war?

....

....

....

....

....

Go online to write and illustrate your own **myStory Book** using the **myStory Ideas** from this chapter.

What is worth fighting for?

After the Civil War, Americans counted their losses, including those who died in the war, the property destroyed, and the money it had cost. Yet for many Americans fighting for what they believed in was worth the cost.

Think about the challenges you face in doing the right thing. **Write** about how you know when something good is worth standing up for.

....

....

....

....

Not all fighting is done with weapons. Hard work and good deeds are other ways to fight. **Create** a poster that shares your opinion of something worth fighting for.

While you're online, check out the **myStory Current Events** area where you can create your own book on a topic that's in the news.

Expanding West and Overseas

THE BIG ?

How did different groups experience the growth of the nation?

Suppose that you could go back in time and travel across the United States in 1880. **Describe** what you see and the people you meet. Then **write** a diary entry about your experiences.

The railroad played an important role in settling the American West.

Homestead National Monument

A Tribute to American Pioneers

my Story Video

"That is one *old* cabin. It looks like it's going to fall down," says Laura. She's talking about the Palmer-Epard Cabin. "A family of *twelve* lived here?" she asks.

Today, Laura is touring the Homestead National Monument with Ranger Merrith Baughman. The national park is in Beatrice, Nebraska. It pays tribute to the Homestead Act of 1862.

"The cabin *is* awfully old, Laura. It was originally built in 1867, but it's not going to fall down," says Ranger Baughman. "It's been moved and restored several times. And, yes, a family of twelve lived in here."

The Palmer-Epard Cabin is actually larger than most homes back then, but is built of the same materials as other homesteader cabins, such as homemade bricks and different kinds of wood.

Laura stands in front of a real homesteader's cabin at the park.

349

Pioneers traveled west on foot, on horseback, and in Conestoga wagons like this one.

On the frontier, people had to make most things themselves. Here, Laura learns how homesteader women made butter.

"What is a homestead?" asks Laura.

"A homestead is 160 acres of public land granted to ordinary people for little money," replies the ranger. "If the families who were awarded homesteads could make a home on the land and remain there for five years, the land would be theirs."

Back in 1863, people came from all over to begin new lives in the United States. For people from Europe, the possibility of owning land was exciting. Land in Europe was scarce and expensive. Farmers in Europe often farmed land owned by others. "They had less freedom to use the land as they wished," explains Ranger Baughman. "Land ownership under the Homestead Act gave these farmers the chance to own their own land and control their own futures," she says.

"So what kind of people applied for homesteads?" asks Laura. The Homestead Act said only that you had to be 21 years of age or a head of a household. So, many people applied for homesteads: women, African Americans, and people who were not even U.S. citizens.

"It was pretty amazing that people who couldn't even vote had the opportunity to own their own land!" says the ranger.

Laura sits at a desk in a frontier schoolhouse. Often several grades were taught together in these schools.

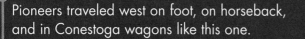

Before electric lights, many homesteaders also made their own candles.

The invention of steel plows, like this one, helped homesteaders to break up the grassy soil to plant crops.

The walking trails through the Freeman homestead wind through the beautiful landscape. The National Park Service has tried to restore this land to what it might have looked like in 1863. "Isn't it pretty?" exclaims Ranger Baughman.

With tall grass prairies and a creek flowing through, this was a great place to farm. In fact, the soils of this region in eastern Nebraska are some of the best in the world for farming.

As Laura and Ranger Baughman explore the exhibit of native plants, Laura asks, "What happened to all these native plants?"

The ranger answers, "When pioneers and farmers came to the prairies, they plowed the land to plant corn, wheat, and other crops. This exhibit shows the native plants that once grew here."

As Ranger Baughman and Laura make their way through the prairie, they finish up their tour at the Heritage Center. The interactive exhibits found here demonstrate how homesteading evolved and changed the landscape of the United States.

Immigration, agriculture, Native American life, and the local environment were all affected by the Homestead Act.

"So many different types of people . . . ," Laura thinks aloud as she explores, "all looking for the same things: freedom and a better life. I wonder what my family would have done?"

Think About It The growth of a nation affects everyone. As you read the chapter ahead, think about how different groups might have experienced the nation's growth in the 1800s. How might the experiences of these groups have been the same? How might they have differed?

Lesson 1

Railroads, Miners, and Ranchers

Envision It!

The Union Pacific and Central Pacific railroads connected in 1869, joining the east and west coasts for the first time.

It is 1860. There are crowded cities in the eastern part of the United States. Families came to these cities from Europe to find a better life. Now many people are deciding to move to the western plains to find more economic opportunity. It is a long, hard trip, but this journey will be the start of a new life.

The Movement From East to West

1. Circle the river that would take someone the farthest west. **Circle** the area that would be most difficult to cross by land.

While the eastern cities were crowded, the western United States offered people plenty of space to live and work. The West also had many resources. There was fertile farmland for growing wheat and other crops. The thick forests provided lumber, while the flat plains offered large grassy areas for grazing cattle. Miners could search for rich deposits of minerals, such as gold and silver.

Getting to the West was not easy, however. Most people went west by stagecoach or wagon, which were slow and dangerous ways to travel.

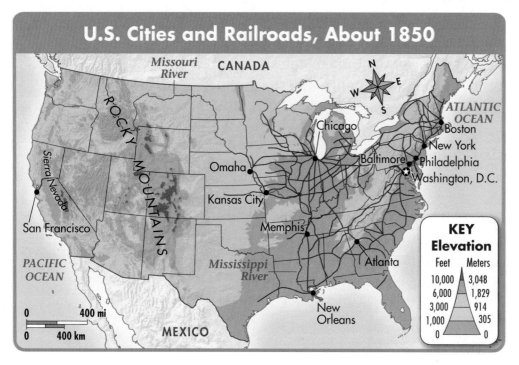

U.S. Cities and Railroads, About 1850

Missouri River

CANADA

ROCKY MOUNTAINS

Sierra Nevada

Chicago

ATLANTIC OCEAN

Boston

New York

Omaha

Baltimore

Philadelphia

Washington, D.C.

Kansas City

San Francisco

Memphis

PACIFIC OCEAN

Mississippi River

Atlanta

New Orleans

MEXICO

KEY
Elevation

Feet	Meters
10,000	3,048
6,000	1,829
3,000	914
1,000	305
0	0

0   400 mi

0   400 km

Write a newspaper headline about this event.

UNLOCK THE BIG

I will know how the expansion of the railroads changed American life.

Vocabulary

pioneer   gold rush
Manifest   cattle drive
  Destiny
transcontinental
  railroad

With so many resources, it's no wonder the federal government encouraged people to move west. These **pioneers,** or early settlers, included farmers, miners, ranchers, and immigrants such as Germans, Irish, and Jewish people from Eastern Europe. In addition, Mormon settlers moved to Salt Lake City, in what is now Utah. Many of these settlers believed in the idea of **Manifest Destiny.** According to this belief, the United States should keep expanding west, across the continent, to the Pacific Ocean.

The pioneers provided an important link between the cities in the East and the open land in the West. In the East, factory workers made goods, such as textiles, to sell to other countries. But these factories needed raw materials, such as lumber and minerals. At the same time, growing cities needed to feed their workers.

The much-needed food, lumber, and other important resources came from the West. But the pioneers soon faced a serious problem. How could they transport goods to the East more quickly? There was no railroad link between the Mississippi River Valley and the Pacific coast. That situation was about to change.

2. ◎ **Compare and Contrast Fill in** the boxes below to compare the resources in the West to the resources in the East.

U.S. Resources

Resources in the West	Resources in the East

A National Railroad System

Many people supported building a **transcontinental railroad**, one that stretched across the country. Congress passed the Pacific Railway Act of 1862, which gave the job of building the railroad to two companies. The Union Pacific Railroad Company would build a railroad west from Omaha, Nebraska. The Central Pacific Railroad Company would build a railroad east from Sacramento, California. The government paid the companies with money and land as they went. As a result, each one raced to finish first.

Many of the workers on both railroads were Chinese immigrants. Their skills with gunpowder made blasting tunnels through the mountains possible.

Four years later, workers from both companies completed the first transcontinental railroad. On May 10, 1869, the two lines joined at Promontory Point, Utah. To celebrate the event, a golden railroad spike was hammered into place. At long last, Americans could travel by rail from coast to coast.

3. Label the modern states that the transcontinental railroad crossed from Omaha to Sacramento.

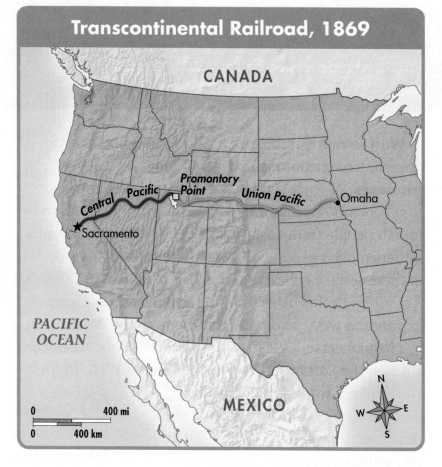

Transcontinental Railroad, 1869

CANADA

Central Pacific

Promontory Point

Union Pacific

Omaha

Sacramento

PACIFIC OCEAN

MEXICO

0   400 mi

0   400 km

N E S W

Trains like this one linked the Mississippi River Valley with the West Coast.

100TH MERIDIAN
247 MILES FROM OMAHA

Mining in the West

The 1849 **gold rush** attracted people to California who wanted to find gold and become rich. Ten years later, more gold was discovered throughout the West. Miners also discovered silver, zinc, copper, and lead.

Sometimes miners' tools were very simple. Some miners shook a tin pan filled with soil and water. With luck, heavier pieces of gold sank to the bottom. New technology also provided tools that improved miners' work. Miners used large amounts of water to separate gold from the soil. Machines, such as the water wheel shown at right, could deliver water up to the stream bank where miners shoveled soil. No matter what process was used, mining was difficult and often dangerous.

Some miners did become rich. Most did not. But large-scale mining damaged the land. For example, drilling created rock dust. Dumping this rock dust into rivers polluted the water and ruined towns and farms.

Often miners and farmers disagreed about the effects of mining on the land. Farmers were worried because certain types of mining destroyed the soil. Mining released poisonous gases into the air. To remove gold, miners used a metal called mercury. Too much mercury poisoned streams and rivers.

4. **Explain** how this water wheel helped improve the work of gold miners.

....

....

....

....

Cowboys and Ranchers

Cattle raised in the West provided beef for people living in the growing eastern cities. At the end of the Civil War, millions of cattle grazed freely across the open Texas plains. The land was better suited for ranching than for farming. But there was one problem. How could ranchers get their cattle to market?

In 1867, the Kansas Pacific Railroad helped solve this problem. The company built a rail line to Abilene, Kansas. After that, cowboys guided huge herds of cattle to Kansas. Then they sold the cattle to buyers from the East, who shipped the herds on the railroad to meat-packing plants in Chicago and eastern cities.

By the 1880s, waves of settlers pushed farther west across the plains, setting up farms. Meanwhile, the new Santa Fe Railroad helped ranches expand farther west. Soon farmers and ranchers were competing fiercely for land in the Southwest.

The Impact of the Railroads

The growing railroad system changed life across America. Raw materials from the West now shipped more quickly to factories and ports in the East. Cowboys no longer guided herds of cattle to market along dusty trails. Now these **cattle drives** ended at railroad towns, where the cattle were carried by train to Chicago and to the coasts. At the same time, railroads carried products made in eastern factories to cities and towns in the West.

Of course, the many new railroads carried people, too. For the first time, passengers could travel by train across the country. Bad weather could no longer slow their trips. Travelers and business people were eager to move by train. After 1869 at least one train from the East and one train from the West ran across the entire country each week.

Train travel helped the West to develop more quickly. More and more Americans lived west of the Mississippi, and more states joined the Union. By 1900 only three western territories remained— Oklahoma, Arizona, and New Mexico. Every month new settlers traveled west by rail to build new lives. They farmed areas with rich land and a good water supply. At the same time, railroads helped other industries develop too. These included the lumber and mining industries.

5. Nat Love was a famous African American cowboy. **Circle** three things in this picture that give clues about what he did for a living.

6. ◉ **Cause and Effect**
By 1920, westward expansion had given Americans access to many resources. In the key, **circle** five resources made accessible to the East by the railroads.

Resources of the United States by 1920

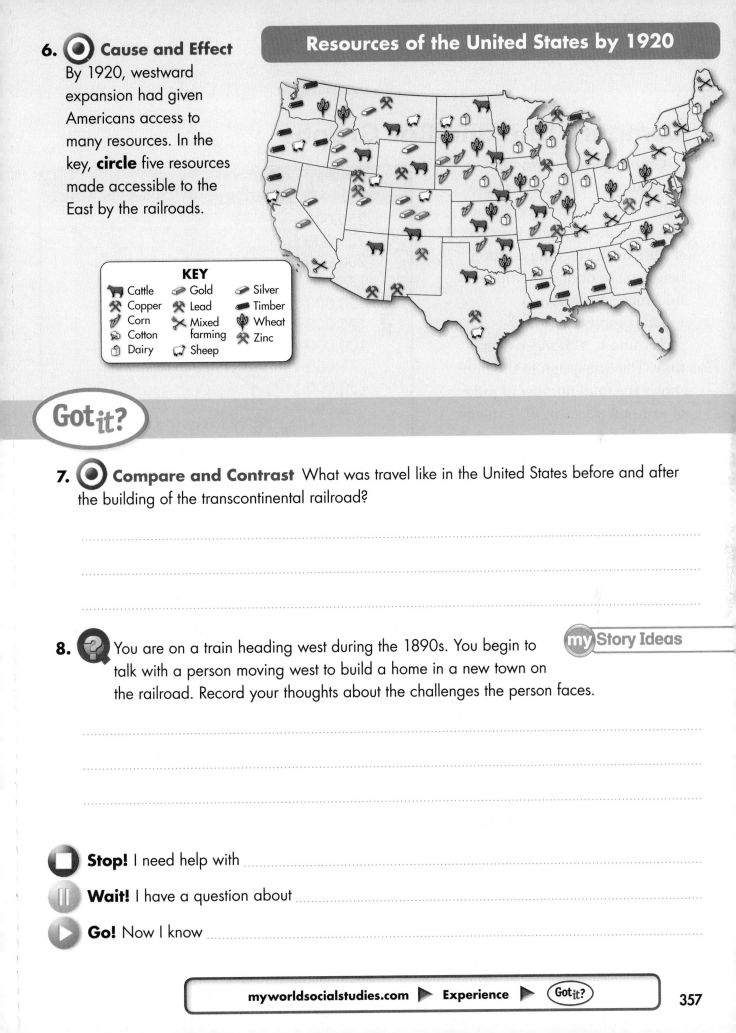

KEY

🐄 Cattle	Gold	Silver
✗ Copper	✗ Lead	Timber
🌱 Corn	✗ Mixed farming	🌾 Wheat
Cotton		Zinc
Dairy	Sheep	

Got it?

7. ◉ **Compare and Contrast** What was travel like in the United States before and after the building of the transcontinental railroad?

....

....

....

8. ❓ You are on a train heading west during the 1890s. You begin to talk with a person moving west to build a home in a new town on the railroad. Record your thoughts about the challenges the person faces.

my Story Ideas

....

....

....

⏹ **Stop!** I need help with ....

⏸ **Wait!** I have a question about ....

▶ **Go!** Now I know ....

Compare Line and Bar Graphs

Graphs show information in a visual way. They help you to better understand facts in what you read, including in your social studies book. Reading a graph helps you to analyze complex information quickly.

Line graphs show how something has changed over time. The line graph to the right shows the total number of miles of railroad tracks in the United States. It presents this information over a period of time, from 1860 to 1910. It helps you see how railroads changed in the United States during this period. Each section of the line shows a change between years.

Bar graphs help you compare the different sizes or amounts of something by analyzing the size of each bar. Look at the bar graph to the right. It shows the miles of railroad track in different parts of the United States in one year, 1870. The numbers on the left side of the graph show the number of miles of track. The labels on the bottom of the graph show a different region of the country. Each bar represents a different region.

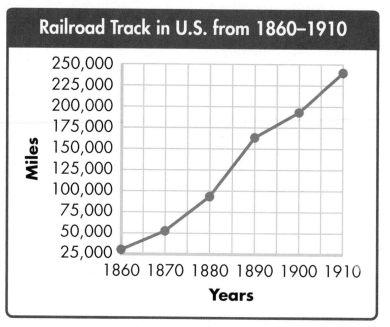

Source: Davis, Hughes, McDougal, *American Economic History.*

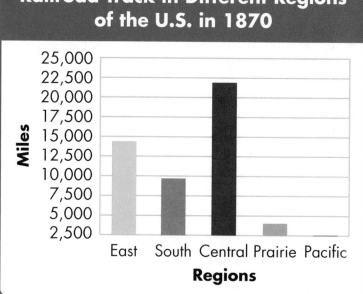

Source: *Historical Statistics,* Series Q 32.

1. Between 1860 and 1880, about how many miles of railroad track were built in the United States? ....

2. Between 1880 and 1900, about how many miles of railroad track were built in the United States? ....

3. Suppose that you wanted to travel by rail in the United States. Could you travel to more places in 1890 or 1860? Explain.

   ....

   ....

4. Study the line graph. What is one generalization you can make about the data in this graph?

   ....

   ....

5. Now look at the bar graph.
   - What part of the country had the highest number of railroad miles in 1870? ....

   - What part of the country had the lowest number of railroad miles in 1870? ....

6. **Apply** Suppose you made a graph recording the amount of rainfall in your community each day for one week. Which type of graph would help you more easily find the day with the most rain? Explain your answer.

   ....

   ....

   ....

Lesson 2

Sodbusters and Homesteaders

Envision It!

RICH FARMING LANDS!
ON THE LINE OF THE
Union Pacific Railroad
Located in the GREAT CENTRAL BELT of POPULATION, COMMERCE and WEALTH, and adjoining the WORLD'S HIGHWAY from OCEAN TO OCEAN.

12,000,000 ACRES
3,000,000 Acres in Central and Eastern Nebraska, in the Platte Valley, now for
We invite the attention of all parties seeking

2,000,000 FARMS of Fertile Prairie Lands to be had Free of Cost

CENTRAL DAKOTA

30 Millions OF Acres

YOU NEED A FARM!

Nineteenth-century railroad posters urged people to settle the West.

A pioneer family stood alone on the Great Plains, looking at miles of flat, empty, wind-swept grassland that stretched far into the distance. They were eager to begin living their dream. What would their future be like?

160 Acres!

To encourage settlers to move west to the Great Plains and to areas beyond, President Abraham Lincoln signed the **Homestead Act** of 1862. Under this law, new settlers received 160 acres of land for a small fee—$18.00. **Homesteaders** also had to build a home on their land within six months. After living there for five years, the land would be theirs.

The federal government hoped the new settlers would turn the West into productive farmland. The land offered in the Homestead Act appealed to Americans and immigrants alike. Immigrants from Sweden, Norway, Denmark, Germany, and Russia wanted to become American farmers, too. They brought their languages, customs, and traditions to their new homes.

1. **Write** one question you might ask this Nebraska homestead family.

....

....

....

UNLOCK THE BIG ?

I will know what it was like to be a homesteader in the 19th-century West.

Vocabulary

Homestead Act   irrigation
homesteader   dry farming
drought   sodbuster

Write why people might move across the country today. Why did they move across the country in the late 1800s?

Homesteading was hard work. Prairie land was flat and open, with few trees, and the thick grass could grow six feet tall. In the summer it was blazing hot. Fierce rain, windstorms, and swarms of grasshoppers could destroy crops. Often, severe **droughts** meant long periods without rain. During the winter, blizzards sometimes trapped people under the deep snow. The freezing cold killed many farm animals.

These hardy pioneers built their homes near hills to protect them from the strong prairie winds. It was also important to live near a railroad. Farmers wanted an easy way to transport their crops and cattle to market.

2. ◎ **Compare and Contrast Complete** the Venn diagram to compare life in your community today with homesteading on the plains in the 1860s.

Comparing Homes

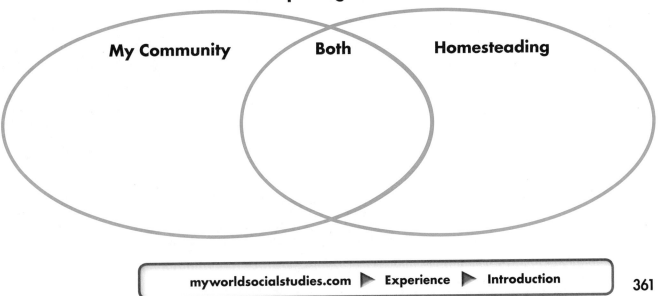

My Community   Both   Homesteading

Adapting to the Environment

Settlers learned to adapt, or change, so that they could live in their new homes. For example, farther west, the land became much dryer, and many kinds of wheat did not grow well there. But immigrants from Russia brought a new kind of winter wheat that could grow better in dry land.

How could farmers find enough water for their crops? Some tapped into the underground supply of water and used irrigation. **Irrigation** directs water from a source to a place that needs it. In one system, pumps gathered water into a pond. Then the water ran through irrigation ditches to the fields.

Other homesteaders used a farming method called **dry farming.** With this method, farmers conserved moisture in the soil during dry weather.

The settlers on the prairie were called **sodbusters** because they had to cut through the thickly rooted grass, or sod, to build their homes and plant crops. Cutting sod bricks was hard work, and building a sod house could take many weeks. Often, settlers built a small, dark shelter into the side of a hill to live in while they built their houses. Sometimes, as the family did in the photo, they built their home right around the original shelter.

McCormick mechanical reaper

Deere steel plow

1830   1840   1850

To build a sod house, settlers cut the sod into bricks. It took 3,000 sod bricks to build a small house. To make the roof, settlers used cedar poles to hold up bundles of mud, grass, and more sod.

Sod houses were not very clean and they were a bit damp. But sod is an excellent insulation. Sod homes were cool in the summer and warm in the winter. Since they were made from dirt, they were even fireproof.

Many homesteaders adapted the land to their own needs. But some could not adapt. Harsh weather, accidents, and sickness were serious problems. Living on the Great Plains could be very lonely, especially during the winter. Some homesteaders gave up and went home, while others moved on to the growing cities on the West Coast.

Settlers built their sodhouses against hills for protection from the weather.

Farming on the Great Plains

Sometimes farmers adapted to their new life by using natural resources. Other times, they used new technology. Inventors built new kinds of machines to help settlers farm their land and keep their crops safe.

Iron plows used in the East didn't work very well in the Midwest. The rich soil stuck to the bottom of the plow. To solve this problem, in 1837 John Deere built a stronger plow made of steel. Another inventor, James Oliver, made a new kind of iron plow in 1869. This plow was less expensive and was long lasting. Best of all, farmers could use it in any kind of soil. Another important farm machine, the mechanical reaper, was invented by Cyrus McCormick in 1831. Large horses pulled the reaper across the fields. Now farmers could harvest crops much faster.

Farmers on the Great Plains faced yet another problem. How could they protect their crops from animals or keep their animals from wandering away? Farmers needed strong fences, but there were few trees or large stones available. To solve this problem, Joseph Glidden invented barbed wire in 1873. Farmers now had a way of enclosing their fields. They could also fence in their cattle.

3. Draw a line to connect each invention to the year when it was invented. **Write** a title for the timeline.

Glidden barbed wire

| 1860 | 1870 | 1880 |

"From Sea to Shining Sea"

Wave after wave of homesteaders pushed across the land toward the Pacific Ocean. By 1900 they had filed claims to own 80 million acres of land. The population of the western United States grew by almost 30 percent. Between 1861 and 1907, seven western territories became states: Kansas (1861), Nebraska (1867), Colorado (1876), North Dakota (1889), South Dakota (1889), Montana (1889), and Oklahoma (1907).

To encourage further settlement, the federal government offered free land in Oklahoma in 1889. People from all across the country traveled there by railroad and wagon. On the morning of April 22, an excited crowd of settlers waited for the signal. At noon, soldiers fired pistols in the air. Then thousands of men and women surged forward to claim their free homesteads.

The Oklahoma land rushes beginning in 1889 helped close the western frontier. By 1890 the United States no longer had a frontier. A new stage in U.S. history was beginning.

4. **Write** two ways in which the settled areas shown on the maps changed between 1850 and 1890.

....

....

....

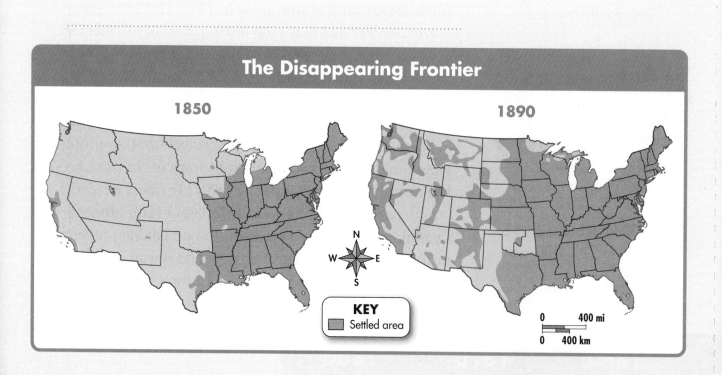

The Disappearing Frontier

1850   1890

KEY
Settled area

0   400 mi
0   400 km

5. Describe how this painting connects with the idea of Manifest Destiny.

....

....

....

....

....

....

....

....

This painting, titled American Progress, was painted by John Gast in 1872.

Got it?

6. ◉ **Make Generalizations** What was one way that homesteaders changed the West?

....

....

7. ❓ On one of the Great Plains homesteads you pass on your train, a farmer is harvesting a huge field of wheat, far more wheat than any family could eat. **Write** an explanation about where all that wheat might go.

my Story Ideas

....

....

....

⬛ **Stop!** I need help with ....

❙❙ **Wait!** I have a question about ....

▶ **Go!** Now I know ....

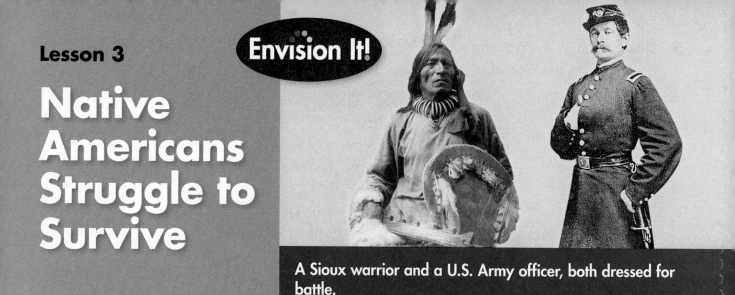

Native Americans Struggle to Survive

Envision It!

A Sioux warrior and a U.S. Army officer, both dressed for battle.

Native Americans had lived on their lands for centuries. At first, a few settlers began to travel onto Native American lands on horseback or by wagon. Then, the transcontinental railroad was built. Soon, thousands of homesteaders were building new homes on the Great Plains and beyond. As more settlers moved west, conflicts with Native Americans increased.

Who Owns the Land?

Native Americans and settlers viewed land ownership differently. Native Americans had a close link to the land and everything on it. Lakota Sioux Chief Crazy Horse said, "One does not sell the land people walk on." He meant that Native Americans did not believe they owned the land. Instead, they respected the natural world and used its resources to provide for their families. For example, Native Americans living on the Great Plains hunted and gathered food. Their homes, called **tepees,** were constructed of wood poles, bark, and animal skins.

Unlike the Native Americans, settlers wanted to own their land. The U.S. government said that after living in their new homes for five years, the land belonged to the settlers.

1. This Native American family of the plains lived in a tepee. **Circle** the parts of the tepee that are made with natural resources.

Same
Different

Describe how the Sioux warrior and the U.S. Army officer are the same and different.

Vocabulary

tepee

reservation

The End of the Buffalo

For centuries, Native Americans on the Great Plains had depended on buffalo for food, clothing, and shelter. No part of a buffalo went to waste. Even the horns became spoons and bowls. Native Americans of the Plains hunted buffalo without destroying the large herds. In 1865, around 15 million buffalo still roamed the West.

When the new settlers arrived, they killed millions of buffalo for their meat and their hides. Eastern hunters shot many at a time for sport. These hunters often also sold the hides of the buffalo they killed.

By 1889, fewer than 1,000 buffalo were left in the United States. The destruction of this precious resource angered Native Americans and hurt their way of life. It also deepened the conflict between the two groups.

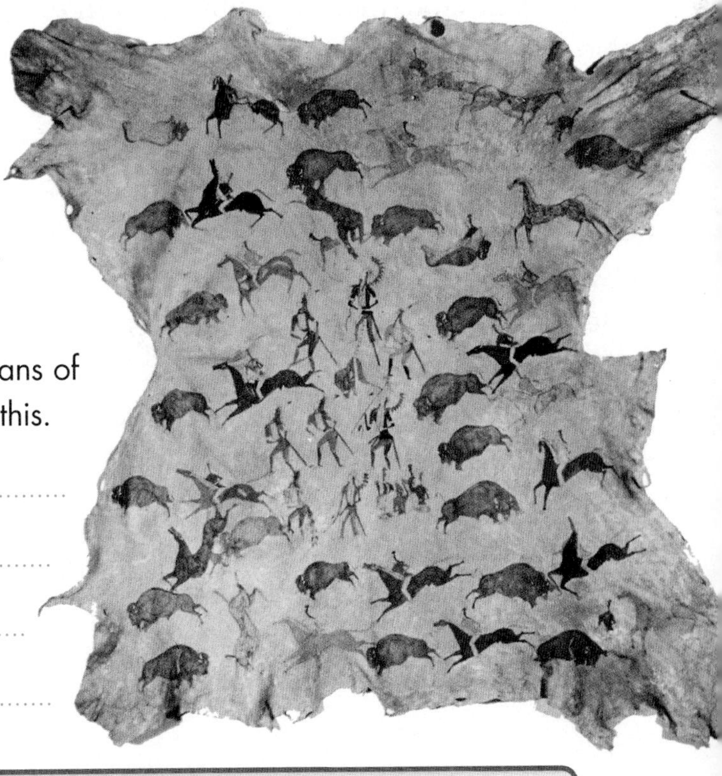

2. **Write** how this buffalo hide shows how important the buffalo was to Native Americans of the Plains. **Circle** the details that show you this.

....

....

....

....

A Growing Conflict

In the early 1800s, Native Americans' rights to large areas of land were unchallenged. Native Americans did what they could to live peacefully with the settlers. Then, in 1828, gold was discovered on Cherokee land in Georgia. Suddenly, this Native American land was very valuable. How could settlers take possession of it?

In 1830, Congress passed the Indian Removal Act. Under this law, the U.S. government gave Native Americans unsettled prairie land. This would become new Indian Territory. Native American groups living east of the Mississippi River, like the Cherokee, were forced to give up their own, more valuable land in exchange.

3. In this photo, Navajo Chief Black Horse, right, and a white missionary are shaking hands. **Write** what they might be agreeing about.

....

....

....

No one asked the Native Americans what they thought about this exchange. From their perspective, why should they leave their villages and farms to travel to this new Indian Territory? Some groups fought the new law in court, but were not successful. Others refused to leave and tried to defend their land.

Between 1830 and 1840, U.S. troops forced 100,000 Native Americans from their homes. Most walked 800 miles to Indian Territory in present-day Oklahoma. More than 4,000 people died on the journey, which is called the Trail of Tears.

4. Why do you think this journey is called the Trail of Tears?

....

....

The Reservation System

After the end of the Civil War, the U.S. government began to pay close attention to western settlement. Leaders wanted Native Americans to relocate to areas of land called **reservations.** To move there, Native American groups had to give up their own land. In exchange, the government said they would pay them in cash, livestock, and supplies. But the government was not always true to its word, and reservation land was usually different from traditional lands. A reservation was often much smaller. Also, it was far away from the group's original home. It might also have completely different resources.

Native Americans from the plains found life on reservations very different from their old ways. For centuries they had followed herds of buffalo. Now they had to stay in one place. Trying to raise crops on the reservation was difficult because the land was often not suitable for farming.

Also, Native Americans did not have many legal rights on a reservation. Their children could be taken away and sent to boarding schools. Were they loyal to the government? If someone suspected they weren't, they could be arrested.

How did the U.S. government keep Native Americans on the reservations? United States soldiers handled that job with military force that eventually led to war.

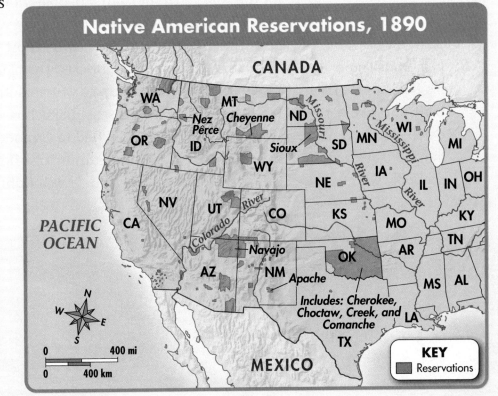

Native American Reservations, 1890

5. Answer the questions about the map.

a. In what states is the Sioux Reservation? ....

b. What river borders the Navajo Reservation on the west? ....

c. What New Mexico reservation is closest to Mexico? ....

Thirty Years of War

From the end of the Civil War to the 1890s, battles raged between Native Americans and the U.S. Army. In 1864, U.S. troops attacked Cheyenne (shye-AN) people living in Sandy Creek, Colorado. Soldiers killed about 400 Cheyenne.

The Sioux (soo) believe that the Black Hills of Dakota are sacred, or spiritually important. When gold was found in the Black Hills, miners rushed there. The result was war.

In 1876, Colonel George Custer led his soldiers against a band of Sioux led by Chief Sitting Bull. The battle took place at the Little Big Horn River in Montana Territory. At the Battle of the Little Big Horn, Colonel Custer and more than 200 U.S. soldiers were killed. The battle was an important victory for Native Americans. But soon the U.S. government sent many more troops to the West to fight.

In 1855, the United States had created a large reservation for the Nez Perce (nez purs) people that included most of the tribe's land in Oregon. But when gold was discovered there, the government wanted to take away most of the new reservation.

In 1877, U.S. soldiers attacked the Nez Perce leader Chief Joseph and a small group of warriors; the Nez Perce War began. For the next five months, soldiers chased Chief Joseph and his people 700 miles as they fled to Canada. But Chief Joseph did not want his people to continue to suffer. With great sadness he finally surrendered, saying, "I will fight no more forever."

6. In this painting of the Battle of the Little Big Horn, **circle** a detail that shows that the Sioux will probably win.

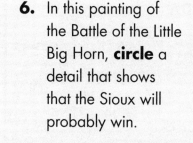

Other Native American Leaders

Sitting Bull had become the principal Sioux chief in 1867. He helped his people by extending their hunting grounds to the west. At the Battle of the Little Big Horn, Sitting Bull led his warriors to victory. After the battle, he and his followers escaped to Canada, but he later returned to the United States. In December 1890, Sitting Bull was killed when reservation police tried to arrest him.

Another Sioux leader, Crazy Horse, had been fighting to preserve his people's way of life since he was a teenager. He fought at the Battle of the Little Big Horn and spent the next winter attacking and being chased by U.S. soldiers during the Great Sioux War. In 1877, he surrendered and was killed by a soldier who claimed Crazy Horse was trying to escape.

The great Apache leader Geronimo (juh-RAHN-ih-moh) was born in Mexico in 1820. In the early 1870s, he and his warriors successfully fought the U.S. Army. The last stage of the Apache wars began in April 1886. More than 5,000 soldiers tracked Geronimo and his followers to their camp in northern Mexico. Geronimo surrendered in September. He died in 1909.

Chief Joseph

7. ◎ **Compare and Contrast**
How were the results of war for Chief Joseph and Geronimo similar?

....

....

....

....

8. Fill in this chart with information about Native American leaders from these two pages.

Native American Leaders

Leader	Group	Actions	Date
Sitting Bull	Sioux	Battle of Little Big Horn	1876
Crazy Horse			
Chief Joseph			
Geronimo			

The Armed Conflict Ends

On December 29, 1890, soldiers attacked a group of Sioux warriors and their families at Wounded Knee, South Dakota. At the time, the warriors were trying to give up their weapons, but U.S. soldiers killed more than 150 of them, including women, children, and the elderly. The battle at Wounded Knee brought the wars between Native Americans and the United States government to a sad and bloody end.

By 1900, most Native Americans lived on reservations in the West. Reservation life remained difficult. It changed Native American cultures and weakened their traditions.

The U.S. government passed a new law in 1885. Under this law, each Native American family received 160 acres of land to farm. After 25 years of living on these acres, the land owners would become U.S. citizens.

9. A Sioux family poses at the Pine Ridge Reservation in South Dakota. **Circle** three items in the photo that show traditional Native American culture. **Write** why you think it was important to Native Americans to maintain their culture on the reservations.

....

....

Many Native American leaders opposed the law. They believed that it would destroy their cultures by attempting to make them more like white people. Also, the law opened up even more Native American land to white settlers.

Sadly, the leaders were right. Native Americans faced many problems trying to become farmers. By 1900, the size of reservation land was reduced further due to new settlement. The traditional cultures of Native Americans were badly damaged.

This monument stands on the site of the battle at Wounded Knee.

Got it?

10. ⊙ **Cause and Effect** What was an important effect of western settlement on Native American people?

....

....

....

11. ❓ As you pass by new communities, you speak to a Native American going to a reservation to see family members. **Write** about her views on how the West has changed.

my Story Ideas

....

....

....

◻ **Stop!** I need help with ....

⏸ **Wait!** I have a question about ....

▷ **Go!** Now I know ....

Study Guide

Lesson 1

Railroads, Miners, and Ranchers

- The United States government encouraged westward migration.
- The transcontinental railroad linked the east and west coasts of the United States.
- Miners and ranchers used the western lands for different purposes.

Lesson 2

Sodbusters and Homesteaders

- The Homestead Act of 1862 encouraged Americans and immigrants to move to the Great Plains.
- Homesteaders adapted to the harsh environment of the Midwest.
- New inventions improved farming and ranching.

Lesson 3

Native Americans Struggle to Survive

- Conflicts between Native Americans and settlers developed over the use of western lands.
- Conflicts led to wars between Native Americans and the U.S. Army.
- Native Americans were removed from their lands to reservations.

Lesson 4

Expanding Overseas

- After the Spanish-American War, the United States gained new territory and became a world power.
- The Panama Canal created a faster sea route from coast to coast.
- The United States acquired Alaska and Hawaii during the later 1800s.

Review and Assessment

Lesson 1

Railroads, Miners, and Ranchers

1. What is one reason why people from the eastern United States moved west during the 1800s?

2. ◎ **Compare and Contrast**
Compare and contrast settlement in the West before and after the completion of the transcontinental railroad.

3. **Write** a sentence explaining why each of the following terms was important to United States expansion west.

a. gold rush

b. Transcontinental Railroad

Lesson 2

Sodbusters and Homesteaders

4. How did the Homestead Act affect settlement on the Great Plains?

5. What is one way that settlers adapted to the environment in the Midwest?

6. How do you think farmers reacted to the invention of the new iron plow in 1869?

Review and Assessment

Lesson 3

Native Americans Struggle to Survive

7. **Circle** the correct answer.
   Who led Native Americans to victory at the Battle of the Little Big Horn?

   A. Chief Joseph

   B. Sitting Bull

   C. Geronimo

   D. Black Horse

8. What was life like for Native Americans before and after they were moved to reservations?

   ....
   ....
   ....
   ....
   ....
   ....
   ....
   ....
   ....
   ....

Lesson 4

Expanding Overseas

9. How did the United States expand its trading power in the nineteenth and early twentieth centuries?

   ....
   ....
   ....
   ....
   ....
   ....

10. **How did different groups experience the growth of the nation?**

    a. What did the idea of Manifest Destiny mean to settlers?

       ....
       ....
       ....

    b. What did settlers' ideas about Manifest Destiny mean to Native Americans?

       ....
       ....
       ....

Go online to write and illustrate your own **myStory Book** using the **myStory Ideas** from this chapter.

How did different groups experience the growth of the nation?

During the late 1800s, the United States economy grew quickly. This growth depended in part on the rich resources of the West. The strong economy supplied jobs and homes for many people. Yet the growth had other effects as well, and some people suffered during this time.

Think about the way the growth of the West affected Native Americans. **Write** about whether the country could have grown without causing harm to their nations and lands.

....

....

....

Now **draw** a sketch for a poster that might have persuaded settlers to get along better with Native Americans in their area.

While you're online, check out the **myStory Current Events** area where you can create your own book on a topic that's in the news.

Inventors and Inventions

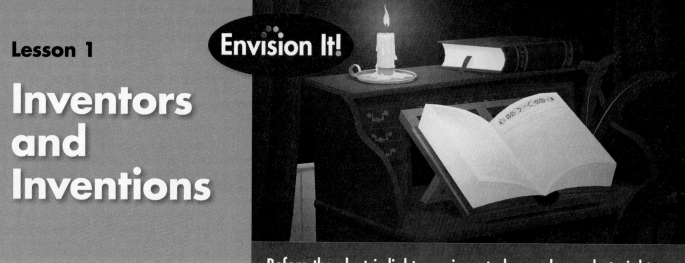

Envision It!

Before the electric light was invented, people read at night by the light of a fire, a candle, or a gas or oil lamp.

1. **Draw Conclusions** **Write** a conclusion you can draw from the information in this chart.

....

....

....

....

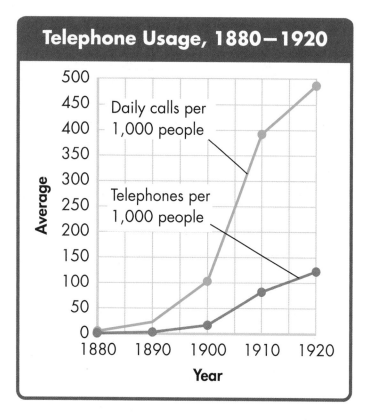

Telephone Usage, 1880–1920

Daily calls per 1,000 people

Telephones per 1,000 people

Average

500
450
400
350
300
250
200
150
100
50
0

1880   1890   1900   1910   1920

Year

The late 1800s was an exciting time. The United States had become a major economic power. In Chicago, Illinois, the first skyscrapers were built. More and more Americans were becoming consumers. A **consumer** is someone who buys or uses goods and services.

Scientists and inventors were creating things that would have a huge impact on the country. And consumers were ready to buy those things.

In 1867 Christopher Sholes invented the first practical typewriter. He also developed the keyboard arrangement we use today. By 1874, typewriters were available in stores.

Inventions such as the typewriter quickly became popular. It was among many inventions that changed life during this period.

Some scientists and inventors looked for ways to feed the growing population. African-American scientist George Washington Carver got Southerners to grow peanuts and sweet potatoes, and he developed many uses for these crops.

UNLOCK
THE BIG
?

I will know that Americans developed new inventions that changed life in the United States and around the world.

Vocabulary
. . . .

consumer

telegraph

investor

profit

Why do you think people came to depend on electric light at night?

New Ways to Communicate

In the mid-1800s, Samuel Morse had invented the **telegraph.** This device sent little bursts of electricity along wires. Morse developed a code based on short bursts (dots) and longer bursts (dashes). The telegraph used this code, called Morse code, to send messages quickly. Americans used the telegraph system for the first time in May 1844.

During the mid- to late-1800s, investors helped develop new inventions. An **investor** is someone who puts money into a business to make a profit. **Profit** is the money an investor earns when the business does well. One investor, Cyrus Field, started a company to lay a telegraph cable across the Atlantic Ocean. It was difficult. But by July 1866, the transatlantic cable made it possible to send telegraph messages to Europe.

Alexander Graham Bell was a teacher. He trained teachers of hearing-impaired students in Boston, Massachusetts. He also worked on a device that would send sound through wires. On March 10, 1876, Bell and his assistant, Thomas Watson, were testing this first telephone. Bell claimed that he called Watson for help using his new machine: "Mr. Watson, come here. I want to see you." This exchange was the first telephone call.

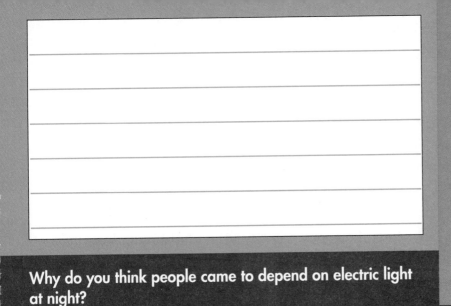

Alexander Graham Bell speaks into one of his telephones.

2. **Explain** why telephones attracted investors.

....

....

Edison's Bright Idea

Thomas Alva Edison introduced the world to a lot of new inventions. Edison set up a research laboratory in Menlo Park, New Jersey, in 1876. He worked with a team of young scientists to solve problems. His was the first research lab of its kind. In 1877, Edison invented a machine that could record sounds and play them back. It was called a phonograph. The phonograph made Edison famous. People called him the Wizard of Menlo Park.

Two years later, Edison made a working light bulb. Inventors had tried for years to make a light bulb that would remain bright for more than a few minutes. At first, Edison couldn't find the right material for the filament—the tiny wire inside the bulb that glows when the light is turned on. Finally, he tried a carbon filament. It worked. On December 3, 1879, he showed his light bulb to the investors of the Edison Electric Light Company.

Edison's light bulb was a great success. However, it would only burn for a few days. An African-American inventor named Lewis Latimer improved the light bulb so it would burn longer. Edison was so impressed, he asked Latimer to join his team.

Before electric lights, people used candles, kerosene, or oil lamps for light at night. But Edison and Latimer's work made the world brighter.

Edison also gave the world movies. In 1888, Edison and another scientist invented a movie camera. They also invented a device for viewing the movies. Edison never stopped inventing. Working alone or with others, he created 1,093 inventions, a world record.

3. Write the name of the invention and the name of the inventor next to the date of the invention.

American Inventions, 1840–1900

1844
telegraph
Samuel Morse

1867

1840   1850   1860   1870

1866
transatlantic cable
Cyrus Field

The Impact of Electricity

Edison had to find a way of getting electricity into homes and businesses. On September 4, 1882, he opened the first electric power station in the United States at Pearl Street in New York City. Electricity produced there traveled through wires to nearby buildings.

At first, the Pearl Street station served just 59 customers. But Americans wanted electricity. Nikola Tesla, a Serbian immigrant, developed the type of electricity that we use today. In 1884, he sold his invention to George Westinghouse, Edison's biggest competitor. Soon, power stations opened in many American cities.

By the 1890s, electric power stations were set up throughout the country. Electricity powered streetlights and electric trolley cars. Inventors created new machines that ran on electric power. Small, private electric companies began to merge into bigger ones. These large companies could create electricity more cheaply. As the cost of electricity dropped, more and more people used it.

Electric lights brighten New York City around 1908.

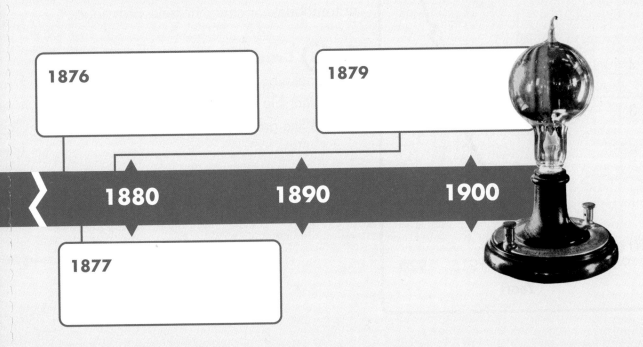

1876	1879

1880 1890 1900

1877

New Ways to Travel

In 1832, people in New York City had a new way to get around. Instead of coaches that bumped along rough streets, they could now ride in streetcars that ran on smooth, steel railroad tracks. Like a coach, a streetcar was pulled by horses, but the tracks made the ride more comfortable and faster. People called this streetcar a horsecar. Riders paid about ten cents for a ride. Horsecars traveled about six to eight miles per hour. Like buses, they made regular stops. They became very popular. By the mid-1880s, more than 400 companies around the nation were carrying 188 million passengers a year over more than 6,000 miles of "street rail" track.

In 1887, Julian Sprague developed a streetcar system in Richmond, Virginia. Sprague's streetcar, or trolley, was half the size of a modern bus. It was powered by electricity. Rides cost only a nickel. An electric streetcar could travel up to 20 miles per hour. Americans liked them better than horsecars. By 1903, there were 30,000 miles of street rail tracks in the United States, and electric trolleys ran on almost all of them.

In 1886, Charles Duryea saw a gasoline engine at the Ohio State Fair. The engine seemed small enough for a carriage or wagon. That sparked an idea. He and his brother built a car with an engine in their Springfield, Massachusetts, workshop. On September 22, 1893, they drove this early car for the first time. People called the first automobiles, or cars, "horseless carriages."

Horse-drawn wagons had to share the road with the new streetcars known as horsecars.

4. **◉ Draw Conclusions Write** a conclusion you can draw about car ownership based on the information in the line graph.

....

....

....

....

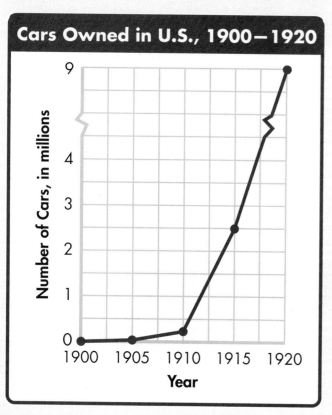

Cars Owned in U.S., 1900—1920

Number of Cars, in millions

9
4
3
2
1
0

1900　1905　1910　1915　1920

Year

Airplanes and Flight

Using trains and trolleys, people were now traveling more quickly. Soon, two American inventors would take to the skies. Brothers Wilbur and Orville Wright ran a bicycle repair shop in Dayton, Ohio. But they dreamed of building a flying machine.

The Wright brothers experimented with kites to learn more about how wings worked. In October 1900, they tested a glider at Kitty Hawk, a small fishing village in North Carolina. A glider has no engine. It just glides, or floats, on the wind. The glider didn't work as well as they hoped, but they didn't give up.

The brothers built a wind tunnel to do experiments. They kept testing and improving their design. The next step was to design a machine with a gasoline engine for power. On December 17, 1903, this new powered machine, Flyer I, was ready.

As five citizens from Kitty Hawk watched with Wilbur, Orville took the controls. Flyer I lifted and flew 120 feet. This first airplane flight lasted just 12 seconds. Then Wilbur flew even farther. By the end of the day, both brothers had flown twice. For the first time, humans had flown a powered machine that was heavier than air. The world would never be the same.

5. **Use** the picture and the text on this page to **write** why you think the Wright Brothers were successful.

....

....

....

The Wright brothers made their first flight in their plane Flyer I.

The Impact of Inventions

Unlike most European countries, the United States is a country of vast distances. Thousands of miles lie between the west coast and the east coast. So inventions that made distances easier to cross became popular quickly. As people began to talk, drive, or fly over long distances, these inventions changed lives and the economy.

Telephones linked more and more people. The Bell Telephone Company was formed to provide telephone service to even more people. The first investors included Alexander Graham Bell, Bell's wife, Mabel, and Thomas Watson, the man who had received the first phone call. Soon, more companies were providing telephone service.

To connect telephones, wires had to be run to a central office. This office was called a telephone exchange. An operator connected calls by putting the two ends of a cord into the correct places on the switchboard. Today, telephone calls are connected automatically. Telephones look much different, too.

Early telephone connections were made by mostly women operators on a huge switchboard.

Inventions Shrink Distances

Talking	Driving	Flying
• In 1877, the Bell Telephone Company was formed. • In January 1878, the first telephone exchange opened in New Haven, Connecticut. • In February 1878, an exchange opened in San Francisco, California. • The telephone dial was invented in the 1890s.	• By 1908, more than 200 companies manufactured cars in the United States. • In 1925, a new word was coined: motel. It was a "motor hotel," or hotel for people on driving vacations. • In 1936, Duncan Hines published the first guidebooks for people traveling by car.	• In the early 1920s, airline companies started. • By the end of 1920s, most U.S. cities had airports. • In 1927, American pilot Charles Lindberg flew alone across the Atlantic. • In 1932, Amelia Earhart became the first woman to fly alone across the Atlantic.

The automobile was another invention that changed life in the United States. Americans loved cars and took to the road in increasing numbers. The automobile industry created many new jobs for American workers. But there were costs, too. With people moving faster, there were more traffic accidents. Do you think the benefits have been worth the dangers?

More and more people wanted to fly, too. At first, passenger planes could not fly at night or over high mountains. Engineers soon solved these problems. Designs improved. Metal replaced wood and cloth in airplane construction.

Airplane uses and designs changed quickly. Jet engines were developed, and then rockets. People began to wonder if they might even be able to travel in space one day. On July 20, 1969, just 66 years after the Wright brothers' first flights, two American astronauts walked on the moon.

> Ours is the commencement [start] of a flying age, and I am happy to have popped into existence at a period so interesting.
>
> —Amelia Earhart, 1928

6. **Write** what you think would be harder to live without, a car or a telephone? Explain.

....

....

....

Got it?

7. ◉ **Summarize** What effect did the telephone have on Americans?

....

....

8. **?** Suppose that you live in New York City at the start of the 1900s. **Write** a short letter to a friend outside the city explaining how you feel about the new ways to travel downtown.

my Story Ideas

....

....

....

⬛ **Stop!** I need help with ....

❚❚ **Wait!** I have a question about ....

▶ **Go!** Now I know ....

Predict Consequences

A consequence is what happens as a result of another event. It is what follows and is caused by an action or event. If you can predict consequences, you can better choose what action to take. Predicting consequences can help you get better results.

You have learned about many inventions. Using those inventions had many consequences. For example, the use of cars led to whole new industries, but also to crowded roads. Do you think people could have predicted these consequences?

Predicting consequences can help you better understand what you are reading. These steps can help you predict consequences.

- Think about what is happening.
- Look for clues about what might happen next.
- Think about what you already know about similar actions and their results or consequences.

Today, new inventions using Earth's resources are being developed. Read this article about solar energy. Then, answer the questions that follow.

Solar Energy

Every day, Earth receives energy from the sun. This energy is called solar energy. Solar energy can't be used up, and it doesn't produce pollution.

The easiest way for people to use solar energy is by collecting the heat. Flat-plate collectors face the sun and heat up. The heat is carried by water or air flowing through the collectors.

However, the sun's energy is weak at Earth's surface. So collectors need to be large.

Look at the flat-plate collectors on the roof of the house in the picture. These can heat the water used by one family.

Try it!

1. What are two important facts about solar energy you learned in this article?

   ....

   ....

   ....

2. What is one invention that uses solar energy? What does it do?

   ....

   ....

   ....

3. What do you think are some possible good consequences of using this invention?

   ....

   ....

4. What do you think would be the consequence of using a solar collector in a place that doesn't get much sun?

   ....

   ....

   ....

5. **Apply** Think about an invention you use every day that is important to you. What do you think would be the consequence of having that invention taken away?

   ....

   ....

   ....

The Impact of Big Business

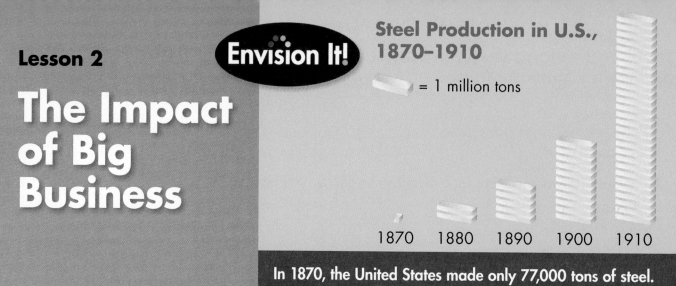

Envision It!

Steel Production in U.S., 1870–1910

= 1 million tons

1870   1880   1890   1900   1910

In 1870, the United States made only 77,000 tons of steel. But in 1910, it produced more than 28 million tons.

In the late 1800s, new inventions were everywhere. New tools made work easier. Some inventions made farming more efficient, but this meant fewer workers were needed on farms. At the same time, other inventions were creating jobs in cities. To fill these jobs, workers from the farms flooded into the cities. The growth of cities is called **urbanization.**

Businesses were growing rapidly. The economy of the United States is a **free enterprise** system. That means people are free to start their own businesses. They are also free to do whatever work they want. Between 1880 and 1900 a lot of people were starting new businesses. The number of factories more than doubled. The number of jobs more than doubled, too.

Business Leaders Take Risks

It was, and still is, risky to start a business. But if you are successful, there are great rewards. One thing that was needed in the rapidly growing cities was steel. An entrepreneur named Andrew Carnegie was determined to supply it. An **entrepreneur** creates and runs a new business and takes on all the risks of the business.

Carnegie's family was poor, so Carnegie began working at a factory at age 12. But he studied hard and made the most of every opportunity. By the time he was 30 years old, he was a wealthy investor. Then he started to make steel.

Risks could be great for entrepreneurs, but rewards could also be great. The size of Andrew Carnegie's home reflects his success.

UNLOCK
THE BIG
?

I will know that the growth of big business had a great impact on life in the United States.

Vocabulary

urbanization	stock
free enterprise	assembly line
entrepreneur	refinery
corporation	monopoly

What kinds of products do you think depend on the strength of steel?

Steel had always been expensive, because it was hard to make. Then in 1856 a British engineer named Henry Bessemer perfected a new way to make steel. The Bessemer process produced good steel at a much lower cost. The steel was processed in huge, egg-shaped metal pots, which could be tilted to pour out melted steel.

In the 1870s, Carnegie became the first person in the United States to build steel plants that used the Bessemer process. But Carnegie didn't stop there. He kept finding new ways to make steel better, faster, and cheaper. When demand for steel increased, Carnegie was ready to supply it.

Carnegie wanted to keep his costs as low as possible. He bought the iron and coal mines that produced the raw materials for steel. Next, he bought the ships and railroads that transported the raw materials. In 1889, he created the Carnegie Steel Company. He helped turn steel into a major American industry. By 1910, the United States made more steel than any other country in the world. Carnegie was rich, but he remembered what it was like to be poor. He gave much of his money to build schools and libraries, and to help others.

1. **Underline** the sentence above that describes what is happening in this steel plant.

2. Under each photograph, **write** the product to which each business person is linked.

Harvey S. Firestone

_____

Henry Ford

_____

William Boeing

_____

Inventions and Businesses

Growing cities needed bigger buildings. The strength of steel made bigger buildings possible. In 1885, the first skyscraper was built in Chicago, Illinois. Soon, tall buildings were going up everywhere.

Automobiles were exciting, but they were expensive. Then, in 1903, American entrepreneur Henry Ford started the Ford Motor Company. The Ford Motor Company is a corporation. A **corporation** is a business owned by investors. Investors buy **stock**, a share of the company, to become partial owners.

Henry Ford had a new idea about how to build cars: the assembly line. With an **assembly line**, a product is put together as it moves past a line of workers. Each worker works on one part of the product before the product moves to the next worker. So more products can be made faster and more cheaply.

In 1908, the Ford Motor Company started to produce one of its most popular cars: the Model T. The Model T was a simple car that many people could afford, and Ford sold millions.

In 1904, the Firestone Tire & Rubber Company, founded by Harvey S. Firestone, started to make tires for cars. Firestone invented a special kind of tire for the Model T, a tire filled with air.

The popularity of the automobile created all kinds of jobs. Workers were needed to build roads, repair engines, and operate gas stations. Others found jobs providing services to tourists traveling by car.

Bigger companies could produce goods at a lower cost, so businesses began to join together. In 1901, banker J.P. Morgan helped create the United States Steel Corporation, which combined the Carnegie Steel Company and several other steel companies.

In 1918, airplanes began to transport mail for the U.S. Post Office. William Boeing's airplane company was chosen to carry mail across the country. The Boeing Airplane Company grew quickly. By 1928, Boeing was one of the largest airplane manufacturers in the world.

Industry and Resources

The country's natural resources also helped the economy grow. Rich farmland produced abundant crops, and industries developed to process and package food. Forests produced wood for lumber that was used to build homes for the growing population. Iron ore from Pennsylvania and the Great Lakes region supplied the steel industry.

There was one important natural resource that Americans needed more and more: oil. Oil helped machines work. So the more industry grew, the more important oil became. Oil was also used to make gasoline to power cars and airplanes.

On August 27, 1859, a drill struck oil near Titusville, in western Pennsylvania. People rushed to the area to drill for more oil. In 1863, entrepreneur John D. Rockefeller built his first oil refinery near Cleveland, Ohio. A **refinery** turns oil into useful products, such as gasoline. Two years later, this refinery was the largest refinery in the region.

Rockefeller started the Standard Oil Company in 1870. He used his profits to buy other oil refineries. By the early 1880s, Standard Oil controlled almost all the oil business in the country. It also owned most of the pipelines that carried oil to the railroads. Standard Oil became a monopoly. A **monopoly** is a company that has control of an entire industry.

Once people started looking for oil, they found it in other parts of the country. In 1901, oil drillers made an incredible discovery. They struck oil at Spindletop, near Beaumont, Texas. This strike was one of the largest in history. One year later, more than 1,000 oil companies operated in that area.

The area around Spindletop became crowded with oil drills.

3. **Write** a newspaper headline about an event at Spindletop, shown here.

....

....

401

Cities and Businesses

Cities linked to important industries grew quickly. People moved to Cleveland, Ohio, to work in oil refineries. They moved to Chicago, Illinois, to work in meat-packing plants and steel plants. They moved to Detroit, Michigan, to make automobiles. Workers found jobs in Philadelphia, Pennsylvania, Baltimore, Maryland, and New York City. Within the cities, workers made clothing in factories or worked in stores and hotels. Some sold food and clothes to the growing population.

Every ten years the government makes an official count of all Americans. This is called a census. The 1920 census showed that, for the first time, more Americans lived in cities than on farms.

Big cities were connected more and more by railroads, airplanes, and highways. Raw materials moved to the cities and finished goods moved out of the cities. Different regions relied on one another more and more.

Although it was an exciting time, problems were developing. The tall buildings and new forms of transportation brought crowding and traffic. Growing industries created pollution. Some businesses were dangerous for workers or people living nearby.

4. How do you think the steel mills affected the city of Pittsburgh? What were the costs and benefits of the steel industry there?

....

....

....

Andrew Carnegie's steel mills were in Pittsburgh, Pennsylvania.

5. ◉ **Draw Conclusions** Study the bar graph. What conclusion can you draw about changes in the U.S. population between 1860 and 1920?

....

....

....

....

....

....

Urban and Rural Population in the U.S., 1860–1920

Years: 1860, 1880, 1900, 1920

Legend: Urban, Rural

Got it?

6. ◉ **Draw Conclusions** Why did people create really big companies?

....

....

....

7. 🔍 Suppose that you have just moved to Detroit to work in an automobile factory. How do you feel about the costs and benefits of your new life?

my Story Ideas

....

....

....

....

⬛ **Stop!** I need help with ....

❚❚ **Wait!** I have a question about ....

▶ **Go!** Now I know ....

Immigration

Beginning in the 1800s, steamships made it faster and cheaper for immigrants to come to the United States.

An Asian immigrant stands in front of his store in New York City in 1903.

Immigrants had always come to the United States in search of freedom and opportunity. But after the Civil War, immigrants started arriving in greater numbers. They came by ship from countries all over the world. The voyage was now easier and faster, thanks to improved transportation.

New Immigrants

There were two major waves of immigrants after the Civil War. The first wave arrived between 1865 and 1890. During that time, about 10 million people moved to the United States. Most of them came from Ireland and countries in northern Europe, such as Germany, Great Britain, Finland, Sweden, and Norway.

The second wave of immigrants arrived between 1890 and 1920. Most came from eastern and southern European countries, such as Poland, Russia, Italy, Austria-Hungary, and Greece. They were called the new immigrants.

People came to America from other countries, too. Some moved south from Canada. Others moved north from Latin America. Still others came from Japan and China.

Most of the new immigrants came from cultures that differed from the cultures of previous groups. Some did not come to stay, but just wanted to make money and return home. It was not an easy time for many Americans, as they tried to compete with the newcomers for jobs, understand the new cultures, and cope with the overcrowding that the huge number of newcomers created.

Vocabulary

diversity	tenement
prejudice	labor union
oppression	melting pot

Write three words to describe what this trip must have been like.

More than 15 million of these "new immigrants" arrived in the second wave. Many immigrants arriving from Europe moved into the industrial cities in the East and Midwest. Immigrants coming from Asia landed on the West Coast and often settled there. Wherever they came from, immigrants brought their languages and traditions with them. These new cultures added to the **diversity,** or variety, of American life.

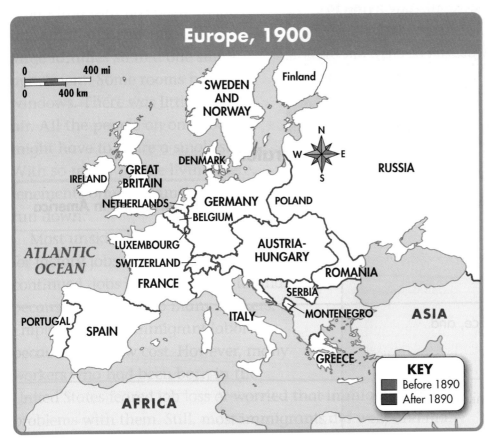

Europe, 1900

0 — 400 mi
0 — 400 km

SWEDEN AND NORWAY
Finland
DENMARK
IRELAND
GREAT BRITAIN
NETHERLANDS
BELGIUM
GERMANY
POLAND
RUSSIA
LUXEMBOURG
SWITZERLAND
FRANCE
AUSTRIA-HUNGARY
ROMANIA
SERBIA
ATLANTIC OCEAN
PORTUGAL
SPAIN
ITALY
MONTENEGRO
GREECE
ASIA
AFRICA

N W E S

KEY
Before 1890
After 1890

1. **Find** the European lands from which most immigrants to the United States came before 1890. **Shade** them in blue. Then find the countries from which most immigrants to the United States came after 1890. **Shade** them in red.

Lesson 1

Inventors and Inventions

- In the late 1800s, Americans were becoming consumers.
- Important new inventions began to change the way people worked, communicated, and lived.
- New forms of transportation were introduced.

Lesson 2

The Impact of Big Business

- Andrew Carnegie and other entrepreneurs created new industries.
- Natural resources in the United States helped the economy to grow rapidly.
- Many Americans moved to big cities to work in industries there.

Lesson 3

THE MELTING POT
THE GREAT AMERICAN DRAMA
BY ISRAEL ZANGWILL

Immigration

- After the Civil War, millions of new immigrants from Europe and Asia arrived in America.
- Life in America could be hard for immigrants.
- Immigrants made many contributions to American life.

Review and Assessment

Lesson 1

Inventors and Inventions

1. Write a sentence to explain why each of the following inventions was important.

a. telephone

....

....

....

b. light bulb

....

....

....

c. airplane

....

....

....

2. How did the development of the electric streetcar affect city life?

....

....

....

3. Choose one of the inventions listed above and explain how it affects life today.

....

....

....

Lesson 2

The Impact of Big Business

4. Use numbers 1, 2, 3, and 4 to arrange the following events in the order in which they happened.

_____ Census shows more Americans live in cities than in rural areas.

_____ Henry Ford starts the Ford Motor Company.

_____ Drillers discover oil at Titusville, Pennsylvania.

_____ Andrew Carnegie starts the Carnegie Steel Company.

5. How did John D. Rockefeller come to control almost all the oil business in the United States?

....

....

....

....

6. Why did the growth of big business affect how and where people lived in the United States?

....

....

....

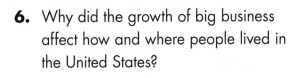

Lesson 3

Immigration

7. **Draw Conclusions** In the chart below, read the facts. Then write a conclusion you can make about immigrant life in America based on those facts.

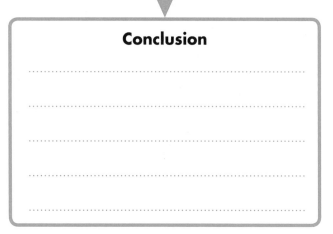

Facts

1. Many immigrants lived in tenements.

2. Work could be hard to find.

3. Some people were prejudiced against immigrants.

Conclusion

....

....

....

....

8. Why did people want to come to the United States?

A. To escape war or prejudice

B. Because they were poor

C. Because of job opportunities in the United States

D. All of the above

9. **What are the costs and benefits of growth?**

Use the photograph and what you have read to think more about the chapter's Big Question.

a. What were some benefits of life in Pittsburgh in the late 1800s?

....

....

b. What were some costs of life in Pittsburgh in the late 1800s?

....

....

c. How would you compare the costs and benefits of growth in Pittsburgh?

....

....

....

....

....

Go online to write and illustrate your own **myStory Book** using the **myStory Ideas** from this chapter.

 # What are the costs and benefits of growth?

American society changed in many ways between 1880 and 1920. Many of our most familiar technologies were developed then, including household electricity and the automobile. At the same time, large numbers of immigrants arrived, swelling our cities and adding new ethnic backgrounds to the "melting pot."

Describe one benefit and one cost of the changes sweeping the country between 1880 and 1920. Then **think** about a change that you have experienced in your own lifetime. What is one benefit and one cost of that change?

....

....

....

Now **draw** an image of something that has changed in your lifetime.

While you're online, check out the **myStory Current Events** area where you can create your own book on a topic that's in the news.

The Progressive Era

This cartoon compares a poor worker and a rich boss. It was made at the start of the 1900s.

The United States was changing rapidly in the early 1900s. New inventions were changing people's lives. Across the country, growing industries created jobs that attracted workers to cities. These changes also created problems for many Americans. However, many groups and people worked to help solve the problems.

Industrialization Leads to Challenges

As new industries grew, more and more Americans worked in large factories. Working conditions in the factories were often very bad. Workers now toiled for ten hours at a time, six days a week. Many factories were unhealthy and even dangerous places to work. Large machines injured untrained workers. There often wasn't enough light or fresh air.

One tragedy showed why new laws were needed to change working conditions. The Triangle Shirtwaist Company in New York City produced clothing. During the day, the main doors were locked to keep workers from stealing. When a fire started on March 25, 1911, workers could not open the doors. Firefighters' ladders could not reach the eighth-floor workshop. Some workers died jumping from windows. Others died when the fire escape collapsed. Most of the 146 who died were young women.

These people gathered in memory of the workers who died in the Triangle Shirtwaist Company tragedy.

LADIES WAIST & DRESSMAKERS UNION LOCAL 25 WE MOURN OUR LOSS

UNLOCK THE BIG ?

I will know that changes in the American economy led to problems that Progressives tried to solve.

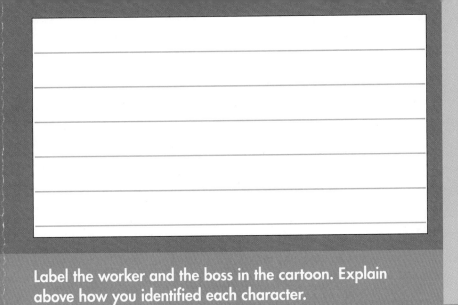

Label the worker and the boss in the cartoon. **Explain above how you identified each character.**

Vocabulary

trust   Progressive
strike   muckraker
strikebreaker   conservation
boycott

In 1900 almost 2 million children worked in factories and mines. Some were as young as five years old. Others worked on the street, selling newspapers or shining shoes. Few poor children, especially those from other countries, had ever gone to school. Americans wanted to change that.

The companies that owned the big factories kept growing. Some of them joined together to form large groups called **trusts.** These trusts could control an industry and drive other companies out of business. As the trusts grew stronger, they had more control over their workers.

As more and more workers moved to cities to find jobs, cities became crowded. Housing was limited. Who would help solve all these problems?

1. **Circle** at least two things in the photograph that you think look dangerous.

In the early 1900s, many American children worked in mills, mines, or factories like this one.

The Labor Movement

By the late 1800s and early 1900s, workers wanted shorter workdays, better wages, and better working conditions. Workers began turning to labor unions for help.

One of the first national labor unions, the Knights of Labor, was organized in 1869. It welcomed factory workers, farmers, women, and African Americans. However, it did not welcome immigrants. It was effective at first, but it attracted radicals, so people left the group. In 1886 a new union replaced it. This union was the American Federation of Labor, or AFL.

The founder of the AFL was Samuel Gompers, a Jewish immigrant who lived in New York City. He described the goals for his union as "pure and simple." He wanted better wages and working conditions for members. Gompers organized the new union by grouping members according to skill. For example, all the carpenters belonged to one craft union. The hat makers belonged to another. These different craft unions were all part of the AFL. By 1904 the AFL had almost 2 million members.

Meanwhile, another union was organizing mine workers. The United Mine Workers relied on the help of Mary Harris Jones. In the 1890s, Jones unionized coal miners in Pennsylvania. Around this time she became known as "Mother Jones." Later, she worked in Colorado and West Virginia. She also worked to end child labor in the Pennsylvania mills.

Mary "Mother" Jones

Unions Demanded Change

Unions wanted more money and better working conditions for their members. However, business owners wanted to keep expenses down to make products affordable. There were also millions of immigrants looking for jobs. Sometimes union leaders tried to achieve their goals by calling a strike. During a **strike**, workers refuse to work, staying away from their jobs until business owners agree to their demands.

Some strikes turned violent. In July 1892, steel workers in Homestead, Pennsylvania, went on strike. Thousands of immigrants eagerly replaced the striking workers. These replacements were called **strikebreakers.** The striking workers attacked the replacements. Armed guards were hired to protect the strikebreakers. By the time the strike ended, several people had been killed or injured in the fighting.

U.S. Union Membership, 1898–1920

Millions of Members

5.0
4.5
4.0
3.5
3.0
2.5
2.0
1.5
1.0
0.5
0

1898 1902 1906 1910 1914 1918

Years

Source: U.S. Department of Commerce, Bureau of the Census

2. Study the line graph. How many workers belonged to unions in 1902? In 1914?

....

....

Workers march in the first Labor Day parade, September 5, 1882, in New York City. In 1894, Congress made Labor Day a national holiday.

Another union strategy was the boycott. During a **boycott**, people agree not to buy goods made by a certain company. When the company agrees to change the way it operates, the boycott ends.

As unions became stronger, working conditions improved. Some cities and states passed laws that shortened the workday to eight hours. Another law made employers responsible for helping injured workers. To help end child labor, Samuel Gompers supported state laws to end cigar production in New York City tenements, because the people living in tenements expected their children to help with the work.

3. Name the book each author wrote and the problem it discussed.

Upton Sinclair

Lincoln Steffens

Ida Tarbell

Solving America's Problems

There were many problems in the late 1800s, including overcrowded cities, big trusts, dangerous factories, and, in most big cities, dishonest politicians. Fortunately, people wanted to solve these problems. Some of the people who tried to find solutions were called **Progressives.**

A group of writers helped spread the Progressives' ideas. These writers were called **muckrakers**, because they uncovered "muck," or shameful conditions in American business and society.

Ida Tarbell showed the danger of trusts in *The History of the Standard Oil Company*, about John D. Rockefeller's oil company. Another muckraker, Upton Sinclair, wrote *The Jungle*. This novel described the horrible conditions in the meat-packing industry. Lincoln Steffens wrote about dishonest public officials in *Shame of the Cities*. Muckrakers focused Americans' attention on these issues, and people began to call for change. The muckrakers also influenced political leaders.

Roosevelt Takes Action

Theodore Roosevelt became president in 1901. He supported many Progressive ideas. His slogan was a "square deal" for all Americans. In 1902, Roosevelt used a law, the Sherman Antitrust Act, to break up many big business trusts into smaller companies. People called Roosevelt a "trust buster."

In 1906, Roosevelt supported two laws that would help make food and medicine safer. One of these was the Meat Inspection Act. For the first time, inspectors checked meat to make sure it was safe. The Pure Food and Drug Act made companies reveal the ingredients in their products.

President Roosevelt sometimes supported striking workers, too. In 1902, he helped coal miners in the state of Pennsylvania win higher wages and a shorter workday.

Achievements of the Progressive Era

Some Progressives wanted to improve life for immigrants and others who might need some help, especially in the cities. In Chicago in 1889, Jane Addams started a settlement house, or center that offers help to needy people. She called it Hull House. It offered English classes and other courses. Working parents could leave their children in a nursery there. Soon, settlement houses opened all over the country.

Progressives supported other laws to change American life. Many workers now worked eight hours, instead of ten or more. President Woodrow Wilson backed laws to end child labor and to protect workers injured on the job. He also declared strikes and boycotts to be legal. Other laws made homes and workplaces safer. Children now had to attend school. Cities built the first playgrounds in crowded neighborhoods.

As government tried to do more, it became more expensive. Congress passed the Sixteenth Amendment in 1913, so the government could tax people's incomes, or wages. The money from this tax helped pay for new programs. Under the Seventeenth Amendment, citizens could elect their senators directly. This gave people more political power.

Hull House grew quickly, adding more buildings and new facilities, such as the playground mentioned above.

4. ◉ **Summarize Complete** these statements about changes during the Progressive Era.

   a. Roosevelt used the Sherman Antitrust Act to break

   up ....

   b. To pay for programs, the government began to tax

   ....

   c. President Wilson declared ....

   .... to be legal.

   d. Jane Addams opened ....

   e. The .... let inspectors
   check meat.

Other Progressive Goals

Progressives often helped people no one else cared about. Julia Tutwiler was born in Alabama in 1841. She supported ways to improve conditions in Alabama prisons. She worked for state inspections of jails and prisons. Tutwiler believed that prisoners should get an education, too. As a result of her efforts, Alabama started night schools in state prisons.

Clara Barton was another important reformer. During the Civil War she had been a nurse. Later she worked to get international laws passed that would help the sick and wounded during war. In 1881, she organized the American Red Cross. When she was 77 years old, she nursed soldiers in Cuba during the Spanish-American War.

Dorothea Dix was another Civil War nurse. For most of her life, she worked to improve the treatment of people who were mentally ill. Their mistreatment in a Massachusetts prison shocked her. After visiting other state prisons, she sent a report to the legislature. Because of this report, the legislature voted to enlarge the state hospital for the insane. For the next 40 years, Dorothea Dix worked to make other states build hospitals for the mentally ill. She also supported better treatment of prisoners.

President Roosevelt, left, visited Yosemite with John Muir, right, in 1903.

Progressives also worked for the **conservation**, or protecting and saving, of the wilderness. In 1872 the government established Yellowstone, the world's first national park. People like John Muir urged the government to establish Sequoia (sih KWOI uh) and Yosemite (yoh SEM uh tee) national parks in 1890. The Muir Woods National Monument in California honors Muir's work.

President Roosevelt strongly believed in conservation. In 1903, he went camping with John Muir in Yosemite National Park. Roosevelt loved the outdoors and worked to protect the country's wilderness areas. In 1905, he urged Congress to create the U.S. Forest Service. President Roosevelt set aside much public land as national forests and parks. By the time he left office, he had protected almost 2 million acres.

National forests are found across the country, but especially in the West.

Got it?

5. **Cause and Effect** How did the work of the Progressives affect the lives of workers in the United States?

....

....

....

6. **Imagine** you are a reporter visiting Hull House for the first time. What is your opinion of what you see there?

my Story Ideas

....

....

....

....

Stop! I need help with ....

Wait! I have a question about ....

Go! Now I know ....

Solve Problems

The Progressives tried to solve political and social problems in the United States. To solve a problem, follow these three steps:

- Identify the problem.
- Gather information about possible ways to solve the problem.
- Identify the solution.

This chart identifies an important problem that presidents Theodore Roosevelt and Woodrow Wilson tried to solve during the Progressive era. Read the steps each president followed to find a solution.

Problem
Large groups of companies, called trusts, controlled entire industries. These trusts could drive out competitors.

Possible Solutions
- There was an 1890 law called the Sherman Antitrust Act. It said trusts should not exist.
- A president can encourage Congress to pass new laws to stop bad practices, such as trusts.
- The president, as head of the executive branch, can make sure that laws are put into action.

Solution
President Roosevelt used the Sherman Antitrust Act to break up trusts. President Wilson urged Congress to pass a new law to prevent trusts.

Upton Sinclair wrote a novel about the horrible conditions in Chicago's meat-packing plants. Complete the chart below to show how President Theodore Roosevelt solved the problem.

> **Problem:**
> The conditions in the meat-packing plants were horrible.

> **Possible Solutions:**
> - Find a way to make these plants safer.
> - Find a way to check up on the plants, to see that they are clean and food is safe.
> - Let people know what they are eating.

> **Solution:**

1. **Apply Think** about a problem affecting your school or community. **Use** a problem-solution chart to show the steps you would follow to solve it.

Unequal Opportunities for African Americans

Envision It!

The word "colored" on the sign above referred to African Americans, who had to face unfair treatment daily.

This protest sign shows how some people felt about Jim Crow laws.

After Reconstruction ended, African Americans faced many difficulties. Harsh laws separated the races in the United States, especially in the South. Even the U.S. Supreme Court did not help to end this unfair treatment. Trying to escape this prejudice, many African Americans moved north to start new lives.

Jim Crow Laws

Between the end of Reconstruction and the mid-1950s, hundreds of laws made segregation legal. Segregation is the separation of people of different races. These laws were known as Jim Crow laws. Southern states passed most of these laws. But some western, midwestern, and northeastern states passed segregation laws, too.

Under Jim Crow laws, white Americans and African Americans led almost completely separate lives. These laws segregated schools, theaters, buses, trains, and other public spaces. Hospitals used by white patients could not treat African Americans. Blacks and whites could not sit together in the same restaurants or use the same restrooms. They could not drink at the same water fountains or visit the same parks. Even cemeteries were segregated.

1. **Summarize** Summarize the ideas in this protest sign.

....

....

....

UNLOCK THE BIG ?

I will know that it was necessary to change the unfair treatment of African Americans.

Vocabulary

civil rights
Great Migration

Since 1870, African Americans had been legally equal. Do these signs support equality? What do they tell you?

In southern states, other laws were passed to keep African Americans from voting. Beginning in 1890, some states required voters to pass a reading test to vote. Because the education of African Americans was often discouraged, many could not pass the test. In other states, African Americans had to pay a voting tax or meet other requirements.

Segregation Limits Opportunities

Segregation limited the civil rights of African Americans. **Civil rights** are the rights all citizens should have under the U.S. Constitution. In 1890, Louisiana passed a Jim Crow law that segregated railroad cars. Two years later, Homer Plessy challenged this law by sitting in a railroad car reserved for white people. After his arrest, Plessy sued Louisiana.

In 1896, the Supreme Court ruled in this case. Most of the justices thought Plessy was guilty. They said that it was legal to separate the races if the facilities for blacks and whites were equal. This is called the separate but equal principle.

One Supreme Court judge disagreed. John Marshall Harlan argued that the Supreme Court's decision was wrong. He believed it would become as hated as the court's decision in the Dred Scott case, before the Civil War.

2. Who do you think might wear this button?

....

....

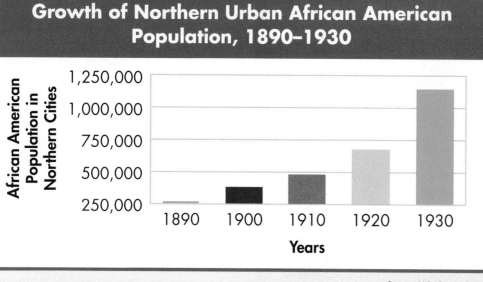

Growth of Northern Urban African American Population, 1890–1930

African American Population in Northern Cities

1,250,000
1,000,000
750,000
500,000
250,000

1890 1900 1910 1920 1930

Years

Source: U.S. Census Bureau

Migrating North

Between 1916 and 1970, about 6 million African Americans moved from farming areas in the South to big cities in the North. This movement is known as the **Great Migration.**

3. Circle the years in the graph in which northern urban African American population was the highest and lowest.

Booming industries in the North and West needed workers. The hope of better-paying jobs and better living conditions drew African Americans to New York, Detroit, Cleveland, and Chicago. They had learned about life in these cities from friends and family who had already moved there. They also read about job opportunities in the *Chicago Defender.* This was an important African American newspaper that encouraged the Great Migration.

Prejudice was only one of the problems that pushed people out of the South. African Americans working as sharecroppers found it hard to escape poverty. Also, many southern farms failed after insects damaged cotton crops in the 1890s.

4. Underline three reasons in the text that tell why African Americans left the South in the Great Migration.

African Americans faced prejudice in the North, too. Some northern states had segregated schools, theaters, hotels, and restaurants. Some African Americans lived together in poor neighborhoods. However, many created thriving communities with successful African American stores, banks, churches, theaters, and businesses. Neighborhoods such as Chicago's Bronzeville and New York City's Harlem became vibrant centers of African American arts and culture.

African American Leaders

Booker T. Washington was the most famous and respected African American leader of his time. He had been enslaved as a child and grew up in poverty during Reconstruction. But he was determined to get an education, and he worked hard to put himself through school.

Ida Wells-Barnett

Washington believed that African Americans needed education before anything else. Useful skills would lead to jobs. Over time these jobs would help African Americans earn better wages and overcome prejudice. He dedicated his life to creating educational opportunities for African Americans.

W.E.B. Du Bois (doo BOYZ) was another important African American leader. His life was very different from Washington's. He was never enslaved. Born in Massachusetts in 1868, he graduated from Fisk University, an African American college in Tennessee. During his long career, Du Bois wrote many speeches, books, and articles. He supported civil rights for African Americans. However, he wanted them right away, without the slower process Washington felt was important.

Mary McLeod Bethune also believed that education was the best way to achieve racial equality and civil rights. In 1904, she founded a school for African American girls in Daytona Beach, Florida. Later her school became Bethune-Cookman College. From 1936 to 1945 she advised President Franklin D. Roosevelt about issues faced by African Americans and other groups.

Ida Wells-Barnett was born in Mississippi in 1862. Her parents had been enslaved. In her speeches and articles, she supported an end to violence against African Americans. After 1895 she lived in Chicago, where she worked for a newspaper. She also founded the first voting rights club for African American women in Illinois. In 1910 she started an organization to help African Americans who traveled North during the Great Migration.

5. What did both Booker T. Washington and Mary McLeod Bethune see as the key to success?

....

New Institutions

Robert S. Abbott founded the *Chicago Defender* in 1905. Over time it became one of the most important African American newspapers in America. You have read that the *Defender* played a part in the Great Migration. Later, during World Wars I and II, the newspaper supported equal treatment for African American soldiers. It also supported ending segregation in the armed forces.

In 1909, W.E.B. Du Bois joined Ida Wells-Barnett and others to start the National Association for the Advancement of Colored People, or the NAACP. This organization wanted to end prejudice and segregation in housing, schools, jobs, voting, and other areas. In 1918, members encouraged President Woodrow Wilson to oppose violence against African Americans. Lawyers from the NAACP argued against segregation laws at the Supreme Court. These lawyers, such as future Supreme Court justice Thurgood Marshall, won the case that ended school segregation in 1954.

Booker T. Washington founded the Tuskegee Institute in 1881. At first, the school taught farming and practical job training to African Americans. For example, students could learn carpentry and printing. In addition, Tuskegee students studied history, science, math, and English. The famous scientist and inventor George Washington Carver did important research at the school. His research helped farmers become more successful.

6. List two topics you think Du Bois might want to write about in *The Crisis*.

....

....

....

....

W.E.B. Du Bois edited The Crisis *magazine, which influenced middle-class African Americans and white Progressives.*

A dozen other colleges for African Americans opened, and older colleges began accepting African American students. However, Tuskegee remained a leader in education for African Americans. In 1943, Tuskegee's fourth president helped start the United Negro College Fund to provide scholarships to deserving students. The Institute became Tuskegee University in 1985.

7. **Describe** what you notice about the students' clothes in this photograph.

....

....

Students at Tuskegee Institute in 1906

Got it?

8. ◉ **Cause and Effect** How did growing industries in the North affect the Great Migration?

....

....

....

9. ❓ You are an African American worker who moved to a northern city in 1910. **Write** a short letter describing your life and what you would like to see change.

my **Story Ideas**

....

....

....

■ **Stop!** I need help with ....

❚❚ **Wait!** I have a question about ....

▶ **Go!** Now I know ....

The Fight for Women's Rights

Envision It!

Women did not always have the right to vote in the United States, but many worked to get this right.

In the early 1900s the United States was changing, and women wanted to be part of that change. New jobs and better educational opportunities made their lives richer. But women's rights were limited, and they still could not vote.

Changing Roles for Women

Most married women in the mid- to late 1800s were homemakers. They stayed at home and cared for their husbands and children. Before they married, many women in cities worked as maids or in factories, mills, and workshops. Better-educated women were teachers. Very poor women kept working after they married. Often, they washed and mended clothes. By 1900, about 4 million women worked in jobs other than farming. Few women worked in the same professions as men.

Life was different for women in rural areas. In the country, pioneer women always shared farm or ranch chores with their husbands. Both women and men had to work to survive. Equal work often resulted in equal rights for rural women.

Between 1900 and 1925, job opportunities for women grew quickly. More women were graduating from colleges and universities. Women still cared for families and homes, but better education made other jobs possible.

The first department stores appeared in the 1800s. These large stores offered many job opportunities for women.

I will know that many people worked to gain equal rights, including voting rights, for women.

Vocabulary

temperance
suffrage
suffragist

Draw a sign or write a slogan about a right or freedom you value and want to protect.

Women worked in large offices or as telephone operators. They became nurses, professors, librarians, and social workers. A few were lawyers, doctors, and writers. But jobs changed for other reasons, too. Washing machines, vacuum cleaners, and other work-saving devices meant fewer jobs for maids, so former maids began working in department stores.

The changing American way of life created more opportunities for work, but also more need for income. Families now bought cars and telephones. They wanted to live in better homes. More women went to work than ever before, and their income helped pay for these new products.

1. **Complete** this Venn diagram to show how women's roles differed and remained the same over two time periods.

Women's Roles

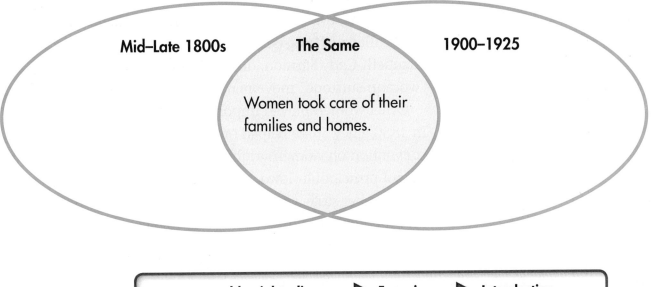

Mid–Late 1800s   The Same   1900–1925

Women took care of their families and homes.

This stamp was issued in 1948 for the 100-year anniversary of the Seneca Falls Convention.

2. Underline the things on this page that women were working to change.

Working for More Rights

In the 1800s, many jobs were closed to women. Married women couldn't own property. Women had nowhere to go if there were problems at home. In the 1800s, the abuse of alcohol was widespread, so often women did have problems in the home. Many women (including Susan B. Anthony) joined the temperance movement. **Temperance** was a call for people to reduce or stop drinking alcohol. Many women also worked to end slavery. In time, women realized that they should also gain more rights for themselves.

In July 1848, two women's rights leaders, Lucretia Mott and Elizabeth Cady Stanton, organized a meeting in Seneca Falls, New York, to discuss women's rights. Almost 250 men and women attended. At the Seneca Falls Convention, Stanton read a statement based on the Declaration of Independence, stating that men and women were equal. She declared that,

> *"[Man] has compelled [woman] to submit to laws, in the formation of which she had no voice."*

Later the convention voted on 12 statements about women's rights. The ninth one demanded that women have the right to vote. Although some were afraid that this demand went too far, the convention approved the statement. The women's suffrage movement was born. **Suffrage** is the right to vote, and people who worked for women's suffrage were called **suffragists.** In 1851, Susan B. Anthony joined Elizabeth Cady Stanton, and the two led what was called the "woman suffrage" movement for 50 years.

Other women played important roles in this movement. In 1850, Lucy Stone helped organize the first national convention on women's rights. Carrie Chapman Catt, a high school principal in Iowa, started working for women's voting rights in her state. Catt joined Susan B. Anthony to support an amendment to the Constitution to give women the right to vote.

Women's Right to Vote

In 1869, Susan B. Anthony and Elizabeth Cady Stanton founded the National Woman Suffrage Association. In that same year Lucy Stone started the American Woman Suffrage Association. Stone wanted state governments to change their constitutions so women could vote in each state. In 1890, the two groups joined, and they worked together for the next 30 years.

These suffragists faced a tough fight. In 1874, the Supreme Court ruled that being a U.S. citizen did not automatically give women the right to vote. Instead, each state should decide women's political rights.

Women had more rights out West. As a territory, Wyoming gave suffrage to women in 1869. When it entered the Union in 1890, it was the first state with full suffrage for women. The small town of Argonia, Kansas, elected Susanna Medora Salter mayor in 1887. She was the country's first female mayor. By 1900 women had full voting rights in Utah, Colorado, and Idaho. Other states followed. In 1917, Jeannette Rankin, a reformer and women's rights leader, became the first woman elected to the U.S. Congress. By 1918, women had the same voting rights as men in 15 states.

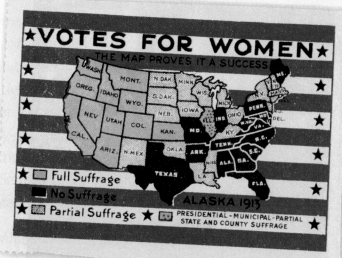

Western and midwestern states were the first to give women the vote, as shown on this 1913 map.

3. **Write** an event in women's suffrage for each year below.

Timeline of Important Events in Suffragist History

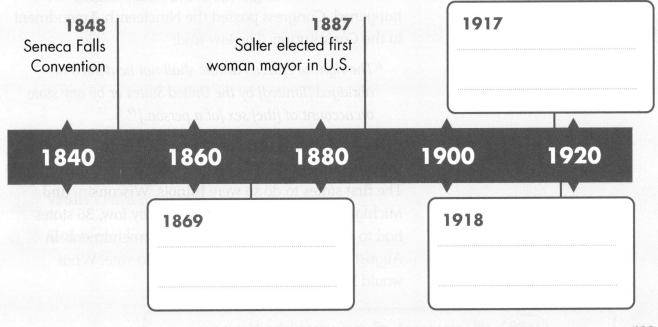

1848
Seneca Falls Convention

1887
Salter elected first woman mayor in U.S.

1917

1840 **1860** **1880** **1900** **1920**

1869

1918

439

Lesson 1

The Progressive Era

- Industrialization led to overcrowding in cities and difficult working conditions in factories.
- Labor unions organized workers to seek better workplace conditions.
- The Progressives worked for political and social reforms.

Lesson 2

Unequal Opportunities for African Americans

- Jim Crow laws legalized segregation in the United States.
- Millions of African Americans moved north during the Great Migration, finding both opportunities and challenges there.
- African American leaders and institutions helped African Americans.

Lesson 3

The Fight for Women's Rights

- In the early twentieth century, more education and job opportunities were open to women.
- Women suffragist leaders led the fight for women's rights.
- The Nineteenth Amendment gave American women the right to vote.

Review and Assessment

Lesson 1

The Progressive Era

1. What effect did industrialization have on workers' lives?

....

....

....

2. **Write** a sentence about what these people did to help others.

a. Samuel Gompers

....

....

b. Jane Addams

....

....

....

3. Why was President Theodore Roosevelt called a trust buster?

....

....

....

Lesson 2

Unequal Opportunities for African Americans

4. What was the purpose of Jim Crow laws?

....

....

5. What are two reasons why African Americans migrated north?

....

....

....

....

6. **Use** the numbers 1, 2, 3, and 4 to arrange the following events in the order in which they happened.

_____ The Great Migration started.

_____ Supreme Court ruled on separate but equal principle.

_____ School segregation ended in the United States.

_____ Booker T. Washington founded the Tuskegee Institute.

Lesson 3

The Fight for Women's Rights

7. **Summarize** What movement started at the Seneca Falls Convention?

....

....

....

....

8. Why do you think the western states were the first states to give women the right to vote?

....

....

....

....

9. Why was the passage of the Nineteenth Amendment important?

   A. It granted all American women citizenship.

   B. It ended segregation in the United States.

   C. It gave all American women the right to vote.

   D. It extended voting rights to all immigrants.

10. **When does change become necessary?**

Use the photograph and questions below to think more about this chapter's Essential Question.

a. What goal did these women have at the beginning of the 1900s?

....

....

b. What does this image suggest about how women felt about women's right to vote?

....

....

c. What kind of change did many women think was necessary to achieve the right to vote?

....

....

....

Go online to write and illustrate your own **myStory Book** using the **myStory Ideas** from this chapter.

When does change become necessary?

You have just read about a time when different groups believed change was necessary. People worked in different ways to bring about changes and improve life for many Americans. Today, there are probably things in your own community or neighborhood that you believe must be changed. Like many Americans at the start of the 1900s, you probably think about how change might happen.

Think about something in your school or neighborhood that you believe must be changed. **Write** about why this change is necessary.

Now **draw** a poster for a campaign to change or solve this problem. On your poster, include reasons for making the change that you support.

While you're online, check out the **myStory Current Events** area where you can create your own book on a topic that's in the news.

Good Times and Hardships

How do people respond to good times and bad?

Identify an event from your life that was very happy or very difficult. Then **write** about how you responded to that event.

....

....

....

....

....

UNEMPLOYED
BUY
APPLES
5¢ EACH

Millions of Americans lost their jobs in the 1930s.

Zora Neale Hurston
A Voice From the South

my Story Video

Zora Neale Hurston loved to make an entrance. When she arrived at a gathering, everyone turned to see her. Smart and full of energy, she charmed people with her humor and her spirit. Those same traits drew people to her writing. Zora Neale Hurston was the most successful African American woman writer of the first half of the 1900s.

During this time, African Americans in the South faced great hardships as a result of discrimination. Racial discrimination is the unfair treatment of a group of people based on their race. Americans in the rest of the country knew little about the lives of these African Americans. Hurston's writing gave them a voice.

Zora Neale Hurston was born in Alabama in 1891 and grew up in the American South. At a young age she moved with her family to a small town in central Florida. The town, Eatonville, had a remarkable history. It was the first official African American town in the nation. Hurston's father helped run the town.

Zora Neale Hurston was a confident person and a talented writer.

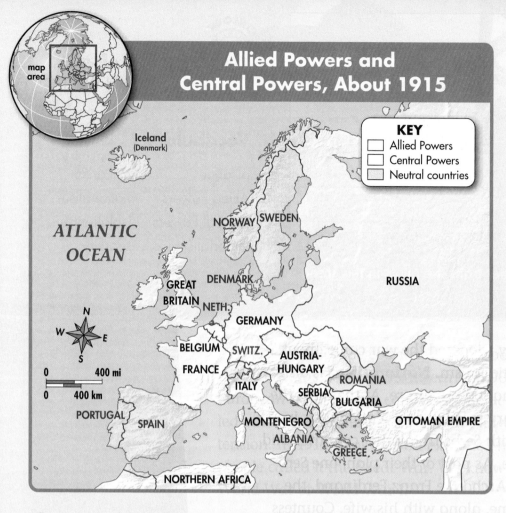

Allied Powers and Central Powers, About 1915

KEY
- ☐ Allied Powers
- ☐ Central Powers
- ☐ Neutral countries

ATLANTIC OCEAN

Iceland (Denmark)

NORWAY
SWEDEN
GREAT BRITAIN
DENMARK
NETH.
GERMANY
RUSSIA
BELGIUM
SWITZ.
FRANCE
AUSTRIA-HUNGARY
ITALY
ROMANIA
SERBIA
BULGARIA
PORTUGAL
SPAIN
MONTENEGRO
ALBANIA
GREECE
OTTOMAN EMPIRE
NORTHERN AFRICA

N W E S

0   400 mi
0   400 km

map area

3. World War I started in 1914. The next year, Bulgaria joined the Central Powers and Italy joined the Allied Powers. More changes came later. **Choose** two colors for the key. Then color in the Central Powers and the Allied Powers to match the key.

The United States Enters the War

At first, Americans showed no interest in fighting what they saw as a European war. They chose to stay neutral. To be neutral is to avoid taking sides. Safe across the Atlantic Ocean, the United States had long followed a policy of **isolationism.** It wanted to stay out of other countries' affairs. This policy reached back as far as the late 1700s when George Washington warned Americans to avoid political ties with other nations.

Two events finally persuaded Americans to join the Allied Powers. The first was the sinking of a passenger ship, the *Lusitania*, by a German submarine in 1915. One hundred and twenty-eight Americans died. Many American citizens now called for war on Germany.

The second event was the Zimmermann Note. This coded telegram asked Mexico to join the Central Powers if the United States declared war on Germany. In return, Germany would help Mexico get back territory it had lost to the United States, including Texas, Arizona, and New Mexico. The note fell into the hands of the British, who decoded it. When it became public, demands for war with Germany grew louder.

Meanwhile, German submarines again attacked and sank several American ships in early 1917. On April 2, U.S. President Woodrow Wilson called for a declaration of war. He said, "The world must be made safe for democracy." On April 6, 1917, Congress declared war on Germany. Within months, the first American troops arrived at the Western front—the battle zone in France. They would help shorten the war.

Trench Warfare

Both sides in the war thought they would win quickly. They were wrong. The war, especially for the soldiers, seemed endless. Territory was won. Then it was lost. Then it was won, and lost, again—over and over.

In the first few major battles along the borders of France, Germany, and Belgium, armies clashed face to face in the traditional way of fighting. But soon leaders realized that too many soldiers were dying. The armies decided to "dig in." Soldiers on both sides dug trenches. These deep ditches often stretched for miles. Troops ate and slept in the trenches, which offered some shelter from enemy gunfire. However, the trenches were muddy and cold, crowded and unclean. Diseases spread easily.

Battles in trench warfare followed a pattern. The infantry, or foot-soldiers, charged up and out of the trenches. Some held a rifle with a long knife, called a bayonet, attached to the tip. Cannons fired constantly from both sides.

Even in the trenches, behind coils of barbed wire, soldiers were not safe. Some of the shells fired at them contained poison gas. Gases such as chlorine caused severe injuries. They choked the throat and burned the eyes. Mustard gas blistered the skin. To survive chemical warfare, soldiers began wearing protective clothing and gas masks.

World War I gas mask

4. **Circle** in the photograph below the following technologies of trench warfare: bayonet, gas mask, barbed wire.

Many battles were fought where neither side won. Often tens of thousands of men would die trying to take over a small area. The battle area between the two enemies' trenches became known as a "no-man's land." It was so dangerous that neither side could control it or would try to capture it.

New War Technologies

Poison gas was a horrifying new weapon. But it was not the only new weapon of World War I. German submarines, called U-boats, could sneak below ships and sink them with torpedoes, or underwater bombs. Airplanes had only recently been invented, in 1903. Eleven years later, fighter planes dropped bombs on enemy targets. They could also attack other planes or troops on the ground with machine guns.

The machine gun became the weapon of choice for defending trench positions. It could fire 600 bullets per minute at targets 1,000 yards away. That was enough to stop an attack by soldiers on horseback or on foot.

The British built a vehicle that machine-gun fire could not stop. It could smash through barbed wire and cross muddy ditches without getting stuck. This armored vehicle ran on metal tracks instead of wheels. It was called a tank.

5. Write how the submarine and the tank changed traditional warfare in World War I.

....

....

....

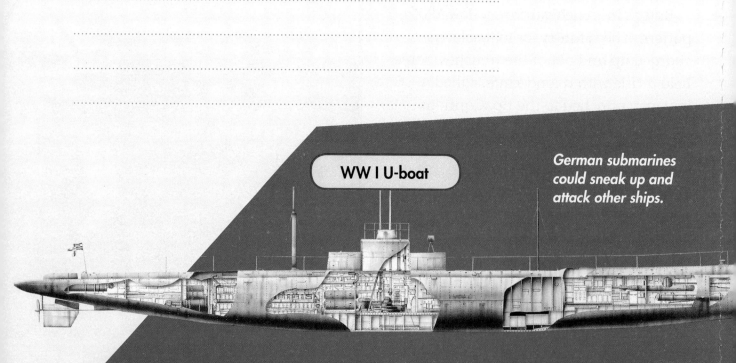

WW I U-boat

German submarines could sneak up and attack other ships.

On the Home Front

While American soldiers fought in Europe, their families and friends worked at home to support their efforts. More than 3 million men served in the U.S. armed forces. That opened up job opportunities for many other Americans.

Workers were needed to build weapons and equipment for the troops. Up to half a million African Americans migrated from the South to find jobs with northern businesses. Around 1 million women worked in factories, offices, stores, and hospitals. Thousands more joined the armed forces in noncombat jobs.

The United States shipped tons of food overseas during the war. As a result, food shortages at home were a problem. Officials such as future President Herbert Hoover, then head of the U.S. Food Administration, urged people to accept "meatless Mondays" and "wheatless Wednesdays."

One solution to the food **scarcity**, or shortage, was a victory garden, also called a war garden. People started growing their own food in their backyards. Some towns set aside areas for community victory gardens.

HELPING HOOVER IN OUR U. S. SCHOOL GARDEN

Posters encouraged Americans, including children, to grow their own food.

WW I tank

Tanks replaced the cavalry, or soldiers on horses. Unlike a horse, a tank can safely cross rough terrain while under fire.

Costs of the War

Finally, the Allies, with the help of about 1,500,000 American troops, won a huge battle in northeastern France. On November 11, 1918, the Central Powers surrendered, ending the war.

Around 116,000 Americans had died and more than 200,000 were wounded in World War I. Human losses suffered by other countries were far greater. Around 8 million soldiers in total lost their lives in the war. Most died in battle, but many were victims of disease.

Another major cost was financial. The United States spent about $33 billion on the war. Much of that came from Americans' purchase of Liberty Bonds. These small loans to the government would later be repaid with a fee called interest.

The Treaty of Versailles

The day the war ended, November 11, was called Armistice Day. An armistice is a cease-fire. In the United States, Armistice Day is remembered as Veterans Day. On this day, we honor all American soldiers, especially those who fought in foreign wars.

6. ◎ **Compare and Contrast** How was the size of Germany different after World War I?

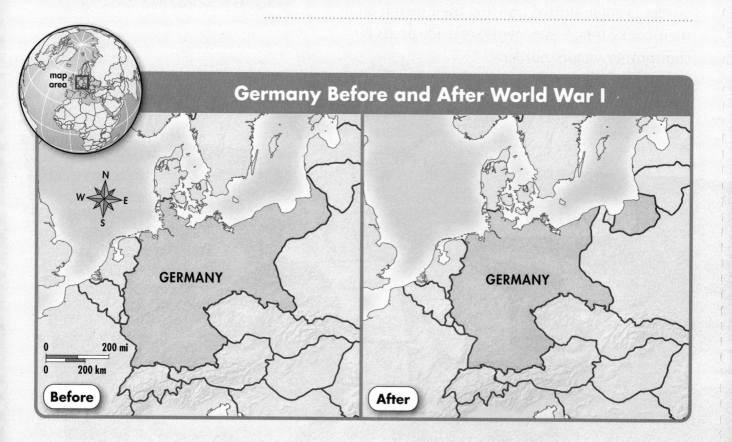

Germany Before and After World War I

Before

After

The official peace treaty was signed on June 28, 1919, in Versailles (vair SYE), France. The Treaty of Versailles punished Germany for its role in starting the war. Germany lost about ten percent of its lands. It had to pay back war costs to the Allied Powers. The treaty also called for creating a League of Nations. The League's member nations would work together for peace.

After the war, Americans wanted a return to isolationism. This feeling prevented the U.S. Senate from approving the Treaty of Versailles. Also, some Americans did not approve of the harsh treatment of Germany. The United States did not join the League of Nations, either. They feared it would force Americans to fight in future foreign wars.

Today, we celebrate Veterans Day on November 11, the day World War I ended. On Veterans Day, Americans honor those who fought and died in foreign wars.

Got it?

7. **◉ Cause and Effect** Which events caused the United States to enter the war?

8. **?** As a teenager during World War I, you receive a letter from a cousin who is on the battlefield. **Write** a passage from the letter that describes his experiences.

my Story Ideas

◼ **Stop!** I need help with ....

❚❚ **Wait!** I have a question about ....

▶ **Go!** Now I know ....

The Roaring Twenties

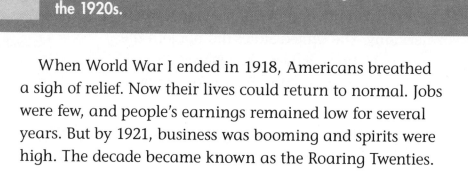

Envision It!

These products were first widely used during the 1920s.

When World War I ended in 1918, Americans breathed a sigh of relief. Now their lives could return to normal. Jobs were few, and people's earnings remained low for several years. But by 1921, business was booming and spirits were high. The decade became known as the Roaring Twenties.

New Products

Entrepreneurs and the industries they started led to the growing U.S. economy. They even produced more goods than consumers wanted, and at a faster rate. **Consumers** are people who buy and use products and services.

Workers on Ford's assembly lines could build more cars faster than ever before.

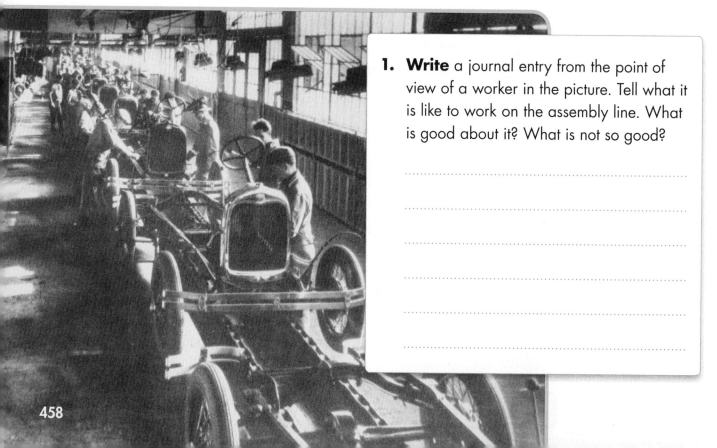

1. **Write** a journal entry from the point of view of a worker in the picture. Tell what it is like to work on the assembly line. What is good about it? What is not so good?

....

....

....

....

....

....

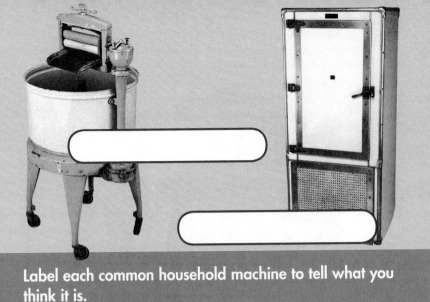

Label each common household machine to tell what you think it is.

UNLOCK THE BIG ?

I will know that the 1920s was a time of progress and plenty for some, but of hardship for others.

Vocabulary

consumer

mass production

mass consumption

Jazz Age

Great Migration

migrant worker

The production of cars rose especially fast during the 1920s. Henry Ford developed an assembly line system to build his Model T cars. In this system, a car started as a frame. The frame moved along a line on a track. Workers at each station on the line added parts to the car. Each worker did just one task, over and over. The assembly line allowed Ford to make large numbers of the same car quickly and inexpensively. This process is known as **mass production.**

Other mass-produced products of the time were radios, washing machines, refrigerators, irons, toasters, and hair dryers. The 1920s became a time of **mass consumption**, or the large-scale demand for goods.

Improvements for Women

For women, the 1920s started on a positive note. After decades of struggle by Susan B. Anthony and others, Congress passed the Nineteenth Amendment, giving women the right to vote. In 1920 it became part of the U.S. Constitution. The law was passed partly in reaction to women's work during the war and in other, new industries.

After the war, most women returned to working in the home. Time-saving new products made housework easier.

As the economy grew, wages rose, and people had more money to spend. They consumed, or used, more goods and services. That helped raise Americans' standard of living, or financial well-being and comfort. This consumption also encouraged the economy to grow even more.

The Culture of the Roaring Twenties

For many Americans, the 1920s "roared" with power and excitement. Traditional ways were cast aside in favor of modern things. It was a time of change.

There is no better symbol of that change than the flapper. Flappers were women who dressed and behaved in a daring manner. They wore shorter skirts, which sometimes rose to the knee. They cut their hair short, in a bobbed style.

The cultural lives of most other Americans also changed. They had more leisure time, so they took longer vacations, attended sporting events, and went to the movies. Silent movies attracted millions of people to buy movie tickets each week. In 1927, the first motion pictures with sound came out. Then movie attendance rose even higher.

At home, families tended to gather around the radio. They could sing along with the latest popular music. They could follow national news, such as the nonstop solo flight of Charles Lindbergh across the Atlantic Ocean in 1927. Many Americans tuned in every night to hear their favorite musical or comedy show. During the day, they might listen to an exciting baseball or football game.

Radio and the movies both helped to create a popular culture that everyone shared. Americans across the country listened to the same songs and saw the same movies. They became fans of the same stars. Actors, such as Charlie Chaplin and Mary Pickford, packed movie theaters. Lindbergh and fellow pilot Amelia Earhart were heroes. Baseball player Babe Ruth and the football player Red Grange were also major celebrities.

2. Some flappers wore eye-catching clothing like this. **Circle** two or more details in this fashion illustration that you think might show 1920s styles.

The Jazz Age

Many musicians also gained fame during the 1920s. The era was also known as the **Jazz Age.** Jazz is a style of music that has roots in traditional African American sounds and rhythms. In the 1920s, jazz became widely known and popular. This was the time when jazz music moved out of small clubs and onto the national stage.

Louis Armstrong did much to bring jazz to a wider audience with his creative trumpet playing. Composer George Gershwin mixed jazz and classical music to create a fresh, modern sound. Bands led by Duke Ellington and Fletcher Henderson got people up on their feet and dancing. Popular dances during the Jazz Age included the Charleston and the Lindy Hop. Both involved quick movements and fancy steps. Young people crowded into dance halls to kick and swing to the lively beat.

Writers, too, caught the excitement of the Jazz Age. In his novel *The Great Gatsby*, F. Scott Fitzgerald looked closely at the modern world. He wrote about the parties, the music, and the people—like himself and his wife, Zelda—who had grown rich in the booming economy. But he saw that the culture of the 1920s was breaking from the past in ways that were not always good. Without traditions to rely on, some people felt lost. Ernest Hemingway also wrote about feelings of loss in the postwar world. His novels include *A Farewell to Arms* and *The Sun Also Rises*.

3. Circle four people mentioned on these two pages. Then, below, **list** their names and what career they were famous for.

Louis Armstrong

Name	Career
Charlie Chaplin	movie star

461

The Harlem Renaissance

In the 1920s, an area of New York City called Harlem became a center for the arts. African American writers, musicians, and painters gathered there to share ideas and to examine their world. These artists explored the experiences of African Americans in the past and in the modern age. This time of great creativity became known as the Harlem Renaissance. A renaissance is a rebirth or flowering of art and learning.

Much of these artists' work promoted pride among African Americans. Many had long been shut out of the American dream, which promised everyone equal rights and opportunities. The poet Langston Hughes claimed the right to share in that dream when he wrote, "I, Too." Through her stories, Zora Neale Hurston showed African Americans as people with goals and problems just like those of all Americans. At the end of the era, Jacob Lawrence told stories of the African American experience through his paintings, like the one on the next page.

This flowering of culture gave a boost to a movement pushing for civil rights. One of the leaders of that movement, W.E.B. DuBois, worked for fair and equal treatment of African Americans.

4. **Write** a sentence to explain who you think "they" are in the poem "I, Too."

....

....

....

....

Movement and Change

African Americans continued to stream from the South after World War I in search of jobs. The flow north grew so large that it was called the **Great Migration.** By the end of the 1920s, more than 1 million had moved north, mainly to cities.

In many ways, life was better in the North for African Americans. They did not have to sit in a special section on buses or in movie theaters. They were not prevented from voting. Wages were higher in the North, too. But African Americans, as a rule, did not move out of lower-paying jobs as fast as white people did.

Factors of the Great Migration

Leave the South	Go to the North
....	....
....	....
....	....

5. **List** three factors that caused African Americans to leave the South. **List** three factors that drew African Americans to the North.

The Migration of the American Negro, Panel No. 1. *This and 59 other paintings by Jacob Lawrence told the story of the Great Migration.*

Migrant workers, like these from Latin America, often faced discrimination in the 1920s.

A Tough Time for Immigrants

Many immigrants from Latin American countries also made little economic progress. In the West and Southwest, great numbers of Latin Americans came to the United States as **migrant workers**, to harvest crops. They moved around with the seasons, never putting down roots. They also faced a wave of anti-immigrant feelings.

Some Americans had long opposed immigration. They thought all immigrants took Americans' jobs. They also thought that immigrants threatened American culture and values. In the 1920s, the Ku Klux Klan were spreading ideas of hatred against African Americans. They also opposed people who had different values and religious beliefs. Anti-immigrant groups gained support, as well.

In 1924, Congress passed the Immigration Act of 1924. It limited the number of people from Asia and Southern and Eastern Europe who could move into the United States each year.

Reforms to the Constitution

During the early 1900s, several changes had been made to the U.S. Constitution. In 1913, two amendments were added. The Sixteenth Amendment gave Congress the power to collect a tax on people's incomes. The Seventeenth Amendment allowed the direct election of U.S. senators by the people. Before this, most senators were elected by state legislatures. In 1920, Congress passed the Nineteenth Amendment giving women the right to vote.

At the same time, Progressive reformers worked for prohibition, or the complete ban, on alcohol. In 1920, the Eighteenth Amendment outlawed the making, selling, or shipping of alcohol anywhere in the United States.

The law stayed in effect throughout the 1920s. Some people still wanted alcohol though, even if it meant breaking the law to get it. Otherwise law-abiding people found ways to get alcohol illegally. Soon criminals were smuggling and selling it. Their competition led to violence. Police spent much time and effort to find and destroy illegal alcohol.

By 1933, however, the country had changed its mind. The Twenty-first Amendment was passed in that year, ending Prohibition.

6. ◉ **Cause and Effect Write** why Prohibition led to crime and violence.

....

....

Police destroy alcohol during Prohibition.

Got it?

7. ◉ **Cause and Effect Write** what you think might have been one cause and one effect of the Seventeenth Amendment.

....

....

....

8. ❓ It's 1925 and you just attended your first jazz concert. **Write** a brief journal entry that describes your response to this new style of music.

my Story Ideas

....

....

⬛ **Stop!** I need help with ....

⏸ **Wait!** I have a question about ....

▶ **Go!** Now I know ....

The Great Depression

Envision It!

During the Great Depression, millions of Americans, like this woman and her family, experienced terrible poverty.

During the 1920s, under presidents Warren G. Harding and Calvin Coolidge, the U.S. economy seemed strong. But in 1929, the year when Herbert Hoover became president, the country went from good times to bad in a hurry. In that year, a long and severe decline in the economy began. This decline became known as the **Great Depression.**

Trouble for Farmers

The U. S. economy seemed to be booming in the 1920s. As the decade passed, though, several signs suggested that the economy was not as strong as it seemed. Trouble was growing in the lives of farmers and factory workers.

Most farmers never fully enjoyed the good times of the 1920s. New technology should have made their work more profitable. Gas-powered tractors and other machinery allowed farmers to grow more crops. But growing more crops turned out to be a problem. The supply of food became greater than people's demand for it.

With new machinery in the 1920s, farmers could grow and harvest more crops than before.

UNLOCK THE BIG ?

I will know the different ways in which Americans responded to the hardships of the Great Depression.

Vocabulary

Great Depression   credit
unemployment   tariff
stock market   Dust Bowl

More Supply, Less Demand

Lower demand caused food prices to fall. Many farmers had taken out loans to pay for their expensive new machines. Now they couldn't make enough money to pay back the loans.

Farmers who didn't buy modern equipment also suffered. Their costs for producing food were too high. They couldn't compete with the larger farms. Farm workers couldn't compete with tractors. It seemed that their labor was no longer needed. In the 1920s, many migrated to the cities to find other work.

These migrants often found that the supply of jobs was limited even in the cities. Companies had built new factories and hired more workers to meet growing consumer demand. But Americans could not consume all the goods being produced. Companies now had to cut production and jobs.

1. ◉ **Cause and Effect**
Fill in three effects of new farm technology.

Effects of New Farm Technology

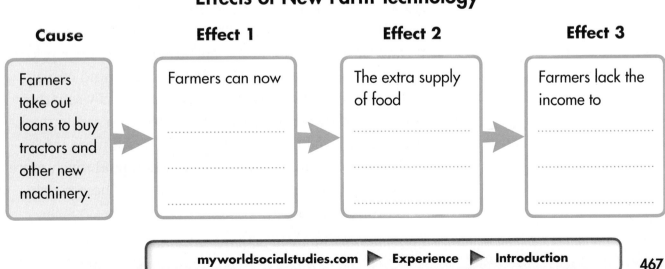

Cause	Effect 1	Effect 2	Effect 3
Farmers take out loans to buy tractors and other new machinery.	Farmers can now	The extra supply of food	Farmers lack the income to

2. This newspaper headline announced the crash of the stock market. **Circle** the words in the newspaper that tell about the crash.

The Stock Market Crash

By the late 1920s, the signs of trouble were clear. Factories were letting workers go or not hiring new workers. **Unemployment**—the condition of being out of work—was rising. Without jobs, Americans could not afford to buy new products. People began to buy less. In March 1929, President Hoover gave his first public address. In the speech, he told the American people:

"I have no fears for the future of our country. It is bright with hope."

Sadly, he was wrong. Seven months later, the stock market crashed. The **stock market** is where people buy and sell stocks. A *crash* is a sudden, steep drop in the prices of stocks. Stocks are shares in the ownership of a company. If a company wants to raise money, it sells stocks. The value or price of a stock generally rises when a company does well, but it falls if the company does poorly.

Buying on Credit

During the 1920s, some people got rich and many others hoped to. People bought stocks hoping to resell them for a big profit. But many did not buy stocks with their own money. Instead, they used **credit**, or borrowed money.

These people expected stock prices to keep rising. Then they could pay back their loans and still make a profit. If stocks prices fell, they might owe more money than their stocks were worth. They could lose everything.

In the 1920s, stock prices rose unusually fast and people invested. Then in the autumn of 1929, stock prices began to fall. Many people worried about losing money, so they sold their stocks. Others panicked. They sold their stocks for whatever price they could get. As a result, stock prices fell by one third. People rushed to sell more stocks, and prices kept falling. Many people had paid much more for their stocks than they were now worth. These people were ruined financially.

The Great Depression Begins

The crash was just one of several causes of what is known as the Great Depression. The Great Depression was the longest and most severe economic decline in United States history.

The economy goes through ups and downs all the time. A depression begins as a normal downturn in the economy. In the late 1920s, the overproduction of goods caused a downturn. The stock market crash and the buying of stocks with borrowed money helped the downturn grow into a depression.

A year after the crash came the first bank panics. Consumers had bought cars and other goods on credit. Now they could not pay their loans. Many banks ran out of funds and had to close. People who had savings in those banks lost them. Customers of other banks raced to withdraw their savings. Many of those banks ran out of cash and had to close, too.

3. Early in the Great Depression, people rushed to this bank to find out if they had lost money. **Write** at least one way you think a bank run like this one could affect a family.

Collaboration and Creativity

Generate New Ideas

When you need to solve a problem it is helpful to have tools you can use to generate, or come up with, new ideas. The first step in generating new ideas is to gather information about the problem. For example, what caused it? Why did it happen? What resources can you use to solve it? Once you have listed the main information about the problem, you can then use these steps to generate solutions.

- **State the problem.** Write, in clear language, exactly what the problem is.

- **Analyze the causes.** Think about how things were before the problem started. What caused the problem or made it worse?

- **Think about the goal of the solution.** Decide what the goal of a solution must be. Ask, "What do we want to accomplish?" or "What would improve this situation?"

- **Brainstorm ideas.** Alone or in a group, list whatever ideas come to mind, even if they seem unrealistic at first. Consider each idea; then keep the best one or two, and delete the others.

The Town of Caznor, 1931

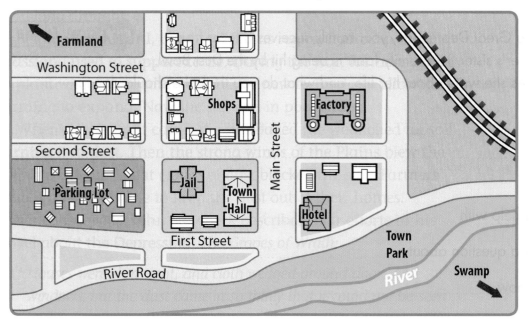

Try it!

The map on the opposite page shows an imaginary town, Caznor, in 1931. The factory in Caznor closed a year ago, and all 30 workers lost their jobs. Now most are homeless, living in shacks in a parking lot. The state has given the town emergency funds, which could help, but the mayor asks you to come up with a way to help the workers. You know some facts. You have a map of the town. Follow the steps for generating new ideas to develop a solution.

1. **Write** a statement of the problem.

   ....

2. **List** the cause or causes.

   ....

   ....

3. **Write** the main goal of your solution.

   ....

   ....

4. **Brainstorm** solutions. On another sheet of paper, **record** all your ideas. Then cut down the list to include only the best one.

5. **Describe** your best solution here:

   ....

   ....

   ....

6. **Apply** Think of a problem in your school or community. Then, follow the steps to generate two new ideas that might solve it.

   ....

   ....

The New Deal

Envision It!

During the Great Depression the federal government hired artists to create public art, such as this mural in California.

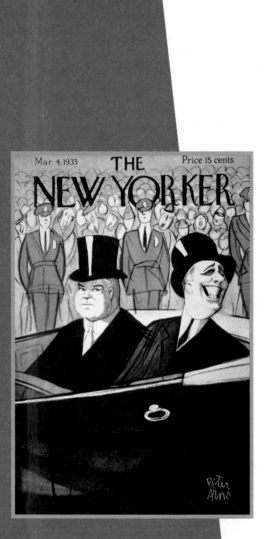

This magazine cover shows a glum Hoover and a cheerful FDR on his inauguration day.

For the first two years of the Great Depression, many Americans suffered. They lost jobs, homes, and hope. The U.S. government did little to help. President Hoover had faith that the economy would bounce back. But the crisis only grew worse. Many people blamed Hoover. In 1932, they would choose a new leader: Franklin D. Roosevelt, also known as FDR.

Roosevelt and the New Deal

Roosevelt realized that Americans were afraid of the future. He also had once feared for his own future. Early in his career he had been a state senator and then Assistant Secretary of the Navy. By 1921, he was a rising star in the Democratic Party. But in that year, he caught the terrible disease, polio.

Franklin Roosevelt survived polio, but his legs were damaged—he would never walk again without help. But he did not give up. He stayed active in politics. In 1928, he was elected governor of New York.

During the 1932 presidential election, Roosevelt told the American people that, if he won, he would use the power of the government to try to solve their problems. He made them a promise: "I pledge you, I pledge myself, to a new deal for the American people." Once elected, the programs President Roosevelt set up to end the Depression became known as the **New Deal.**

UNLOCK THE BIG ?

I will know that the purpose of the New Deal was to improve people's lives during the Great Depression.

Vocabulary

New Deal
First Hundred Days
Social Security

List three things that you think the artist is trying to express in the mural.

Immediately, Roosevelt tried to give the American people hope. In his first presidential speech he told them, "The only thing we have to fear is fear itself." He would work right away to restore confidence in the economy. His New Deal programs would take aim at the major problems facing the nation.

1. **Write** what you would say as president to give the American people hope for the future.

President Roosevelt used the power of radio to speak directly to the American people.

New Laws

On his second day as president, March 5, 1933, Roosevelt took a bold step. To deal with bank panics, he declared a "bank holiday." For four days, all banks would be closed. Each bank would only reopen when it was judged to be stable.

Soon, Roosevelt also gave the first of his "fireside chats." He spoke on the radio directly to the American people. Through these informal talks, the president kept the public informed about the progress of the New Deal. He hoped to lift their spirits.

Much happened in the first three months of Roosevelt's presidency. This period, from March to June, became known as the **First Hundred Days.** During this time, the president worked with Congress to pass many new laws. The new laws focused on three goals: relief, recovery, and reform.

Relief measures aimed to help the unemployed. One of them, the Civilian Conservation Corps (CCC), put 250,000 young men to work right away. They built roads, planted trees, and did other work on public lands. By 1941, the CCC had employed more than 2 million people.

The goal of the recovery programs was to boost the economy. A major recovery project was the Tennessee Valley Authority (TVA). One task of the TVA was to control flooding in the region of the Tennessee River Valley. Another job was to provide electricity to the people of the region. Workers did both by building dams and power plants.

2. Circle the names of three states in the Tennessee Valley that benefitted from the TVA.

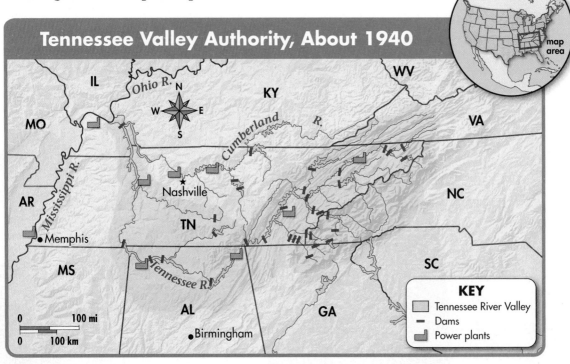

Tennessee Valley Authority, About 1940

IL
Ohio R.
N
W E
S
MO
KY
WV
VA
Cumberland
R.
AR
Nashville
TN
NC
Mississippi R.
Memphis
MS
Tennessee R.
SC
0   100 mi
0   100 km
AL
GA
Birmingham

KEY
Tennessee River Valley
Dams
Power plants

More New Deal Reforms

Some New Deal reforms were meant to prevent future problems, like those that had caused the Great Depression. The Banking Act of 1933 improved banking practices. One of its most important features was the Federal Deposit Insurance Corporation (FDIC). This agency insures bank deposits up to a certain amount. It ended bank panics, since people trusted that their savings were safe. In 1934, the Securities and Exchange Commission (SEC) was formed to protect people in the stock market. That is still the SEC's main job.

The FDIC, TVA, and CCC, as well as a dozen or more other programs, were all put in place during the First Hundred Days. Some, including the FDIC and the TVA, still exist. The CCC ended in 1942.

After the First Hundred Days, the New Deal produced many other programs. Later in 1933, Congress passed the Social Security Act. **Social Security** is an insurance system to help support the disabled and provide funds to retired people. Today, this program still provides benefits to millions of retired, disabled, and other Americans.

Other programs included the Works Progress Administration (WPA), created in 1935. This agency, like the CCC, put jobless people to work—more than 8 million in all. They built roads, bridges, parks, airports, and public buildings. The WPA also employed many writers, actors, and artists. It ended in 1943.

ILLINOIS
NATIONAL YOUTH ADMINISTRATION

GIRLS – ARE YOU INTERESTED IN A JOB?
FIND OUT WHAT AN OCCUPATION HAS TO OFFER YOU IN PAY- EMPLOYMENT-SECURITY AND PROMOTION
FREE CLASSES IN OCCUPATIONS
ON   AT
THE SUBJECT WILL BE

Wm. J. CAMPBELL, STATE DIRECTOR

Posters like this one encouraged women to learn new job skills.

3. **Cause and Effect**
Fill in the effect that each program had on Americans.

New Deal Programs	Purpose
CCC and WPA	
TVA	
FDIC	
SEC	

479

Lesson 4

The New Deal

8. Why was the New Deal established and what were the three main goals of its programs?

....

....

....

....

....

....

9. Circle the correct answer.

The New Deal agency that helped bring an end to bank panics was called the

A. FDIC.

B. SEC.

C. TVA.

D. CCC.

10. Fill in the blank with the correct word.

The New Deal .... the role of the U.S. government in the economy.

11. **How do people respond to good times and bad?**

The period covered in this chapter was one of ups and downs. Use these questions to think more about this chapter's Big Question.

a. What do victory gardens suggest about how Americans responded to World War I?

....

....

....

b. How did consumption of goods change between the 1920s and the 1930s?

....

....

....

c. How did President Roosevelt respond to the Great Depression?

....

....

....

....

....

Go online to write and illustrate your own **myStory Book** using the **myStory Ideas** from this chapter.

How do people respond to good times and bad?

In a 30-year period, from the beginning of World War I through the Great Depression, the United States experienced war, peace, good economic times, and very bad economic times.

Think about what you might have enjoyed had you lived during the good times of the 1920s. **Write** about how you would have expressed your enjoyment.

....

....

....

....

....

Now **write** how you might have experienced the Great Depression.

....

....

....

....

....

....

While you're online, check out the **myStory Current Events** area where you can create your own book on a topic that's in the news.

World War II

my Story Spark

What is worth fighting for?

You may know someone or have seen news stories about men and women who are serving in the military. Why do you think people are willing to take on this dangerous job?

....

....

....

....

This is the memorial for the American navy ship, the USS Arizona, in Pearl Harbor, Hawaii. The ship was sunk when the Japanese attacked in 1941, killing 1,177 crew members. The sunken ship lies below the memorial.

USS ARIZONA BB 39

World War II
Those Who Were There

my Story Video

"What stories am I going to hear?" Katelyn wonders as she gets ready for her interviews. Today she's talking with people who lived through World War II. She has lots of questions for them and is excited to learn from those with first-hand knowledge. As she enters the Veterans of Foreign Wars, or VFW, Center, she sees a variety of friendly faces.

People who lived during World War II are getting more difficult to find as the years go by. Katelyn understands that this is an extraordinary opportunity for her.

"It's so nice to meet you all," she says. "They are older than my grandparents," she whispers. "This is really cool; we're going to learn a lot!"

Right away Katelyn is greeted by Gigi, an energetic and friendly woman. "I was about your age when the war started," Gigi says. "I remember two main things: the beginning and the end. But I did have loads of fun in the middle."

Katelyn meets Gigi, who lived during World War II.

During the war, top female players like Gigi were recruited for the All-American Girls Professional Baseball League.

Frank's VFW hat shows that he is a life member. The VFW works to help those who serve in the military.

Mo, top, before a mission; Frank, below, in uniform

Expecting to hear war stories, Katelyn is pleasantly surprised by Gigi's first words. "I met new people and had a wonderful time," Gigi continues. "It was about baseball for me."

"Baseball?" Katelyn asks. "Yep!" Gigi replies. "One day I got home from school and a man had come to our house asking my parents if they would allow me to play baseball. I'd been scouted pitching for our church league. They wanted me to be the pitcher for their team! I was ecstatic."

Most baseball players had joined the military and were off at war. To help keep spirits high, it was decided to start a women's league. Gigi spent two wonderful years playing baseball. "We knew the war was necessary, and playing baseball was one way for us to help fight!"

Next, Katelyn meets Frank. Frank was in the Navy during the war. His main job was to fix and maintain the ships. He faced many difficult days as a sailor out at sea. But it's the memory of how he felt when the war ended that he remembers best. "I was aboard an aircraft carrier on V-J Day."

"I'm sorry," Katelyn interrupts. "What's V-J Day?"

"That stood for 'Victory over Japan,'" he says. "I was so grateful to be able to get off that ship and be in Times Square in New York City."

You can almost feel the excitement as Frank continues. "You see, my mother lived on Long Island. Among 2 million people there at Times Square, I bumped into her. Can you believe it?"

Neither Frank nor his mom knew the other was there. It was the first time they had seen each other in three and a half years. "We had a grand old time!" Frank says.

Mo poses at base camp between bombing runs.

These medals were awarded to Mo during the war. The medal on the left is the Distinguished Flying Cross, given for heroism.

Before Katelyn can stop smiling, she's introduced to Moylan, known to his friends as "Mo." An Air Force veteran, Mo was a pilot during World War II. His memory of the war is a little different from Gigi's or Frank's.

"When I first started to fly in combat, we had to fly 25 missions. The planes were being shot down so easily, completing 25 missions didn't seem very possible," he says. After Mo survived the first 5, though, he thought 20 might not be so bad. "Then they changed the quota to 30 missions. Now that seemed impossible!"

Mo received many medals at the end of the war for his bravery. He was honored to accept those awards, but remembering the friends who died is still difficult.

"I was part of the air strike force against the Germans on D-Day, one of the most important days of the war. We helped the ground troops land on the beaches of Normandy, France. I am very proud of that fact."

"It sounds like you played a big part in helping us win the war!" says Katelyn. "Thank you, Mo!"

As Katelyn turns to leave, she says, "I'm really honored to have met such fascinating and courageous people. They helped this country during such a difficult time in history. I'm really glad people like Gigi, Frank, and Mo felt freedom was worth fighting for!"

Think About It The experiences of these people during the war were different. But they all contributed to the war effort because they believed it was important. As you read the chapter ahead, think about what you would fight for and how you might have helped during World War II.

Katelyn's new friends, Mo, Frank, and Gigi

World War II Begins

Envision It!

It was December 1941. The American naval base in Hawaii had just been attacked by the nation of Japan.

After World War I, the United States returned to its prewar policy of isolationism. It chose not to get involved in foreign affairs. It even reduced the size of its armed forces. Americans wished never to go to war again. But events in Europe soon drew the United States into another global conflict.

Dictators Rise in Europe

The Great Depression of the 1930s had caused hard times everywhere. People in some countries blamed their governments. They began looking for strong leaders to take control and fix the problems. Some even turned to dictators. A **dictator** is a ruler who has total power over a country.

One such dictator was Benito Mussolini [beh NEE toh moo soh LEE nee] of Italy. Italy had been one of the victors of World War I. But the country had lost many lives in that war. It had also lost a lot of money and had gained little from the Treaty of Versailles that had ended the war. This angered many Italians.

Mussolini came to power in 1922. His party was called the Fascists, which gave us the word *fascism*. **Fascism** is a movement that gives all power to the government and does away with individual freedoms. It uses the military to enforce laws. Mussolini took control. He banned elections and ended free speech.

Italian dictator Benito Mussolini inspired great crowds.

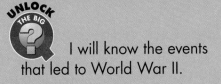
Vocabulary

dictator
fascism
Axis
Allies
Lend-Lease Act

Write a list of actions the United States could have taken to protect itself from more attacks.

An even more dangerous dictator was Adolf Hitler. He and his political party, the Nazis, gained control of Germany in 1933. The Nazis turned the country into a fascist state. Hitler was its supreme leader.

Germans, too, were unhappy with the Versailles treaty. It stated that they were guilty of starting World War I. It had forced Germany to make payments to the victors of the war. It had also taken away some of Germany's land. Hitler vowed to get back that land, and more. To do so, he began rearming Germany and increasing its troop levels.

1. Adolf Hitler led rallies to win support from huge crowds. **Write** why you think so many people followed a dictator like Hitler.

....

....

The Axis and the Allies

Mussolini set out to expand Italy's territory. In 1935, he took over the African country of Ethiopia, then made an agreement with Hitler. The two fascist countries planned to conquer other countries. They called their new alliance the **Axis.** Japan would later join the Axis. By 1937, Japan had invaded China and controlled much territory in the Pacific.

Starting in 1936, German armies began taking lands that the nation had lost in World War I. The leaders of Britain and France urged Hitler to stop his aggression, but they did not try to block him. The British and French people did not want to go to war again. Britain and France were known as the **Allies.**

2. Study the map. On which continents did the Axis have control?

....

....

World War II, 1939–1945

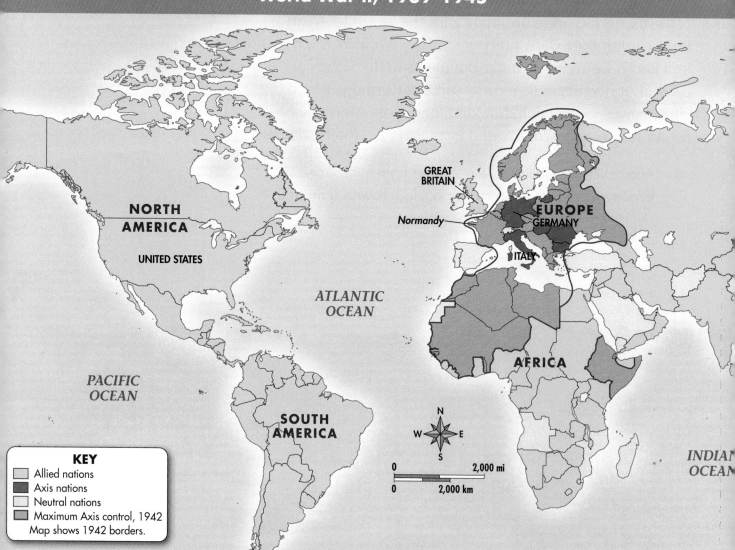

NORTH AMERICA

UNITED STATES

ATLANTIC OCEAN

PACIFIC OCEAN

SOUTH AMERICA

GREAT BRITAIN

Normandy

EUROPE
GERMANY

ITALY

AFRICA

INDIAN OCEAN

N
W E
S

0   2,000 mi

0   2,000 km

KEY
- Allied nations
- Axis nations
- Neutral nations
- Maximum Axis control, 1942
Map shows 1942 borders.

In 1938, Germany took control of its neighbor, Austria. In 1939, Hitler prepared to invade Poland. Britain and France said they would fight if Hitler went ahead with his plans. In September, Nazi forces moved into Poland. The Allies then declared war on Germany. World War II had begun.

The Germans easily defeated the Polish army. A few months later, Hitler decided the time was right to invade France. First, his armies defeated the smaller and weaker countries west and north of Germany. British troops sent to block the Germans were forced to retreat. In May, the German army swept across northern France, all the way to the English Channel.

Then, in June 1940, German forces struck the heart of France. The French capital, Paris, fell. In less than three weeks of fighting, Germany had conquered France. Italy now declared war on the Allies, too.

3. ◉ Sequence **Underline** and **number** the dates and other time clues on these two pages that show the sequence of events that led to the start of World War II.

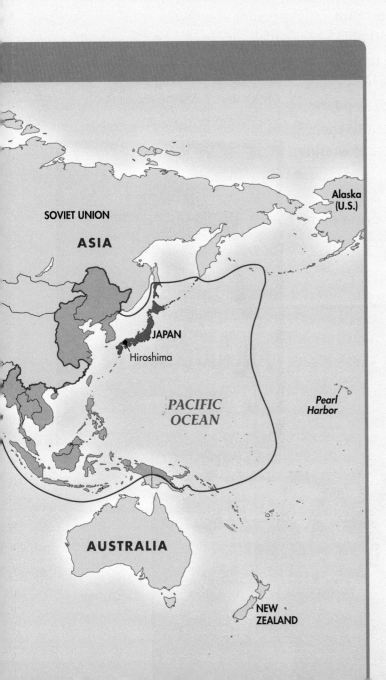

In 1939, the Allies declared war on Hitler's Germany.

The United States Debates Going to War

Great Britain now stood alone against Hitler. The British defense of their island nation is called the Battle of Britain. It took place mostly in the air. For months, night after night, German planes dropped bombs on London and other British cities. British fighter planes shot down many bombers, but the pounding continued.

Britain's prime minister, Winston Churchill, asked U.S. President Franklin Roosevelt for help. Many Americans still wanted to stay out of the conflict. With the Atlantic Ocean between them and Europe, they felt secure. Others, though, feared what might happen if Hitler were able to defeat the British. What would keep him from attacking the United States?

Roosevelt decided to take action, but still remain neutral. In September 1940, he sent Britain 50 old destroyers, a type of warship, to help defend its coastline. Then in March 1941, Roosevelt signed the **Lend-Lease Act.** This bill allowed the United States to sell, lend, or give ships, planes, tanks, and other equipment to the Allies. Many Americans worried that this action would draw the country into war.

Meanwhile, Congress passed the Selective Service Act. This law required more than 1 million young men to serve in the military by the fall of 1941. The United States built up its army, air force, and navy.

During the Battle of Britain, people in London looked for shelter from air raids, or bombings, in the city's subway system, called the Underground.

Hawaii and Pearl Harbor

Hawaii

Pearl Harbor

JAPAN UNITED STATES

Hawaii

PACIFIC OCEAN

0   100 mi
0   100 km

4. Find Hawaii on the globe. Then look at the photo of the U.S. naval base at Pearl Harbor, which shows rows of American warships. **Write** a caption explaining why the Japanese might have chosen to attack the United States at Pearl Harbor.

The Attack on Pearl Harbor

By the spring of 1941, the British had won the Battle of Britain. The Germans had been stopped at the English Channel. But in the Pacific, Japan was steadily grabbing more land. It now controlled much of China and Southeast Asia.

Japan depended on the United States for many of its resources, including oil. But in July 1941, Congress banned all trade with Japan. As a result, tensions rose between the two countries. In Japan, the military ran the government. Leading general, Hideki Tojo (hee DAY kee TOH joh), believed that the U.S. Navy stood in the way of Japan's complete control over East Asia. Japan decided to attack the U.S. Pacific fleet.

On December 7, 1941, Japan launched a surprise attack on the U.S. Navy base at Pearl Harbor, Hawaii. The first Japanese bombers arrived early in the morning. They had taken off from the decks of aircraft carriers far out at sea. The Japanese sank or damaged 18 American warships and destroyed nearly 200 planes. More than 2,300 soldiers and sailors from the base died.

On December 8, President Roosevelt told Congress:

Yesterday, December 7, 1941—a date which will live in infamy [shame]—the United States of America was suddenly and deliberately attacked by naval and air forces of the Empire of Japan.

That same day, Congress declared war on Japan. The attitude of Americans quickly shifted. Now most of them supported joining the war.

Germany Attacks the Soviet Union

Hitler's armies had easily moved west across Europe. But all that time, Hitler had his eye on a large area of rich farmland far to the east. The land was in Russia, then called the Soviet Union. In 1941, Hitler would try to claim it for Germany.

The Soviet Union was ruled by Joseph Stalin. Stalin, himself a brutal dictator, did not trust Hitler. In 1939 he and Hitler had made an agreement not to attack each other. That agreement had allowed Hitler to send his full forces west to conquer France. He did not have to worry about fighting the Soviet Union on a second front in the east. The pact had also left Stalin free to invade Finland, which he did in 1940.

In June 1941, Hitler broke the agreement with Stalin. He began an invasion of the Soviet Union. Hitler sent 3 million German troops, backed by 3,000 tanks and 2,500 planes, against the Soviets. The Germans destroyed much of the Soviet army and forced the remaining Soviet troops to retreat.

As the Soviets retreated, they burned crops and destroyed railways and factories. The goal of this "scorched-earth" policy was to leave nothing behind for the Germans to claim.

5. Label each leader on these two pages *Axis* or *Allies* to show which side his country fought on in the war.

Benito Mussolini

....

Joseph Stalin

....

Hideki Tojo

....

Franklin Roosevelt

....

The Germans still pressed forward. By November they had nearly reached Moscow, the Soviet capital.

Stalin needed help. He had never been friendly with Britain or the United States. But now he was forced to turn to them for equipment and supplies. The United States, through the Lend-Lease Act, gave the Soviet Union a loan of $1 billion to buy what it needed. Soon, the Soviet Union would become an important member of the Allies.

The Soviet scorched-earth policy slowed the advance of the German army. Then the Soviet winter, with its heavy snows and bitterly cold temperatures, stopped the Germans completely. Soviet forces were able to drive them back. In a few months, the Soviets had pushed the German troops well away from Moscow.

Adolf Hitler

....

Winston Churchill

....

Got it?

6. ◉ **Sequence Number** the events below from 1 to 4 to show the correct sequence in which they happened.

_____ Japan bombs Pearl Harbor.   _____ France falls to German forces.

_____ The Battle of Britain starts.   _____ Germany invades Poland.

7. ? In the attic of an old house, you and your friends find some newspapers from the late 1930s. One headline reads, "Hitler's Troops Continue to Advance." **Write** what you say to your friends to explain the headline.

my Story Ideas

....

....

⬛ **Stop!** I need help with ....

❙❙ **Wait!** I have a question about ....

▶ **Go!** Now I know ....

Analyze Historical Visuals

Look at the photo below. What is your first reaction? You might say, "It's a picture of some soldiers." That is true. But it is more than that. When you analyze visuals from history, like this photo, you can uncover important details. Historical visuals can help you learn more about the period you are studying.

To analyze a historical visual, follow these steps:

1. Identify what you see. What, exactly, is in the picture? Note people, objects, and major details.

2. Describe the action. What is going on in the picture?

3. Determine the mood. Does the picture express sadness, happiness, or some other emotion?

4. Link the picture with any nearby text. If there is a caption, how does it help you understand the picture?

5. Use your experience and what you have learned to draw a conclusion about the meaning or importance of the picture.

Analyze the historical picture on the opposite page. Follow the steps and answer the questions.

1. **Identify** what you see in the visual.

   ....

   ....

   ....

2. **Describe** any action you see in the visual.

   ....

3. **Determine the mood** of the visual.

   ....

   • What does the mood suggest to you about the soldiers?

   ....

4. Suppose that near the photograph is a caption or text heading that says "Americans Ship Out." **Draw** a conclusion about what is going on in this picture.

   ....

   ....

A poster advertising war bonds

5. **Apply** The U.S. government raised money by selling war bonds. What conclusions can you draw from this poster?

   ....

   ....

   ....

World War II at Home

Envision It!

During World War II, Americans did many things to help the war effort. These boys are collecting metal to recycle.

During the war, the U.S. government printed posters like this one to encourage women to take jobs in war industries.

Starting in 1941, many autoworkers learned a new trade. Their factories were converted to wartime use. The workers stopped making cars and started making planes or tanks or bombs. The assembly line of one auto plant near Detroit, Michigan, turned out a new plane every two hours. By the end of the war, about 200,000 companies had switched from producing consumer goods to military ones. This was just one of many changes that the war caused on the American home front.

Helping Win the War

Food and fuel became scarce during the war. Soldiers needed food. Their planes, tanks, and ships needed fuel. Other goods became scarce, too, as more goods were needed to help the war effort. Americans at home had to learn to get by without some things and with less of others.

The U.S. government tried to make sure that everyone had equal shares of scarce goods. In 1942, it set up a rationing system. **Rationing** is a system that limits the amount of scarce goods people can buy. President Roosevelt told Congress, "…where any important article becomes scarce, rationing is the democratic, equitable [fair] solution."

Rationed foods included sugar, butter, meat, eggs, and canned goods. Tires and gasoline were also rationed. Highway speed limits were lowered to save fuel.

UNLOCK THE BIG ?

I will know that Americans at home during World War II played an important role in the war effort.

Vocabulary

rationing

war bond

internment camp

Draw a poster or write a slogan aimed at getting Americans involved in the war effort at home.

Americans also helped the war effort by recycling. War industries needed metal, paper, and rubber. To do their part, children held "scrap drives." They went from door to door, collecting scrap materials. People contributed metal cans, tin foil, old cooking pots, piles of newspapers, and old tires.

Much of the food grown on American farms was shipped overseas to feed the Allied troops. As they had done in World War I, Americans made up for food shortages by planting victory gardens. These vegetable plots popped up in backyards and public spaces all over the country. In 1943, Americans planted about 20 million victory gardens.

Americans also supported their country by lending it money. The cost of fighting the war was about $350 billion. Taxes paid some of the cost, but the government borrowed the rest. It did so by selling **war bonds.** By purchasing bonds, Americans lent money to the government. People later earned money called interest on these bonds. More importantly, buying bonds helped to fund the war.

Victory gardens helped free up food for the troops and provided Americans at home with fresh food.

1. **Draw** a check mark next to the activity on these pages you think had the greatest impact on the war. **Explain** your choice.

....

....

....

....

The Battle for Europe and North Africa

The German invasion of the Soviet Union had stalled outside Moscow in December 1941. But the Germans did not give up. Soon they had the Soviets on the defensive again. Now the German goal was to conquer the Soviet city of Stalingrad. The Battle of Stalingrad was one of the turning points of World War II.

The battle started in September 1942. The German army entered the city but met fierce resistance. Soviet troops defended every house on every block. Then, in November, a large Soviet force managed to break out of the city. Soon they had the German army surrounded. With winter coming on, the German troops were trapped. The battle ended in February 1943, when the invading Germans surrendered. Finally, the Soviets started pushing the rest of the German forces out of their country. Germany would never conquer the Soviet Union now.

In 1942, Axis forces held all of North Africa except Egypt. That June, Axis troops invaded Egypt. They aimed to take over the Suez Canal, a key Middle East shipping route. In October 1942, a British army unit forced the Axis troops to retreat. Again, it was a major victory for the Allies.

The next month, Allied troops landed in North Africa and started moving east. The British in Egypt moved west. The Axis troops were caught in Tunisia, between the two Allied forces. A series of hard battles followed. In May 1943, the Allies forced about 250,000 Germans and Italians to surrender.

Now the Allies were free to cross the Mediterranean Sea to invade Italy. The Allied campaign to take Italy began on the island of Sicily. By August 1943 the Allies controlled the island. Next, they began heavily bombing Italian cities on the mainland.

2. Study the photo below. **Explain** how the Russian climate affected the attacking Germans.

....

....

....

....

....

German troops trudge through snow after the Battle of Stalingrad.

The Allied invasion and constant bombing by air brought big changes. Mussolini resigned. In September, the Italians surrendered. A month later, the new Italian government declared war on Germany, its former ally.

At the same time, American and British bombers were hitting targets inside Germany. One raid on the city of Dresden killed about 45,000 German people.

3. Sequence **Draw** a line from the timeline entries for 1942 and 1943 to the locations on the map where each event happened.

World War II in Europe and Africa

1941
December—German advance stalls near Moscow

1942
September—Battle of Stalingrad begins

1943
May—250,000 Germans and Italians surrender in Tunisia

1944
June—Allies enter Rome

1942
October—British stop Axis forces in Egypt

1943
August—Allies secure Sicily

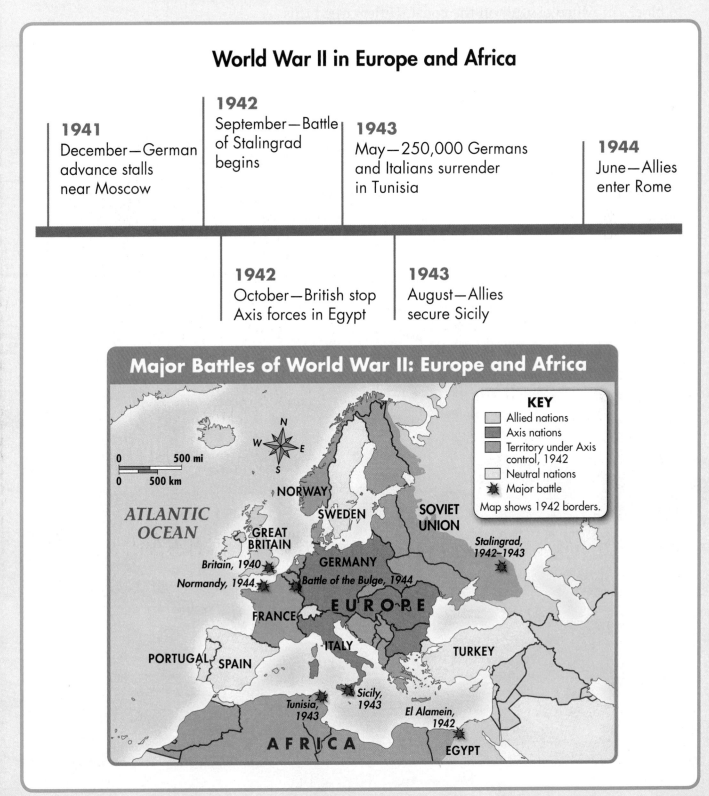

Major Battles of World War II: Europe and Africa

KEY
- Allied nations
- Axis nations
- Territory under Axis control, 1942
- Neutral nations
- ✴ Major battle

Map shows 1942 borders.

ATLANTIC OCEAN

NORWAY
SWEDEN
SOVIET UNION
GREAT BRITAIN
Britain, 1940
Normandy, 1944
Battle of the Bulge, 1944
GERMANY
Stalingrad, 1942–1943
EUROPE
FRANCE
PORTUGAL
SPAIN
ITALY
TURKEY
Tunisia, 1943
Sicily, 1943
El Alamein, 1942
AFRICA
EGYPT

0   500 mi
0   500 km

N W E S

The Normandy Invasion

The Allies were making progress. But Germany still controlled most of western Europe. It was time for the Allies to push into the center of Europe and free it from German forces. Doing that would not be easy. By now, Germany had big guns in place all along the Atlantic coast of France. It also had half a million troops prepared to block an Allied assault on the coast. Hitler called this his "Atlantic Wall."

Once the Allies decided to invade, the planning began. American general Dwight D. Eisenhower was made Supreme Commander of all Allied forces in Europe, and directed the operation. Secrecy was the key to success. The Germans knew an invasion was coming; they did not know exactly when or where.

Eisenhower chose a 60-mile section of Normandy in northern France for the Allied invasion. This part of France lies directly across the English Channel from Great Britain.

Invasion at Normandy, 1944

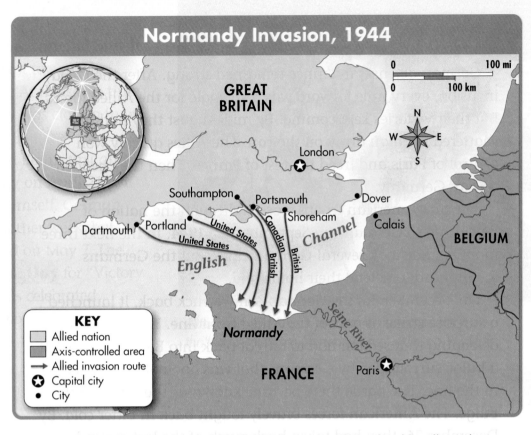

Normandy Invasion, 1944

GREAT BRITAIN

London

Southampton • Portsmouth • Dover
Portland • Shoreham
Dartmouth • United States • Canadian • Calais
United States • British • BELGIUM
English • Channel
Normandy • Seine River

FRANCE • Paris

KEY
- Allied nation
- Axis-controlled area
- → Allied invasion route
- ★ Capital city
- • City

4. **Circle** the route of the Allied invasion. **Write** why the Allies chose Great Britain as the place from which to launch their attack.

....

....

Eisenhower gathered more than 150,000 troops in Britain. He had about 4,000 ships and boats prepared, too. By the spring of 1944, the invasion forces from the United States, Canada, and Britain were finally ready to cross the English Channel.

The Allies hit the beaches at Normandy on June 6, 1944, known as **D-Day.** They faced a line of German guns and 70,000 soldiers. This part of Hitler's "Atlantic Wall" did not stop the Allies, but it cost them dearly. Many soldiers were killed or injured.

The battle for one area was the most deadly. The spot was code-named Omaha Beach. Americans coming ashore there had to make their way from their ships to the shore. Carrying gear and weapons, they had to run across minefields on the beach, where explosives were hidden in the sand. They had to get through tangles of barbed wire. Then they had to climb over a concrete wall. All the time, they faced a storm of German gunfire.

The Americans showed great courage and willpower. They fought through the German defenses and pushed inland. By July, the Allies had brought ashore more than 1 million troops.

Concentration Camps

The Nazis began rounding up Jews and placing them in ghettos. A **ghetto** is an area in a city where members of certain minority groups are forced to live. Jewish ghettos had existed in European cities and towns for centuries. But under the Nazis they now had a special purpose. Jews were held in ghettos until they could be sent to concentration camps.

The concentration camps had begun as prisons to hold political enemies of the Nazis. When Hitler started conquering new lands in 1938, he moved the Jews from those lands to the camps. Jews from Poland, France, and many other countries ended up in these places. Besides Jews, other groups considered inferior by the Nazis were put in the camps. After he invaded the Soviet Union, Hitler also filled camps with Soviet prisoners of war.

The Nazis began to locate concentration camps near factories. Prisoners were forced to work as slave laborers. Many were worked to death. Others died from beatings, disease, or lack of food.

In January 1942, the Nazis made a secret decision. They called it the "Final Solution" to the "Jewish problem." They would kill all the Jews in Europe. Several concentration camps in Poland were set aside as places for killing Jews. They became death camps. Many prisoners were killed as soon as they arrived.

Germany's government forced Jews and other groups into concentration camps.

The killing in the death camps was carefully planned and well organized. Jews were transported by train to a camp. They were herded into rooms that would then be filled with poison gas. At the largest death camp, Auschwitz (OWSH vihtz) in Poland, up to 8,000 Jews were killed each day.

Resisting the Nazis

Life in the ghettos was very harsh. Disease and starvation were common. The Warsaw ghetto in Poland was the largest. About 450,000 people lived there. The Nazis built a 10-foot wall around it to keep people from escaping.

Beginning in July 1942, the Nazis began regularly taking Jews from this ghetto to the death camps. By September 1942, nearly 300,000 Warsaw Jews had been killed. The remaining Jews decided to fight back, even though they had few weapons and they did not know if the rumors of the death camps were true.

When the Germans came to kill them in April 1943, the Warsaw Jews fired on them. This rebellion, called the Warsaw Ghetto Uprising, lasted nearly a month. By the end, the ghetto was in ruins and the remaining Jews were killed or sent to concentration camps.

Jews in many other ghettos fought back as well. They also resisted the Nazis from hiding places in the forest and even in the death camps themselves.

The Experience of Anne Frank

Anne Frank, a Jewish girl in the Netherlands, also resisted. When the Germans invaded, Anne and her family went into hiding in an office building of her father's. For two years in hiding, Anne kept a diary. The diary shows that she remained hopeful. She wrote, "In spite of everything I still believe that people are really good at heart." In 1944, the Nazis found the Franks. Anne ended up in a concentration camp, where she died of an illness at age 13.

Non-Jewish friends had helped Anne and her family. They had brought them food and other necessities. Across Europe, others resisted the Nazis by aiding Jews. Some helped Jews escape. Others hid them in their own homes.

This monument to the Warsaw Ghetto Uprising stands in that city today.

This is Anne Frank's original diary. It was published in English in 1952.

Anne Frank

Survival and Freedom

Millions of Jews died in the concentration camps. But some survived. They hoped and prayed that one day they would be free again.

In 1944, the Soviet army began to push into Poland. The Nazis tried to cover up their genocide as they retreated back to Germany. They destroyed some of the camps. They forced prisoners to march away, or they simply murdered them. But much evidence of their "Final Solution" remained.

In July 1944, the Soviets found thousands of Jews and others at the Majdanek (mye DAH nek) death camp in Poland. It was the first of many camps they would liberate, or make free. In April 1945, Americans and other Allies began to liberate camps in Germany.

For months after liberation, surviving Jews remained in the camps. Most could not return home. By now, their houses had been taken over by others. Many were not welcome back in their own towns.

I even find myself trying to deny what I am looking at with my own eyes. Certainly, what I have seen in the past few days will affect my personality for the rest of my life.

—U.S. soldier Harold Porter

2. **Write** a list of the emotions you see in this photograph.

....

....

Prisoners being set free from a concentration camp

Many Allied countries limited the number of Jewish immigrants they would accept. In time, however, the United States and other nations changed policies. Public pressure also built to let surviving Jews move to their historic homeland in the Middle East. In 1947, the United Nations voted to establish the Jewish state of Israel there.

Many Holocaust survivors settled in Israel, the United States, and elsewhere. Wherever they went, they made sure that people understood the Holocaust's lesson that good people must act against hatred. Today, memorials to Holocaust victims exist worldwide. They all make the same point: Nothing like the Holocaust should happen again.

3. This is the Holocaust Memorial in Miami Beach, Florida. **Write** why memorials to the Holocaust are important.

....

....

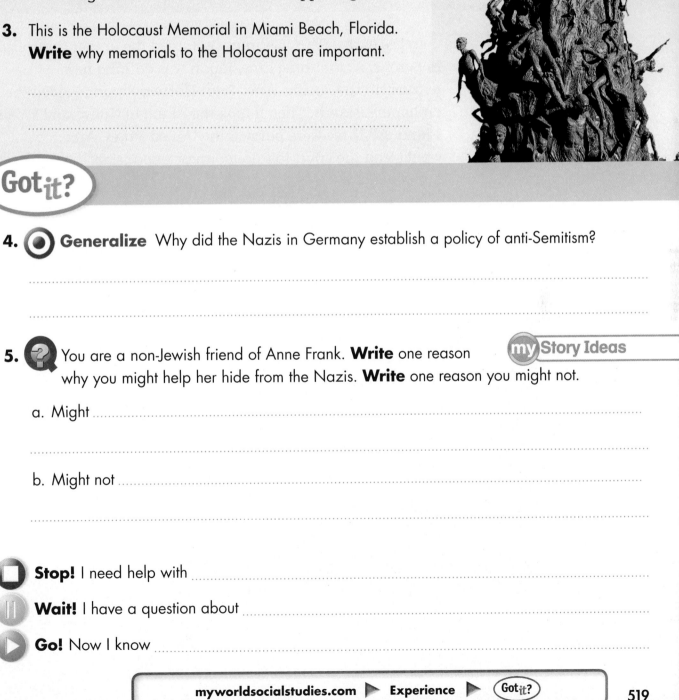

Got it?

4. (◉) **Generalize** Why did the Nazis in Germany establish a policy of anti-Semitism?

....

....

5. (?) You are a non-Jewish friend of Anne Frank. **Write** one reason why you might help her hide from the Nazis. **Write** one reason you might not.

(my) **Story Ideas**

a. Might ....

....

b. Might not ....

....

(■) **Stop!** I need help with ....

(❚❚) **Wait!** I have a question about ....

(▶) **Go!** Now I know ....

World War II in the Pacific

Envision It!

The World War II aircraft carrier *Enterprise* supported up to 90 planes and had a crew of more than 2,000.

In the early 1940s, Germany enlarged the area it controlled in Europe. At the same time, Japan was gaining new territory in the Pacific. After Pearl Harbor, Japan invaded the Philippine Islands. Then it took the island of Guam and Wake Island. All three were parts of the United States. America would lead the effort to stop Japanese expansion.

War in the Pacific

Warfare in the Pacific was different from warfare in Europe. Unlike in Europe, the war in the Pacific was fought mostly by naval forces. Japan was a nation of several islands. It controlled land from China, south through Southeast Asia. Much of Japan's growth was the result of its taking over other islands in the Pacific Ocean. The aircraft carrier would be at the center of many of the battles. The long-range bomber, too, would play a key role in the Pacific theater of the war.

In April 1942, U.S. Navy fliers launched the first air attack on Japan. They dropped bombs on Tokyo, Japan's capital. The attack did not do widespread damage, but it showed the Japanese people that their homeland was not secure.

Vocabulary

island hopping
atomic bomb

Why do you think aircraft carriers were important in fighting the war in the Pacific?

In May 1942, Japan took control of the Philippines. The American commander there, General Douglas MacArthur, left that island nation in March. Most of his troops were captured by the Japanese. He made a famous promise to those he left behind: "I shall return!"

Many people wondered if the Americans would really ever return. The Japanese forces seemed unstoppable. But few in Japan thought that beating the United States would be easy. One Japanese admiral wrote in early 1942:

This war will give us much trouble in the future. The fact that we have had a small success at Pearl Harbor is nothing.

The battle of Midway in June 1942 proved him right. It was a fierce battle over a tiny island, but it changed the course of the war.

Japan wanted to push the Americans out of Hawaii. But between the Japanese fleet and Hawaii lay Midway Island. There, the American forces took a stand against the Japanese. In a four-day clash of aircraft carriers and fighter planes, the United States earned its first victory. Japan's expansion in the Pacific had been stopped.

1. Navies and aircraft clashed at the battle of Midway in the Pacific. **Write** a caption that tells why this battle was a turning point.

....

....

....

....

From Island to Island

In late 1942, Japanese leaders still dreamed of enlarging their empire. They wanted to claim the big prize of the South Pacific: Australia. But the island of Guadalcanal helped to end that dream. The fight with the Allies for that island lasted more than five months. After losing much of their navy there, the Japanese retreated in February 1943.

The U.S. military then went on the attack. American forces drove the Japanese off island after island. The fighting was fierce nearly everywhere. The Allies often had superior air and sea power. However, those alone could not capture an island. To do that they also needed ground forces. Ground forces meant the U.S. Marines.

The Marines were troops who were trained to fight both on land and at sea. Yet, on the jungle islands of the Pacific, the Marines lost many men. On some islands, the Japanese troops hid in tunnels and caves. These hideouts could not be overcome without great loss of life. But these battles had to be won. Otherwise, the Allies could not defeat Japan.

To win in the Pacific, the United States had to invade a series of islands.

2. Underline sentences in the text that describe why it was hard for American troops to capture a Pacific island.

The Allies needed a new strategy, or plan. They came up with the idea of **island hopping.** When they came to a heavily guarded island, U.S. bombers would pound it day after day. Ground troops would pass it by, moving on to an island that was less well defended.

By island hopping, the Allies caused Japanese food and supplies to begin running out. This gradually forced the Japanese forces to retreat to their home islands.

However, some islands could not be "hopped." For example, pounding the Philippines with bombs would have been too destructive to this crowded island nation. Therefore, winning those islands back from Japan became a long, hard struggle. In 1944 General MacArthur did return to the Philippines. But it took his forces nine months to overcome the Japanese. They finally succeeded in July 1945.

Two other islands also proved very hard to win. The nearer the Allies got to Japan's home islands, the more fiercely the Japanese fought. The battle of Iwo Jima took more than 6,000 American lives. More than 12,000 American soldiers died taking Okinawa. But those victories in 1945 brought the Allies major steps closer to ending the war with Japan.

3. ◉ **Sequence** Which happened first, the battle at Iwo Jima or the battle of Midway?

....

....

....

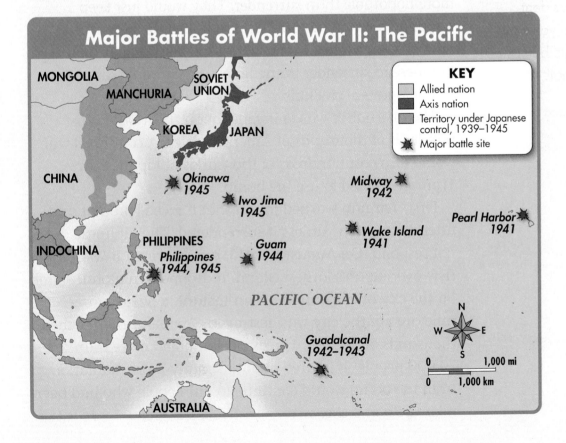

Major Battles of World War II: The Pacific

MONGOLIA
MANCHURIA
SOVIET UNION
KOREA
JAPAN
CHINA
INDOCHINA

KEY
◻ Allied nation
◼ Axis nation
◼ Territory under Japanese control, 1939–1945
✸ Major battle site

Okinawa 1945
Iwo Jima 1945
Midway 1942
Pearl Harbor 1941
Wake Island 1941
PHILIPPINES
Philippines 1944, 1945
Guam 1944
Guadalcanal 1942–1943
AUSTRALIA

PACIFIC OCEAN

N W E S

0   1,000 mi
0   1,000 km

A Dangerous New Weapon

While American troops fought in Europe and the Pacific, a different kind of challenge was taking shape at home. Scientists were trying to create the first **atomic bomb.** Their secret work was given the code name the Manhattan Project.

The idea of engineering an atomic bomb went back to 1939. In that year, scientist Albert Einstein sent President Roosevelt a letter. He explained that a new source of energy might be used to create "extremely powerful bombs." He hinted that the Germans might be making such a weapon.

Two years later, the U.S. government approved the project. Scientists around the country worked on it. The first test of the atomic bomb took place in July 1945 in the desert of southern New Mexico. The explosion was a shocking success.

Hiroshima and Nagasaki

President Roosevelt died in April 1945. Now it was up to the new President, Harry S. Truman, to make a hard choice. He had to decide whether to drop an atomic bomb on Japan.

Truman knew that most Japanese believed death was more honorable than surrender. They would just keep fighting, never giving up. Truman hoped the powerful new weapon could end the war quickly. It would force the Japanese to surrender immediately. But it would also kill many Japanese civilians.

The alternative was to invade Japan. That would cost hundreds of thousands of American lives. A continued war would also cost hundreds of thousands of Japanese lives. Truman decided to use the bomb.

First, Truman warned Japan that it faced "prompt and utter destruction" unless it surrendered. The Japanese did not respond. On August 6, 1945, an American B-29 bomber flew over Japan's largest island. It dropped an atomic bomb on the city of Hiroshima. In an instant, a four-square-mile area of the city was destroyed. Temperatures reached thousands of degrees. The explosion killed more than 70,000 people. It injured about as many more. Radiation from the bomb would continue to kill people who had been near the bomb site.

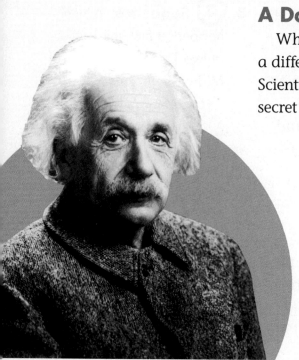

Albert Einstein was a German Jew who fled the Nazis. His theories led to the discovery of atomic energy.

4. If you were President Truman, would you have used the atomic bomb? Why or why not?

....

....

....

....

....

....

Hiroshima after the atomic bombing

On August 9, U.S. forces dropped another atomic bomb, this time on the city of Nagasaki. The results were just as devastating. On August 14, Emperor Hirohito (hihr oh HEE toh) agreed to the Allies' terms for surrender.

That date became V-J Day, for "Victory Over Japan." The formal surrender, and the end of World War II, came on September 2, 1945.

5. **Complete** the Venn diagram to compare and contrast the fighting tactics, or methods, during World War II in Europe and the Pacific.

World War II Tactics in Europe and the Pacific

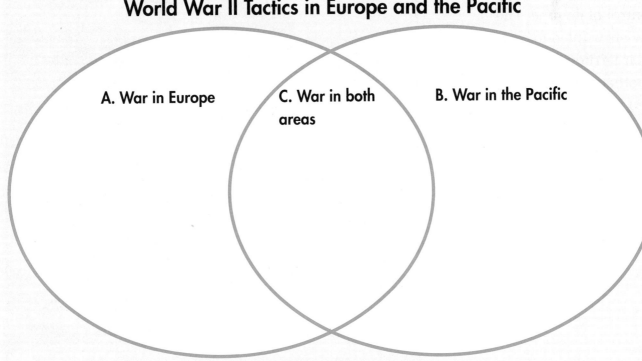

A. War in Europe

C. War in both areas

B. War in the Pacific

The Effects of the War

The human cost of World War II was terribly high. As many as 60 million people may have died as a result of the fighting. Although the exact number is hard to estimate, half probably died serving in the armed forces. The other half were civilians, or people not in the military.

The United States lost about 298,000 people. Great Britain lost about 388,000, and France lost 810,000. China lost more than 11 million, mostly civilians. Japan lost almost 2 million, and Germany about 4 million. Nearly 7 million Polish people died. More than half of them were Jews killed in the Holocaust. The estimated number of Soviet war deaths was 18 million.

The economic cost of the war is harder to determine. Governments probably spent more than $1 trillion to fight the war. But that figure does not cover the property destruction linked to the war.

To help restore order, British, Soviet, and U.S. forces remained in Germany. However, while Britain and the United States worked to make the parts of Germany they controlled independent, the Soviet Union kept control of its zone. The Soviets wanted to expand their territory. Not wanting another war, the Americans and British gave in to this.

6. **Study** this map. Which country benefited the most from changes to national boundaries as a result of World War II?

....

....

Europe After World War II

KEY
- Soviet Union before World War II
- Land gained by the Soviet Union
- Occupation zones in Germany

Map shows 1945 borders.

ATLANTIC OCEAN

SWEDEN
FINLAND
NORWAY
0 — 400 mi
0 — 400 km
GREAT BRITAIN
DENMARK
IRELAND
SOVIET UNION
GERMANY · Berlin
NETHERLANDS British Zone Soviet Zone POLAND
BELGIUM
U.S. Zone CZECHOSLOVAKIA
LUXEMBOURG
French Zone
AUSTRIA HUNGARY
SWITZ.
FRANCE ROMANIA
YUGOSLAVIA
BULGARIA
ITALY
SPAIN ALBANIA
GREECE TURKEY

A New Role

By the end of the war, the United States had proven itself to be an important world leader. It could no longer return to its prewar isolationism.

The United States was willing to help Germany and Japan recover from the war. However, the Soviet Union, a former ally, would soon become a powerful enemy in a future and very different kind of war.

Joseph Stalin, Harry Truman, and Winston Churchill were allies during World War II. Afterwards, their alliance broke down.

Got it?

7. **Cause and Effect** Why did the Allies develop the Pacific strategy of island-hopping?

....

....

....

8. A friend of yours cannot understand why the United States used the atomic bomb. What do you say?

my Story Ideas

....

....

....

Stop! I need help with ....

Wait! I have a question about ....

Go! Now I know ....

Lesson 1

World War II Begins

- World War II began when Hitler's German army invaded Poland.
- Japan's attack on Pearl Harbor brought the United States into the war.
- Near Moscow, Soviet troops stopped German expansion eastward.

Lesson 2

World War II at Home

- Americans rationed goods, held scrap drives, and bought war bonds.
- African Americans and women found new opportunities in the workforce and in the armed forces.
- Many Japanese Americans were forced into internment camps.

Lesson 3

World War II in Europe

- The Allies pushed Axis forces east across North Africa and then north through Italy. Mussolini resigned and Italy joined the Allies.
- On D-Day, Allied forces invaded Europe at Normandy in France.
- Germany surrendered after Allied troops reached Berlin.

Lesson 4

The Holocaust

- Under Hitler, Jews in Germany and the lands it held faced genocide.
- The Nazis sent millions of Jews to their deaths in concentration camps.
- Many Jews resisted, but few survived the Nazi "Final Solution." Those who did survive were liberated by invading Allied soldiers.

Lesson 5

World War II in the Pacific

- At the battle of Midway, the United States stopped Japan's expansion.
- By island hopping, Americans pushed back Japanese forces.
- Scientists working on the Manhattan Project built the first atomic bomb. The United States used two bombs against Japan to end the war.

Review and Assessment

Lesson 1

World War II Begins

1. **Write** the name of each group.

   a. The group led by Mussolini

   ....

   b. The alliance between Italy, Germany, and Japan

   ....

2. Why did most Americans support going to war after the Pearl Harbor attack?

   ....

   ....

Lesson 2

World War II at Home

3. **Write** a sentence to describe one effect the war had on each group of Americans.

   a. African Americans

   ....

   ....

   b. Women

   ....

   ....

   c. Japanese Americans

   ....

   ....

Lesson 3

World War II in Europe

4. How did radar help the two sides during the war?

   ....

   ....

5. **Sequence** Number the following events 1 to 4 to show the order in which they happened.

   _____ Battle of Stalingrad starts

   _____ Battle of the Bulge starts

   _____ V-E Day

   _____ Allies invade Italy

6. Why was D-Day so important to the Allies?

   ....

   ....

   ....

   ....

7. **Circle** the letter of the correct answer. Bombers were used mainly to

   A. transport troops over long distances.

   B. attack submarines way out at sea.

   C. bomb enemy factories and cities.

   D. bomb enemy troops on the battlefield.

Lesson 4

The Holocaust

8. What Nazi policies led to *Kristallnacht*?

....

....

....

9. Why did the Germans try to hide what they were doing in the death camps?

....

....

....

Lesson 5

World War II in the Pacific

10. What might have happened if the Japanese had won the Battle of Midway?

....

....

....

11. How did island hopping help the Allies win the war?

....

....

12. **What is worth fighting for?**

Use the questions below to think more about this chapter's Big Question.

a. Why were so many Americans willing to fight in World War II?

....

....

....

b. Why were Americans at home willing to deal with rationing?

....

....

....

c. Why did Japanese American soldiers fight in the U.S. Army?

....

....

d. Why did the Jews in the Warsaw ghetto fight the German Nazis?

....

....

....

Go online to write and illustrate your own **myStory Book** using the **myStory Ideas** from this chapter.

What is worth fighting for?

Nations took part in World War II for different reasons. Some fought because they believed in a dictator's promises or to gain land and resources. Others fought to defend their homeland and to defend their belief in individual worth and freedom.

Think about why people are fighting wars today. **Write** about causes that are worth fighting for today.

....

....

....

....

....

Now **draw** a home page of an Internet blog where you might express your feelings about a cause worth fighting for.

While you're online, check out the **myStory Current Events** area where you can create your own book on a topic that's in the news.

Chapter 15

The Cold War

What are the responsibilities of power?

Congratulations! Your classmates have just elected you class president. What will you do if you disagree with what your classmates ask of you?

President Richard Nixon talked with U.S. troops on his trip to South Vietnam during the Vietnam War, 1969.

Ronald Reagan
and the Berlin Wall

my Story Video

The huge concrete barrier looked like a prison wall. At more than 12 feet high, it was capped with barbed wire. Along its length, soldiers guarded it carefully. They made sure that no one tried to climb it and escape to the other side. The wall cut across the city of Berlin, dividing the old capital of Germany into two zones: the Communist zone and the democratic zone. The Berlin Wall was more than just a boundary line. It was the symbol of a divided world.

On June 12, 1987, U.S. President Ronald Reagan stood in front of this wall. He was about to make a speech that would change the history of the Cold War, a long period of international tension between Communist and democratic countries. This "war" was "cold" because the United States, which led democratic countries, and the Soviet Union, which led communist nations, never fought each other directly.

President Reagan believed that democratic countries would triumph over communism. This idea helped get him elected President in 1980. Ronald Reagan had other ideas and qualities that appealed to voters, as well.

REAGAN FOR PRESIDENT!

The Marshall Plan

In June 1947, Secretary of State George Marshall proposed a plan for rebuilding Europe and strengthening its economy. He described this plan by saying that, "Its purpose would be the revival of a working economy in the world." Marshall explained that the countries that chose to take part would draw up the program. The United States would pay the costs. The recovery program became known as the Marshall Plan.

Seventeen countries met in July 1947 to figure out what they needed. The Soviet Union was not one of them. It accused the United States of using the Marshall Plan to try to take over Europe. The countries of Eastern Europe that were under Soviet influence refused to participate.

In 1948, Congress approved the Marshall Plan. President Truman signed it into law. Over the next four years, the United States provided about $13 billion in aid to Europe. This money was used to rebuild houses and factories and to provide machinery, food, and supplies. As a result, industries grew and trade increased.

The Marshall Plan also strengthened the bond between the United States and Western Europe. That would be important in the years to come. The United States would need support as it clashed with the Soviet Union.

Supplies of sugar from the United States arrive at the Royal Victoria Docks in England as part of the Marshall Plan.

2. **Write** three effects of the Marshall Plan in the empty boxes below.

Effects of the Marshall Plan

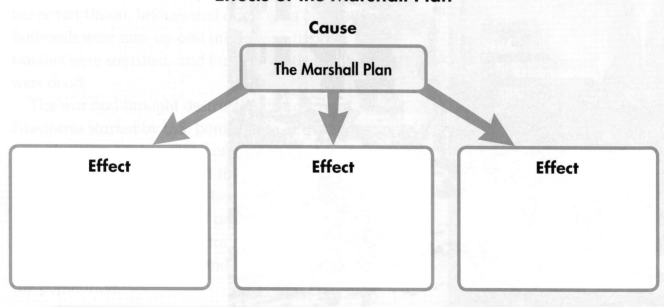

Cause

The Marshall Plan

Effect

Effect

Effect

worldsocialstudies.com ▶ Experience ▶ Introduction

The United Nations

After World War I, the Allied countries had created the League of Nations. The United States did not join. Ultimately, the League proved too weak to stop World War II.

Now many countries, including the United States, said they were eager to form a new world organization to promote peace. On October 24, 1945, they founded the United Nations, or UN. The UN Charter states its goals:

"to save succeeding generations from the scourge of war, . . . to reaffirm faith in fundamental human rights, . . . to promote social progress and better standards of life . . . ."

The UN would soon be tested. Relations were growing worse between the Soviet Union and the West. The *West* refers to the countries that opposed Soviet expansion after World War II. It includes the United States and the countries in Western Europe.

In 1947, President Truman announced the Truman Doctrine. It stated that the United States would protect any nation from invasion or control by an outside power. This was a warning to the Soviet Union.

The United Nations headquarters in New York City today

3. **Write** a sentence to put the goals of the UN Charter into your own words.

....

....

....

....

Communism and Capitalism

Communism is an economic and political system developed on a national level in the Soviet Union. In a communist country, the government owns all the land and most industries, in the name of the people. However, communism tends to limit personal freedoms. **Capitalism** is an economic system that encourages citizens to own businesses and property. A capitalist and democratic nation, like the United States, also protects personal freedoms. Most countries in the West were capitalist democracies.

The Soviet Union gained strength after the war. It became a powerful rival of most Western nations. Differences in ideology, or belief, led to conflict. One stated goal of communism is to overthrow capitalist countries. After the war, the Soviet Union and the West soon became enemies.

A Divided Europe

As World War II was ending, the Soviet army fought its way across Eastern Europe into Germany. After the war, the Soviets set up communist systems in the countries of Eastern Europe. As a result, Europe was divided between capitalism in the West and communism in the East.

Former British leader Winston Churchill described this divided world. In a famous speech in March 1946, he said, "An Iron Curtain has descended across the Continent." The **Iron Curtain** meant the closing off of Eastern Europe from Western Europe. Soon real concrete and barbed wire would divide these two parts of Europe.

Winston Churchill delivered his speech about a divided Europe in Fulton, Missouri in 1946.

4. ◉ **Fact and Opinion** In what way does Churchill's quote express a fact? Support your answer.

....

....

....

....

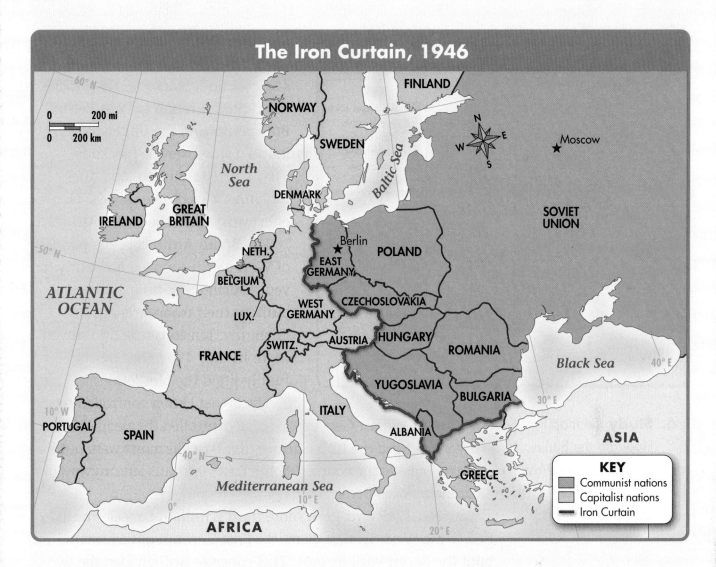

The Iron Curtain, 1946

(Map of Europe showing the Iron Curtain)

Countries and labels shown on the map: FINLAND, NORWAY, SWEDEN, North Sea, DENMARK, IRELAND, GREAT BRITAIN, NETH., BELGIUM, LUX., ATLANTIC OCEAN, Baltic Sea, Moscow, SOVIET UNION, Berlin, EAST GERMANY, POLAND, WEST GERMANY, CZECHOSLOVAKIA, SWITZ., AUSTRIA, HUNGARY, FRANCE, ROMANIA, Black Sea, YUGOSLAVIA, BULGARIA, ITALY, ALBANIA, PORTUGAL, SPAIN, GREECE, ASIA, Mediterranean Sea, AFRICA

KEY
- Communist nations
- Capitalist nations
- Iron Curtain

Western countries feared the Soviet armies on the other side of the Iron Curtain. In 1949, the West formed a military alliance. It is called the North Atlantic Treaty Organization, or NATO. If one NATO country was attacked, the others pledged to come to its aid. In 1955, the countries east of the Iron Curtain signed their own treaty. It was called the Warsaw Pact. Warsaw Pact countries, too, promised to help defend one another.

The Berlin Airlift

Germany had been split into zones after the war. The Soviets controlled East Germany. The French, British, and Americans controlled West Germany. The capital, Berlin, was split in a similar way. But the city itself lay 110 miles inside East Germany. The roads into Berlin passed through Soviet-held land.

5. **List** the countries that the Iron Curtain bordered.

....

....

....

....

....

....

Divided Berlin, 1945–1990

0 — 8 mi
0 — 8 km

KEY
- American zone
- British zone
- French zone
- Soviet zone
- City border
- Berlin wall

Berlin

East Berlin

West Berlin

N W E S

In June 1948, the Soviets tried to cut off the West's access to Berlin. They set up a blockade. No vehicles could pass through to West Berlin. But Britain and the United States found a way over the blockade. They started flying in food, fuel, machinery, and other goods. This effort was called the Berlin Airlift.

The Berlin Airlift kept the people of West Berlin supplied for nearly a year. During that time, both sides built up their troop strength in Germany. Tensions rose and stayed high. In May 1949, the Soviets finally lifted the blockade.

The Soviet Union controlled the government of East Germany. It also controlled the people. Like everyone behind the Iron Curtain, the East Germans were not free to travel outside the country. Some East Germans left anyway, escaping to West Berlin.

Between 1949 and 1961, more than 2 million East Germans fled to the West. To stop them, the East German government built the Berlin Wall in 1961. This concrete wall divided the two parts of Berlin. Barbed wire sat on top of the wall. Armed guards watched it day and night.

By the 1980s, the government had added electrified fences. Still, over the years, about 5,000 East Germans risked their lives to cross the wall into the West.

The Soviet Union worked to keep control of Eastern Europe. It also tried to expand communism into other parts of the world. For example, it backed communist governments in China and North Korea. The United States opposed Soviet efforts wherever it could.

6. Study the map. How did the Berlin Wall separate West Berlin from the rest of East Germany?

....

....

....

....

East German troops stand guard as the concrete wall is erected in 1961.

A New Kind of War

The two sides did not fight a traditional war. Usually, their struggle did not involve weapons. They fought this **Cold War** for about 40 years.

The clash over Berlin was typical. A crisis would put the two sides on edge. But they did not attack each other directly. Sometimes they might fight a "hot war" indirectly by supporting two opposing groups in other countries. For the most part the Americans and Soviets fought the Cold War with propaganda.

Propaganda is the spreading of ideas or beliefs to gain support for a cause. The United States used a radio network in Europe to spread anti-communist propaganda to countries behind the Iron Curtain. The Soviet Union used propaganda to influence its own people and those in other countries.

СЛАВА ОТВАЖНЫМ СЫНАМ РОДИНЫ!

This propaganda poster boasts of Soviet power and achievements.

Got it?

7. ⊙ **Sequence Circle** the event that happened last.

building of the Berlin Wall   founding of NATO   signing of Warsaw Pact treaty   Berlin Airlift

8. It is 1961, and you have a job as a reporter for a magazine with a feature titled "Cold War Diary." You are sent around the world to witness important events. Your first assignment is to describe the Iron Curtain.

my **Story Ideas**

....

....

....

....

⬤ **Stop!** I need help with ....

⏸ **Wait!** I have a question about ....

▶ **Go!** Now I know ....

Students practiced the safety drill "duck and cover" to prepare for a nuclear attack.

The Arms Race

During the Cold War, the United States and the Soviet Union competed in an arms race. An **arms race** is a contest to build more and better weapons than those of your enemy. Both sides continued to make atomic bombs, or nuclear weapons.

In the 1950s, Americans feared a nuclear war between the Cold War superpowers. They realized that Soviet planes could drop nuclear bombs on the United States. The Soviets could also send nuclear weapons on rockets.

Americans began to prepare for a nuclear attack. Some built underground bomb shelters in their backyards. They stocked the shelters with food and other supplies. In schools, students learned how to "duck and cover" in case of attack. This was a drill in which students practiced ducking under their desks and covering their heads for protection.

The Cuban Missile Crisis

Americans' fears almost came true. The nation of Cuba lies about 90 miles off southern Florida. In 1959, Fidel Castro led a revolution in Cuba. Then he formed a communist government. The Soviets supported him. In 1962 the Soviet Union secretly began to install nuclear weapons in Cuba. These weapons had the power to reach many cities in the United States.

On October 14, 1962, American spy planes took photos of the weapon sites being built. President John F. Kennedy sent the U.S. Navy to blockade Cuba. Navy ships prevented any more weapons from reaching the island. In addition, Kennedy demanded that the Soviets remove the sites that were already there.

2. Write an effect of the arms race in each box.

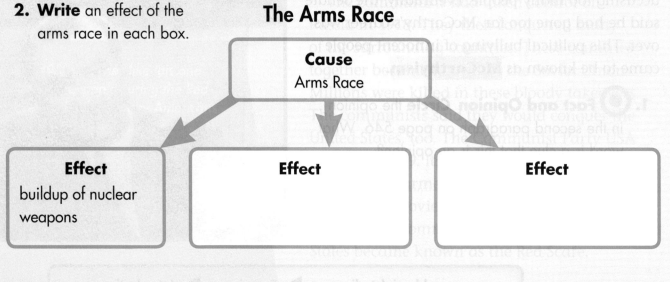

The Arms Race

Cause
Arms Race

Effect
buildup of nuclear weapons

Effect

Effect

This incident was called the **Cuban Missile Crisis.** It lasted for nearly two weeks. Kennedy and Nikita Khrushchev, the Soviet leader, exchanged messages. Meanwhile, the American people wondered what would happen if the Soviets did not back down. Would there be a nuclear war?

Finally, on October 28, the Soviets agreed to Kennedy's demands. In return, the United States pledged never to invade Cuba. The crisis was over. But both sides realized how close they had come to war. They created a telephone "hot line." In this way, the leader of each side could call the other directly to stop another crisis.

The Cuban Missile Crisis did not end the tension over nuclear weapons. Instead, it led to an idea that would shape the future relationship of the two superpowers. The idea was called "Mutual Assured Destruction," or MAD. It was based on the knowledge that each superpower could destroy the other in a nuclear war. According to the theory of MAD, neither side would dare use their nuclear weapons on the other.

An American family sits in an underground bomb shelter.

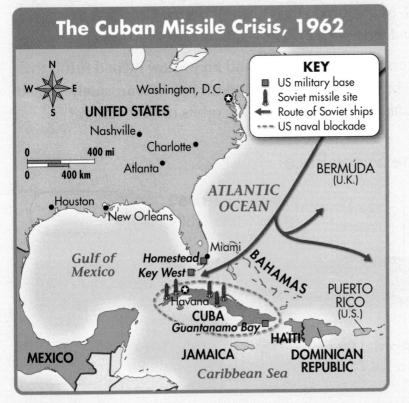

The Cuban Missile Crisis, 1962

KEY
- ■ US military base
- Soviet missile site
- ← Route of Soviet ships
- --- US naval blockade

Washington, D.C.
UNITED STATES
Nashville
Charlotte
Atlanta
Houston
New Orleans
BERMUDA (U.K.)
ATLANTIC OCEAN
Miami
Gulf of Mexico
Homestead
Key West
BAHAMAS
PUERTO RICO (U.S.)
Havana
CUBA
Guantanamo Bay
HAITI
MEXICO
JAMAICA
DOMINICAN REPUBLIC
Caribbean Sea

0   400 mi
0   400 km

N W E S

3. About how far would a missile from Cuba have had to travel to hit Washington, D.C.?

....

549

The Soviet launching of Sputnik 1 made front-page news.

The Space Race

While the arms race continued, another "race" began. The space race would eventually send American astronauts all the way to the moon and back.

The space race started with a satellite called *Sputnik*, which the Soviet Union launched in October 1957. This 184-pound scientific satellite stayed in Earth's orbit for just a few months. But it marked the beginning of the Space Age and the space race between the United States and Soviet Union.

The *Sputnik* launch took the United States by surprise. Now American scientists scrambled to catch up. In 1958, the U.S. government created the National Aeronautics and Space Administration, or NASA, to plan U.S. missions to space.

However, the Soviets had a big head start. One month after *Sputnik 1*, they sent the first living creature, a dog named Laika (LAY kah), into orbit. Then, in April 1961, the Soviets sent the first human into space. Cosmonaut Yuri Gagarin (gah GAH rhin) successfully made one full orbit of Earth in *Vostok 1*.

Two months later, President Kennedy announced to Congress:

"I believe that this nation should commit itself to achieving the goal, before this decade is out, of landing a man on the moon and returning him safely to the earth."

4. Label each event on the timeline as either a U.S. or Soviet achievement.

American competitive spirit and know-how helped fulfill this goal. In February 1962, U.S. astronaut John Glenn safely piloted the *Friendship 7* craft through three orbits around Earth.

The Space Race

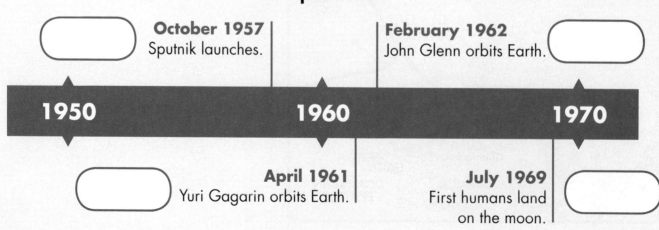

October 1957
Sputnik launches.

February 1962
John Glenn orbits Earth.

1950   1960   1970

April 1961
Yuri Gagarin orbits Earth.

July 1969
First humans land
on the moon.

Americans Reach the Moon

Many other U.S. space flights followed. NASA used them to figure out how to land an American on the moon. On July 16, 1969, NASA was ready. People world-wide watched on television as a rocket blasted off. The *Apollo 11* spacecraft carried three astronauts named Neil Armstrong, Edwin "Buzz" Aldrin, and Michael Collins.

Four days later, on July 20, Armstrong and Aldrin boarded a landing craft named *Eagle.* They flew it to the moon's surface. Armstrong then became the first person to walk on the moon. Aldrin soon joined him. The three astronauts returned safely to Earth on July 24. On the moon, they left an American flag and a plaque that said, "We Came In Peace For All Mankind."

Astronaut Edwin "Buzz" Aldrin on the moon in 1969

Got it?

5. **Draw Conclusions** If Senator McCarthy had never made his claim about communists in the U.S. government, would there have been a Red Scare in the 1950s? Explain.

....

....

....

6. You are asked to report on the Cuban Missile Crisis. **Explain** how the president handled the crisis. Also describe what ordinary families fear about these events.

my Story Ideas

....

....

....

Stop! I need help with ....

Wait! I have a question about ....

Go! Now I know ....

Cold War Conflicts

Envision It!

The Vietnam Veterans Memorial, also known as "The Wall," lists the names of Americans killed in the Vietnam War.

In the Korean War, American soldiers fought alongside South Koreans against North Koreans and their ally, China.

During the Cold War, the United States and the Soviet Union did not fight each other directly. But their conflict did sometimes lead to proxy wars. A *proxy* is a stand-in or substitute. In these **proxy wars,** capitalist and Communist forces battled each other. The United States helped one side; the Soviet Union helped the other. The Korean War and the Vietnam War were proxy wars. Since these wars took place in Asia, communist China was also involved.

The Korean War

After World War II, Soviet forces occupied northern Korea. United States forces occupied southern Korea. By 1950, both superpowers had pulled out. But the Soviets continued to support the communist government in North Korea.

On June 25, 1950, the North Korean army invaded South Korea. The United Nations ordered it to withdraw. However, it did not. The **Korean War** had begun.

Right away, President Harry Truman sent U.S. troops to assist the South Korean army. They would later be joined by troops from 15 other countries. These soldiers would fight as a United Nations force. The battlefront was pushed back and forth across Korea. First, the North Koreans overran almost all of the south. Then UN forces pushed the North Koreans back.

UNLOCK THE BIG ?

I will know that the United States felt a responsibility to fight against the spread of communism.

Vocabulary

proxy war   Vietnam War
Korean War   Tet Offensive
guerrilla

Why do people build war memorials?

The North Koreans retreated north almost to their border with China. Then China entered the war, and Chinese troops drove the UN forces out of North Korea. In January 1951, the Chinese entered South Korea. But the fighting had weakened the northern armies.

UN troops again surged forward. By March, they had retaken all of South Korea. This time, they chose not to invade North Korea. In July, both sides began peace talks. The negotiations dragged on for two years.

Finally, on July 27, 1953, the fighting ended. Korea was divided into two nations, as it remains today. The dividing line is at the 38th parallel, or line of latitude. U.S. and South Korean troops still guard this border.

As far as the United States was concerned, the war was a success. The United States had stopped the spread of communism into South Korea. The United States paid a high price for the victory, however. More than 36,000 Americans died in the war.

1. **Look** at the countries in white. **Color** the democratic country one color and the communist country another. Use the colors in the key. Also **circle** the 38th parallel.

Korea Divided

0   200 mi
0   200 km

CHINA

Beijing ★

Yalu River

NORTH KOREA

Pyongyang ★

Sea of Japan (East Sea)

38° N

★ Seoul

SOUTH KOREA

Yellow Sea

Pusan

JAPAN

KEY
☐ Communist country
☐ Democratic country

N
W   E
S

The Vietnam War

The country of Vietnam was also split after World War II. The communists of North Vietnam started fighting to unify the country under a Communist government. The Soviet Union and China supported this goal. They helped communists in the north arm guerrillas in South Vietnam.

Guerrillas are fighters who do not fight directly but make surprise raids or quick attacks from under cover. They usually fight in small bands. The guerrillas battling the government of South Vietnam were a mix of South Vietnamese and the North Vietnam army. Together, they were known as the Viet Cong.

Most people in South Vietnam did not want communism. The United States feared what might happen if South Vietnam fell to the communists. Maybe Vietnam's neighbors, such as Cambodia and Laos, might also fall, like dominoes in a line. Americans called this effect of one nation after another falling to communism the "domino theory." To help prevent this, the United States sent the South Vietnamese weapons and money. It also sent special soldiers to help train South Vietnam's army.

Then, in 1964, President Lyndon Johnson ordered bombers to attack North Vietnam. The next year, American combat troops joined the conflict. By 1968, half a million American soldiers were fighting in the **Vietnam War.**

South Vietnam is a hilly land covered with thick jungle. Viet Cong guerrillas could hide in the jungle, fire on American troops, and then escape. The Americans often did not see their enemy or know where the shots were coming from. To destroy the Viet Cong's cover, the Americans sprayed the chemical Agent Orange. It killed the vegetation.

American bombers also destroyed roads and bridges in North Vietnam. They hit the main routes that brought North Vietnamese soldiers and supplies south. They also bombed Viet Cong bases in South Vietnam. Bombs often fell on villages, killing civilians.

American troops in Vietnam

This antiwar rally was held in Washington, D.C. in 1969.

Protests at Home

In 1968, the North Vietnamese launched a widespread attack on South Vietnam. They struck at major cities, towns, and military bases. It happened during the Vietnamese holiday of Tet, and it took the Americans by surprise. This attack is known as the **Tet Offensive.**

The Tet Offensive was a turning point in the war, in favor of North Vietnam. U.S. and South Vietnamese forces quickly won back most of the lost areas. But the Tet Offensive proved that the Viet Cong were still strong. The war was far from over.

Even before the Tet Offensive, many Americans at home had begun to question the United States' role in Vietnam. On television, they could see how brutal the war was. They were shocked to see how many American soldiers were injured or killed. The Tet Offensive was a sign that the war was only going to get worse.

Antiwar protests were now common. College students held rallies against the conflict. In 1970, President Richard Nixon announced that the U.S. had bombed Viet Cong bases in Cambodia. At this, protests increased. Then, a protest at Kent State University in Ohio turned deadly. Troops were called in to keep order. But during the event, soldiers shot and killed four unarmed protesters. Americans were horrified.

2. **Fact and Opinion**

Write two statements about the antiwar rally. **Make** one statement a fact and the other an opinion.

....

....

....

....

....

....

The End of the Vietnam War

In May 1968, peace talks began. They continued for years with little progress. In 1969, President Nixon started relying more on the South Vietnamese to fight the war. He withdrew 25,000 American soldiers. By the end of 1971, the U.S. troop level in Vietnam was below 200,000.

In January 1973, the peace talks finally ended in a cease-fire. That allowed the United States to pull all its combat troops out of Vietnam. But the U.S. withdrawal did not stop the fighting between North and South Vietnamese soldiers.

By 1975, the North Vietnamese had taken control of some regions of the South. In April 1975, with the capital city, Saigon, about to fall to the North Vietnamese, South Vietnam surrendered. The nation was then unified as the communist country of Vietnam.

3. The United States entered the Vietnam War to stop the spread of communism. U.S. soldiers risked their lives to carry out that mission. **Write** how this photo captures the hardships of war.

....

....

....

....

The Vietnam War caused a lot of death and destruction. Bombs smashed whole villages and towns. Chemicals like Agent Orange destroyed the countryside. Millions of Vietnamese soldiers and civilians were killed. Thousands of South Vietnamese fled their country in small, flimsy boats. Many immigrated to the United States.

The Vietnam War cost the United States a great deal, as well. Along with large sums of money, more than 58,000 Americans died and many more were wounded in this war.

South Vietnamese people struggle to enter the U.S. embassy for safety from North Vietnamese forces as the last U.S. troops leave Vietnam in 1975.

Got it?

4. ⊙ **Fact and Opinion Write** two sentences about the Korean War. **Make** the first one a fact and the second one an opinion.

....

....

....

5. ❓ In 1968, you take a dangerous trip to Vietnam to report on the war there. **Report** on what officials and soldiers tell you.

my Story Ideas

....

....

....

⬛ **Stop!** I need help with ....

⏸ **Wait!** I have a question about ....

▶ **Go!** Now I know ....

The End of the Cold War

Envision It!

A series of ping-pong matches between the Chinese and American teams improved relations between the two countries.

In the 1950s, the Cold War was a struggle between the two superpowers and their allies. In the 1960s, some things changed. Allies of the United States grew stronger and more independent. The Soviet Union split with its major ally, China, over several issues. Also, the United States and the Soviet Union began to get along better. They even started discussing limiting the production of nuclear weapons.

Arms Control

The arms race was dangerous and costly. The United States and the Soviet Union both knew this, but they were not sure how to stop it.

After the Cuban Missile Crisis in 1962, the two nations took small steps. In 1963, they agreed to ban nuclear tests under water, in the air, and in space. Only underground tests would be allowed.

In 1968, they agreed, by treaty, not to spread nuclear weapons to other countries, although many nations were building their own. Today, nearly every country in the world has signed this treaty. But neither agreement slowed the arms race.

1. **Circle** any countries that you are surprised to see on the chart. Why do you think so many countries want nuclear weapons?

....

....

Nuclear Powers	
Country	Date Nuclear Weapons Acquired
United States	1945
Soviet Union	1949
Great Britain	1952
France	1960
China	1964
Israel	*1968
India	1974
Pakistan	1998

Source: Federation of American Scientists

*Unofficial; Israel does not publicly claim to have nuclear weapons.

UNLOCK
THE BIG
?

I will know that American leaders worked to try to end the Cold War.

Vocabulary

arms control
embargo
diplomacy

Write how sports can bring together people from different cultures.

In 1967, President Lyndon Johnson met with the Soviet leader, Leonid Brezhnev. They talked about **arms control,** or limiting the production of weapons. Their discussion began what were called the Strategic Arms Limitation Talks, or SALT.

Under President Johnson, arms control did not get much past the talking stage. When Richard Nixon became president, there was more concrete progress. In May 1972, President Nixon traveled to the Soviet Union. He was the first U.S. president to visit the capital, Moscow. There, he and Leonid Brezhnev worked out and signed SALT I.

Nixon and Brezhnev shake hands after signing SALT I.

The SALT I agreement accomplished three things. It froze the number of certain kinds of nuclear weapons at the existing numbers. Neither nation would produce more than it already had. It also put a cap on the number of missiles that could be launched from submarines. SALT I also stated that each side would destroy a given number of older nuclear weapons.

In 1979, the SALT II agreement put even more limits on the number of missiles each side could produce. But it did not stop the arms race. Real progress on reducing nuclear arms would not start until the 1980s.

Tensions Rise and Fall

The quest for arms control brought the United States and the Soviet Union closer. That helped ease tensions during the Cold War. Improving U.S.–Soviet relations was a key part of American foreign policy. But it was not the only part.

In 1972, before he went to the Soviet Union, President Nixon became the first U.S. president to go to China. China had been a fierce rival and enemy of the United States. Nixon's goal was to establish friendly ties with this growing communist power. He met with Mao Zedong, China's leader, and he walked along the Great Wall. The Chinese treated him well.

Nixon's trip was possible because of actions the United States had already taken. In 1969, the United States loosened restrictions on travel by Americans to China. In 1971, it ended an **embargo,** or ban, on trade with that nation, too. The Chinese responded with a surprising invitation.

In 1971, they asked the U.S. ping-pong team to come to China. The next year the Chinese team visited the United States. Journalists called it "ping-pong diplomacy." **Diplomacy** is the art of handling relations between nations.

In 1971 the United States proposed that China take a seat in the UN Security Council. At the time, the seat was held by an American ally, Taiwan.

Taiwan was also known as Nationalist China. Anti-communist Chinese had fled there and separated from mainland China. American recognition of Taiwan as the rightful government of China was a very sore point when Nixon arrived. During his visit, Nixon accepted that Taiwan was a part of China. The U.S. says China should only take control peacefully.

2. China invited President Nixon and First Lady Pat Nixon to an official dinner in 1972. How does the picture show an improved relationship between China and the United States?.

....

....

....

....

....

....

Nixon's trips were great diplomatic successes. He helped bring about friendlier relations between the United States and the world's two most powerful communist countries. Tensions remained fairly low. Then, in December 1979, the Soviet Union invaded the central Asian nation of Afghanistan.

The Soviets' goal was to keep Afghanistan's communist government in power. But that government had little support from its people. Soviet troops took control of most cities. Rebel guerrillas, the *mujahedin* (moo zjah heh DEEN), controlled the countryside.

The United States supported the mujahedin. President Jimmy Carter cut grain sales to the Soviets. He stopped sales of technology to them, as well. In 1980 the Olympic Games were held in Moscow, but the United States refused to send its athletes. The Cold War had regained some of its old chill.

Soviet Invasion of Afghanistan, 1979

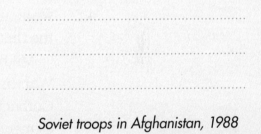

✪ Moscow

SOVIET UNION

MONGOLIA

TURKEY

CHINA

IRAQ

IRAN   Kabul ✪
AFGHANISTAN

PAKISTAN

INDIA   BURMA

map area

KEY
✪ Capital
➡ Soviet troops

N
W   E
S

0   600 mi
0   600 km

3. **Look** at the photograph. **Write** why fighting in Afghanistan was so difficult.

....

....

....

Soviet troops in Afghanistan, 1988

Gorbachev (left) and Reagan (right) chat during an official meeting in the Soviet Union in 1988.

Reagan and Gorbachev

U.S. President Ronald Reagan took a strong stand against communism. He called the Soviet Union "an evil empire." He also spent billions of dollars on new weapons and on building up the U.S. military. Reagan thought the Soviets had a weak economy. His actions pressured them to spend more money on arms than they could afford.

In 1983, Reagan announced a new program called the Strategic Defense Initiative, or SDI. Its goal was to build a defensive shield over the United States to protect the country against a nuclear attack. It would use high-tech weapons to shoot down incoming nuclear missiles. Critics said that SDI was too expensive and would not work. The program was never fully developed.

During the Reagan years, however, the United States did make progress in arms control. Reagan did not want just to limit arms. He wanted to reduce them. In 1982, Strategic Arms Reduction Talks (START) began. They led to a new agreement with the Soviets. START called for both superpowers to begin destroying nuclear weapons. In 1991, President George H. W. Bush signed START for the United States. Mikhail Gorbachev signed it for the Soviet Union.

Mikhail Gorbachev played a key role in ending the Cold War. In the mid-1980s, he led the Soviet Union into a new era. Gorbachev was a reformer. He introduced some basic capitalist elements to the Soviet economy. He allowed some democratic freedoms. He tried to open the Soviet Union to the outside world.

The spirit of reform spread from the Soviet Union to other communist countries under Soviet control. In 1989, communist governments began to fall in Eastern Europe and within Soviet states. Democratic governments took their place. In Poland, Hungary, and elsewhere, the people started freely electing their own leaders. Gorbachev did not try to stop them.

4. ◉ **Fact and Opinion** **Find** and **circle** one opinion expressed by President Reagan on this page.

The Berlin Wall Comes Down

East Germany was another Soviet-controlled country where the people now demanded reform. In 1987, President Reagan had visited West Berlin in East Germany. In a speech near the Berlin Wall, he addressed the Soviet leader: "Mr. Gorbachev, tear down this wall!" he said. This challenge reminded the world that the wall was a barrier to freedom for the people of East Germany.

On November 9, 1989, East German leaders were forced to open the wall. They allowed free passage into West Berlin. By the end of 1990, East Germans and others had torn down much of the wall. They had also freely elected a new government. For years, the Berlin Wall had been a symbol of a divided Europe. Now it became a symbol of the power of people to claim their freedom.

5. **Circle** one person in the picture. **Write** what you think that person is feeling at this moment in history.

....

....

....

Germans break down the Berlin Wall, which divided their nation for almost 30 years.

563

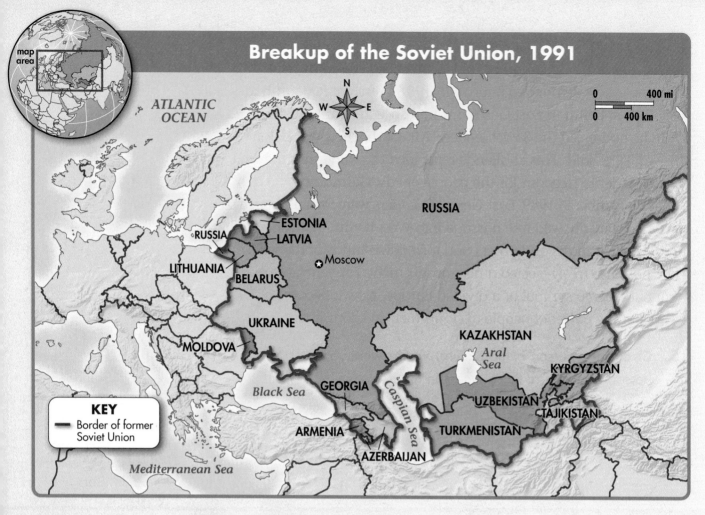

ATLANTIC OCEAN

N W E S

0   400 mi
0   400 km

RUSSIA

ESTONIA
RUSSIA
LATVIA

★ Moscow

LITHUANIA
BELARUS

UKRAINE

MOLDOVA

KAZAKHSTAN

Aral Sea

KYRGYZSTAN

Black Sea
GEORGIA

Caspian Sea

UZBEKISTAN
TAJIKISTAN

KEY
— Border of former Soviet Union

ARMENIA

AZERBAIJAN

TURKMENISTAN

Mediterranean Sea

6. Look at the map. **Write** the names of the countries that came from the old Soviet Union.

....

....

....

....

....

....

....

....

The End of Communism and the Cold War

In 1990, the Cold War was clearly ending. Gorbachev began to withdraw troops from the nations the Soviets had controlled in Eastern Europe. East and West Germany were reunified into a single Germany. The United States and the Soviet Union looked for ways to improve their relations.

Communism had been strong and long-lived in the Soviet Union. The Communist Party there was still powerful. Some Soviet officials saw Gorbachev's reforms as a threat to their influence and way of life. In 1991, they tried to overthrow him. Their plot failed.

Several republics within the Soviet Union decided to secede, or leave. The Soviet Union had been made up of 15 republics, or separate states. These republics wanted to form democratic governments and become independent. By the end of 1991, they achieved this goal. The Soviet Union had ceased to exist.

7. ◉ **Fact and Opinion Circle** one opinion on this page. **Underline** one fact.

8. Add two important events and dates about the end of communism in Europe to the time line.

The End of Communism

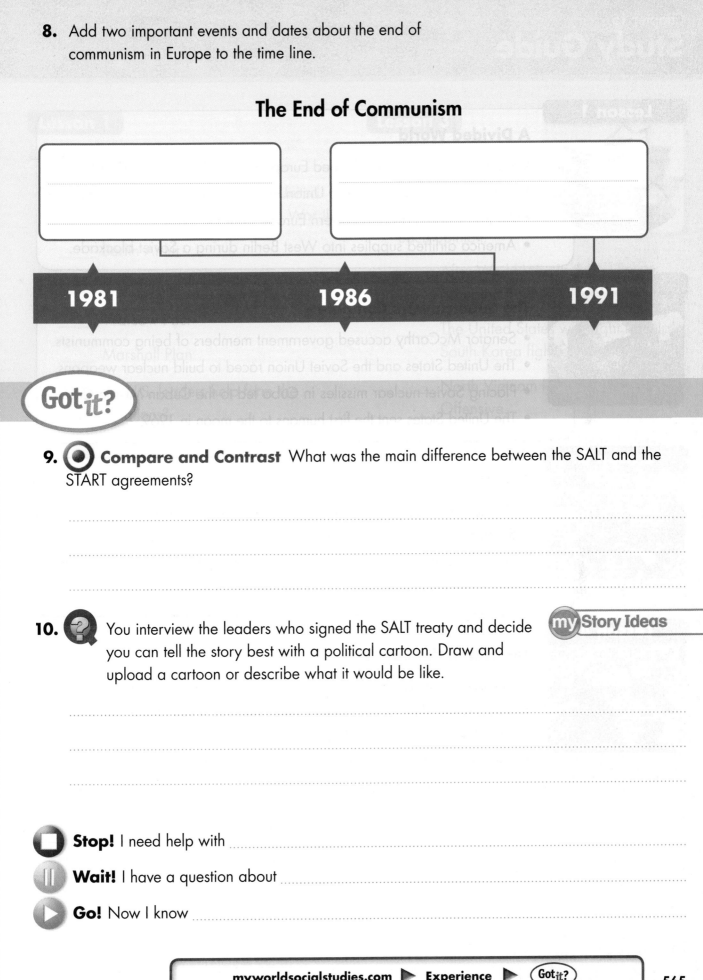

| 1981 | 1986 | 1991 |

9. **Compare and Contrast** What was the main difference between the SALT and the START agreements?

....

....

....

10. You interview the leaders who signed the SALT treaty and decide you can tell the story best with a political cartoon. Draw and upload a cartoon or describe what it would be like.

my Story Ideas

....

....

....

....

Stop! I need help with ....

Wait! I have a question about ....

Go! Now I know ....

Chapter 16

America Changes

THE BIG ? When does change become necessary?

Describe something in your school or community that you think should be changed. What could you do to help bring about the change?

....

....

....

....

....

Germans celebrate the fall of the Berlin Wall in 1989. It had split the city of Berlin since 1961. The event signaled the end of the Cold War.

National Voting Rights Museum
Making a Difference

my Story Video

Denisha' lives in Montgomery, Alabama. Ever since her recent visit to nearby Selma, she's been curious about the National Voting Rights Museum and Institute. This museum is located near the foot of the Edmund Pettus Bridge, which played an important role in history.

Sam Walker is a tour guide at the museum, and he is going to show Denisha' around today. "Hi, Mr. Walker. Thanks for having me," Denisha' says with a smile. "Welcome to the museum," replies Mr. Walker.

Right away, Denisha' notices a large display of plaster casts of footprints. "What are those?" she asks. "This is the foot soldiers' hall of fame room. The museum was created to remember the sacrifice and work of the foot soldiers of the Voting Rights Movement," explains Mr. Walker. It pays tribute to the people who took part in the 1965 Selma to Montgomery marches for voting rights.

Denisha' stands in front of an old voting booth. Many people fought and suffered for the right to vote.

571

At the museum, imprints representing the feet of civil rights marchers are on display.

Stirring images capture the tension and power of the civil rights marches.

This monument celebrates Martin Luther King, Jr., one of America's great civil rights leaders.

Denisha' remembers the Fifteenth Amendment to the Constitution. It granted the right to vote to all men, regardless of race or color. That was almost a hundred years before the voting rights marches! Mr. Walker tells Denisha' that having the right to vote and being able to vote were very different things. In some cities and towns, the local governments made it difficult for African Americans to register to vote.

Many people thought this was unfair, and Denisha' understands why. "Having the right means you should be able to vote," she says. "I think I might have wanted to march back then, too."

Organizers called for a march after a young man named Jimmie Lee Jackson was shot and killed at a civil rights demonstration. The march was planned to protest his death and to call for voting rights. It was supposed to go from Selma to the state capitol building, 50 miles away.

On Sunday, March 7, 1965, about 600 people gathered in Selma at the Pettus Bridge. The protesters crossed the bridge and saw a line of state troopers blocking the road ahead. Alabama's governor, George Wallace, had ordered the troopers to stop the march. When the protesters tried to continue, the troopers threw tear gas and attacked the marchers. This terrible day became known as "Bloody Sunday."

"There were two types in the Movement...those who were just in the Movement and those whom the Movement was *in* them"

- Bob Mants, SNCC member and March Leader on Bloody Sunday

The museum features important and meaningful quotations from civil rights leaders about the events of that time.

Denisha' and Mr. Walker discuss the famous events pictured in this display.

"Dr. Martin Luther King, Jr. then called for anyone who felt what happened was wrong to go to Selma and join them for another march," says Mr. Walker. "Lots of people of all colors went to Selma after that. They were very eager to march," he continues. However, a judge issued an order delaying the march. Dr. King led marchers to the bridge but went no further.

Eventually, the judge decided that the protesters had the legal right to march. He also ruled that they had to be protected. "Governor Wallace refused to provide protection, however. So the President of the United States nationalized the Alabama National Guard," explains Mr. Walker. "This meant they took their orders from him, and not the governor!"

On March 21, 1965, the marchers started from the Pettus Bridge for the third time. "Days later, on March 25, 1965, 25,000 people walked up to the steps of the Alabama capitol building to protest the death of Jimmie Lee Jackson and not being able to vote," says Mr. Walker. "That moment had a huge impact on both civil rights and voting rights."

As Denisha' walks through the museum and views displays, she realizes, "Sometimes change is necessary and people can make a difference." Today she learned that because the marchers focused attention on African Americans' struggles to vote, Congress later passed the Voting Rights Act. As her visit ends, Denisha' says, "I hope I am brave enough to face changes just like these people were!"

Think About It Based on this story, why do you think the protesters were determined to cross the bridge? As you read the chapter ahead, think about times when change becomes necessary.

Postwar America

PARK IN THEATRE

After World War II, cars made it easier and more fun for Americans to do many things, such as going to movies.

When World War II was over, Americans were ready for change. Soldiers came home, and families were reunited. Marion Gurfein had not seen her soldier husband for three years. Almost 60 years later she remembered the day he returned from the war. ". . . [T]he door opened and there was Joe and I guess that was one of the greatest moments of my life." Then she turned to introduce him to his daughter, who had been born while he was away fighting.

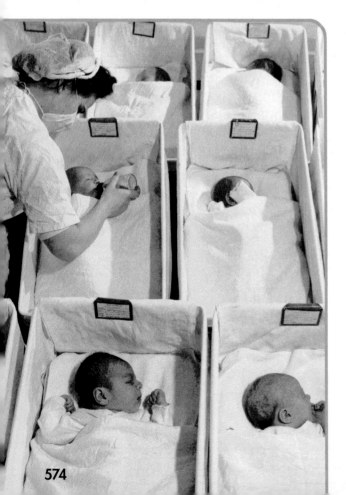

A nurse feeds babies in a typically full maternity ward in the 1950s.

Boom Years

During the war, millions of soldiers had put their lives on hold as they fought for freedom. Now they were ready to enjoy it. So were Americans who had been at home.

Many **veterans**, people who have fought in a war, wanted to start families. So many babies were born in the years from 1945 to 1964 that historians call this wave of births after World War II the **baby boom.** About 76 million babies were part of the baby boom. All these new families needed new houses, more goods, and more services. These were "boom times" for the economy, as well as for the population.

1. What were some of the effects of the "baby boom"?

....

....

Vocabulary

veteran
baby boom
credit card

G.I. Bill of Rights
suburb

_____

Today computers make life easier for many Americans. List some ways computers make your life easier.

The Changing Workplace

During World War II, many women took factory jobs usually held by men. By the end of the war, women made up one third of the workforce. When veterans came home, however, they took their jobs back. Soon, most women were once again at home, working as housewives and mothers.

There was no shortage of jobs. Manufacturing grew, because employed Americans could afford to buy more. In this booming economy, American consumers had a high standard of living. During the war, scarce items like meat, rubber, and gasoline had been rationed, or given out sparingly. Now people wanted plentiful goods that went with their new modern lives, including cars, washing machines, televisions, and refrigerators.

Credit cards helped them pay for these goods. A **credit card** lets a user charge goods and services and pay for them later. Users pay a fee if they do not repay the charge within a certain time period.

By the end of the 1950s, the U.S. economy was changing. It had been based on manufacturing since the Industrial Revolution. By 1960, more and more people were starting careers in service industries such as sales, teaching, or medicine.

2. **Circle** things in this picture that are a sign of the booming economy.

7. Write why you think appearing on television was important for Elvis Presley's career.

....

....

....

....

....

Elvis Presley (far right) appeared on The Ed Sullivan Show in 1956.

American Popular Culture

In the 1950s, new technology let people across the country share culture. Television and portable radios helped. Musicians, sports figures, and actors became major national stars. Some even became popular in other countries.

A new kind of music, called rock-and-roll, swept the nation. Rock-and-roll used old-style country and western sounds. It added in the rhythm and blues of African American music. In the mid-1950s, its most famous performer was Elvis Presley. Presley appeared on *The Ed Sullivan Show* in 1956. About 60 million people watched. It was the largest TV audience up to that time.

Throughout the 1950s, many African American rock-and-rollers became world-famous. Musicians such as Chuck Berry and Little Richard helped make rock-and-roll popular. In 1959, Detroit's Motown Records became a center of African American popular music. Motown helped bring African American music to a world-wide audience.

In the 1960s, folk singers began to sing about the need for political and social change. One of the most famous folk singers was Bob Dylan. Dylan protested old ways and urged listeners to think seriously about the nation's problems.

The 1960s also saw popular singers like the Beatles, Johnny Cash, Hank Williams, and Aretha Franklin rise to stardom. These artists and their music still influence popular music and culture today.

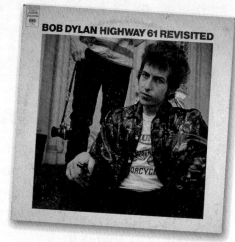

Bob Dylan sang about the changing times.

Got it?

8. ● **Main Idea and Details** Cars were important in the growth of suburbs. **Write** at least two details to support that idea.

....

....

....

....

9. ❓ You are a reporter working in postwar America. **Describe** the most important changes in American life caused by new technology.

my Story Ideas

....

....

....

⬛ **Stop!** I need help with ....

⏸ **Wait!** I have a question about ....

▶ **Go!** Now I know ....

Make a Difference

How can you make a difference? Your first step should be to identify the problem you want to help solve. What problems do you hear about in the news? What problems do you see around you every day?

Your next step is to develop a solution. What will you need to do to solve the problem. Who can help you?

Finally, it's time to put your plan into action. Share your plan with people to get them involved. A huge movement can start with just a few people.

Now read about an elementary school student who used these simple steps to make a big difference.

When Brandon Keefe was in elementary school, he decided to make a difference. One day he visited the Hollygrove Children's Home, a place for children in trouble. His mother volunteered there. Brandon found out that Hollygrove wanted to start a library. But they did not have money to buy books. Brian thought about all the books he had at home. He could give away those he had already read. So could his friends.

The next day at school, Brandon talked to his classmates. He suggested that they hold a book drive.

They would collect books for Hollygrove. Brandon asked his classmates and teachers to help. They made fliers. They gave speeches at school. Soon they had collected almost 900 books for Hollygrove.

Brandon's idea led to an organization called BookEnds. Robin Keefe, Brandon's mother, founded BookEnds more than ten years ago.

BookEnds helps students organize book drives. They give books to places that need them. So far they have donated about 2 million books to almost 500,000 children.

How did Brandon Keefe make a difference?

1. What problem did Brandon identify?

....

....

2. What solution did he develop?

....

....

3. How did Brandon put his plan into action?

....

....

....

....

4. Apply How can you make a difference? Work in a small group to identify a problem in your school or in your community. Think of at least one solution that you can all agree on. Then describe how this solution would make a difference to your fellow students or the people in your community.

....

....

....

....

....

....

Civil Rights

Envision It!

Before the mid-1950s, many African American students and white students attended separate schools.

Thelma Williams grew up in the South before World War II. It was a time and place where African Americans and white Americans were kept separate in many ways. "There were these hard separation lines that you simply did not cross," Ms. Williams remembered. In the postwar years, those lines of separation were strong. But they were about to weaken.

A Long History of Segregation

The United States Constitution guarantees civil rights to free Americans of all races. **Civil rights** are basic freedoms and protections, such as the right to a fair trial. In the late 1800s, African Americans were being denied their civil rights. This was especially true in the South.

In 1896, the Supreme Court judged a now-famous legal case, *Plessy* v. *Ferguson*. It said that separation of races in public places was legal if the facilities, though separate, were equal. This ruling made racial segregation, or separation, legal.

Laws that separated black and white Americans were called Jim Crow laws. Segregated facilities, like drinking fountains, were common before civil rights reform.

DRINKING FOUNTAIN
WHITE   COLORED

UNLOCK THE BIG ?

I will know how African Americans struggled for civil rights.

Vocabulary

civil rights   sit-in
discrimination   freedom ride
integration

Why might it be difficult to make segregated schools equal?

Look at the map. It shows where segregation was required or allowed by 1952. Even in places where segregation was not the law, African Americans often faced **discrimination,** or the unfair treatment of people based on race or gender.

African Americans built strong communities across the nation. They ran successful businesses. There were African American colleges, clubs, and theaters. African American scientists, entertainers, and authors were famous for their achievements. Nonetheless, segregation isolated African Americans. In reality, "separate but equal" did not work.

1. **Circle** the states where segregation was outlawed. **Check** the states that had no laws about segregation.

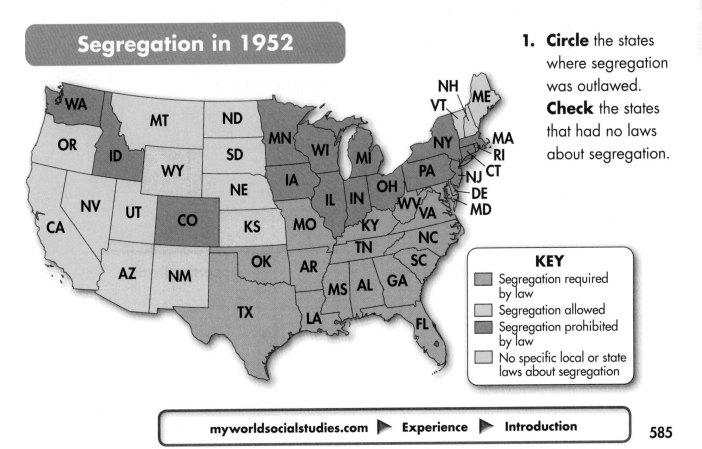

Segregation in 1952

KEY
- ▢ Segregation required by law
- ▢ Segregation allowed
- ▢ Segregation prohibited by law
- ▢ No specific local or state laws about segregation

Breaking the Color Barrier

On April 15, 1947, Jack Roosevelt Robinson stepped onto the field at Dodger Stadium in Brooklyn, New York. It was a historic moment. African Americans had played in their own Negro League since the late 1800s. No African Americans had been allowed to play in Major League Baseball. Dodgers' manager Branch Rickey hired Jackie Robinson from the Negro League. Robinson was a brave and an outstanding player, and he now broke the "color barrier." He faced terrible racism from white players and fans. Ridding the nation of prejudice was not easy; but more change was coming.

Jackie Robinson

A year later, President Harry Truman issued an executive order. He stated that "there shall be equality of treatment and opportunity for all persons in the armed services without regard to race, color, religion, or national origin." The U.S. armed services were, officially, no longer segregated.

Like Robinson, other African Americans were also breaking down the color barrier. In 1950, Ralph Bunche became the first African American to win the Nobel Peace Prize. In that same year, Gwendolyn Brooks became the first African American poet to win the Pulitzer Prize. Meanwhile, something larger was going on. The National Association for the Advancement of Colored People (NAACP) was planning to overturn *Plessy* v. *Ferguson.*

2. ◎ **Main Idea and Details** **Fill in** the chart using examples from this page and the next.

The Color Barrier

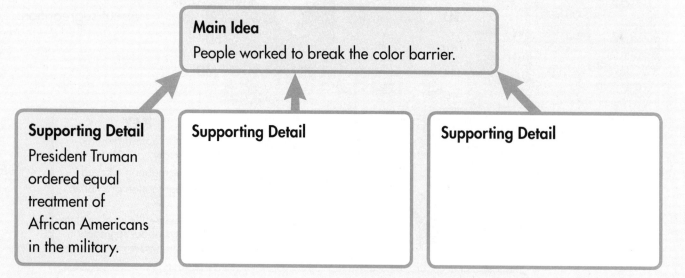

Main Idea
People worked to break the color barrier.

Supporting Detail
President Truman ordered equal treatment of African Americans in the military.

Supporting Detail

Supporting Detail

Ending School Segregation

In the early 1950s, the NAACP asked for legal trials in Kansas, South Carolina, Virginia, and Delaware. All the trials claimed that separate education was not equal education. Eventually, these court cases went to the Supreme Court. Together they were called *Brown* v. *Board of Education of Topeka*. Topeka is a community in Kansas.

The lawyer for the NAACP was the gifted Thurgood Marshall. Marshall spent his career fighting segregation, arguing 32 cases before the Supreme Court and winning 29 of them.

At the center of the *Brown* case was a young girl named Linda Brown. She lived in Topeka and went to an all-African American school far from her house. Why couldn't Linda go to the all-white school close to home?

In 1954, the Supreme Court agreed that she could. It said that "separate educational facilities are inherently [basically] unequal." This decision changed American life.

It would be years before **integration,** or the mixing of different groups, came to all American schools. But the *Brown* decision had improved civil rights for millions of African Americans.

3. A mother and daughter sit on the steps of the Supreme Court Building after the *Brown* decision. **Write** how that decision was similar to Jackie Robinson joining the major leagues.

....

....

....

....

....

....

The Montgomery Bus Boycott

In the 1950s, Montgomery, Alabama, was one of the most segregated cities in the nation. However, the movement for change would come to Montgomery, too.

A woman named Rosa Parks was in the local NAACP. Parks challenged one of Montgomery's Jim Crow laws. The law said that African Americans had to sit in the back of public buses. On December 1, 1955, Parks refused to move to the back of a bus. She was jailed for it.

In response, African Americans in Montgomery organized a boycott of city buses. A majority of Montgomery's bus

Rosa Parks

riders were African American. In the end, the bus company was forced to give in and let everyone sit where they wished on the city's buses, or go out of business.

The boycott's leader was a 26-year-old minister named Martin Luther King, Jr. "We have no alternative but to protest," King said. He understood that the African American community could no longer be patient "with anything less than freedom and justice."

Peaceful but powerful protests like the Montgomery bus boycott were at the heart of King's belief in nonviolence. He urged peaceful resistance to injustice, not violence. "Nonviolence is a powerful and just weapon," he said. "It is a sword that heals." Martin Luther King, Jr. shaped the nation's civil rights movement with this belief in nonviolence.

Protests Spread

Over the next ten years, the strength of the civil rights movement grew. School integration began slowly, however. Arkansas was one of the few states to start integrating schools. In September 1957, nine African American students were ready to integrate Central High School in the city of Little Rock. But the governor of Arkansas refused to let them begin classes. Violence erupted. Finally, President Eisenhower sent 1,000 U.S. Army soldiers to Little Rock. They were ordered to protect "the Little Rock Nine" at school.

Meanwhile, African Americans and white supporters tried to integrate other public places. In 1960, four African American college students in North Carolina staged the first **sit-in.** They sat quietly at a whites-only lunch counter. The manager asked them to leave, but they refused. Soon, sit-ins were happening in cities across the South.

Nonviolence was sometimes met with violence. In the summer of 1961, 13 civil rights protestors went on the first freedom ride. On **freedom rides**, African American and white protesters rode buses together to integrate bus lines. The Freedom Riders were often in danger from those who did not want segregation to end. Rider John Lewis was 21 years old that summer. He remembered the violence. "I thought I was going to die," he said after his bus was burned and he was beaten.

But the protests continued. In Birmingham, Alabama, in 1963, children and adults, including Martin Luther King, Jr., marched and went to jail to protest segregation. Reverend Fred Shuttlesworth was a leader of the African American community in Birmingham. To bring about change, he said, you might have "to suffer for what you believe in . . . . That's what the movement is all about."

4. Write how people in this photo depended on courage to create change.

....

....

....

....

The Little Rock Nine

Martin Luther King, Jr. preached nonviolence.

New Civil Rights Laws

On August 28, 1963, Martin Luther King, Jr. stood on the steps of the Lincoln Memorial in Washington, D.C. He called the crowd of more than 200,000 people in front of him "the greatest demonstration for freedom in the history of our nation." In the most famous part of his "I Have a Dream" speech, King said that day,

"I have a dream that my four little children will one day live in a nation where they will not be judged by the color of their skin but by the content of their character."

In March 1965, King led protests in Selma, Alabama, to demand voting rights. Protesters marched from Selma to the state capitol in Montgomery. The protesters were met with tear gas and beatings. The event, known as Bloody Sunday, was televised. People from around the world were angered by this treatment of peaceful marchers.

Just a few months later, Congress passed the Voting Rights Act of 1965. When he signed it, President Lyndon Johnson called it "one of the most monumental laws in the entire history of American freedom."

The victories of the 1960s were powerful. But tragedy struck when Martin Luther King, Jr. was assassinated in 1968. Today, his birthday, January 15, is a national holiday.

5. African American leader Malcolm X believed African Americans should gain their rights "by any means necessary." **Write** how his approach differed from Martin Luther King, Jr's.

....

....

....

....

The Movement Continues

Strengthened by the civil rights movement, African Americans achieved new successes. Thurgood Marshall became the first African American justice on the U.S. Supreme Court in 1967. In 1968, Shirley Chisholm was the first African American woman elected to Congress. Mae Jemison became the first African American woman astronaut to reach space in 1992. The list of achievements goes on and on.

In 2008, Americans elected the first African American president, Barack Obama. Obama spoke in Selma before his election. Honoring the civil rights movement, he told the crowd, "I am here because somebody marched."

Mae Jemison

Got it?

6. ⊙ **Sequence** **Choose** five important events in the civil rights movement. **List** them below, with their dates, in the correct sequence.

....

....

....

7. ⍰ You are a reporter in the 1960s. **Write** three questions you would ask a civil rights leader. **my Story Ideas**

....

....

....

■ **Stop!** I need help with ....

❙❙ **Wait!** I have a question about ....

▶ **Go!** Now I know ....

From the Great Society to Reagan

In 1970, Americans celebrated Earth Day for the first time.

Lyndon Johnson became president after the assassination of President Kennedy. He and his vice president, Hubert Humphrey, were later elected to office in 1964.

"Let Us Continue.."
–LYNDON B. JOHNSON

a Better Deal for You and America...

JOHNSON   HUMPHREY

ELECT Johnson AND Humphrey

VOTE LIBERAL COLUMN "C"

On November 22, 1963, President John F. Kennedy was assassinated. The nation was in shock. Kennedy had been a popular president, and now a new president had to carry on his work.

The Great Society

Lyndon Johnson, Kennedy's vice president, became president on the same day Kennedy was assassinated. Along with leading a grieving nation, Johnson needed Congress to pass key laws. One was President Kennedy's civil rights bill. President Johnson got it passed. The 1964 Civil Rights Act said that there could be no discrimination in jobs and no segregation in public housing.

President Johnson did not stop there. He wanted to use his power as president to help more people. In a speech in 1964 he gave his plan a name: **the Great Society.** "The Great Society rests on abundance and liberty for all," he said. "It demands an end to poverty and racial injustice . . . . But that is just the beginning."

Americans showed Lyndon Johnson that they approved of his plans. They elected him president in 1964, with the biggest majority in U.S. history. President Johnson created an Office of Economic Opportunity. It managed programs like the Job Corps, which trained young people in job skills.

Draw a poster to announce the next Earth Day. Include an Earth Day slogan or symbol.

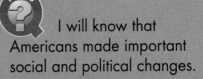

I will know that Americans made important social and political changes.

Vocabulary

the Great Society

minority group

affirmative action

impeach

President Johnson's war on poverty included the Food Stamps Program to help poor people afford food. Members of the Volunteers in Service to America (VISTA) program worked on many projects, such as building homes and fighting illiteracy, to help less-fortunate Americans.

Congress passed bills to reform health and education. Medicare and Medicaid were designed to provide assistance to older or disadvantaged citizens. Other programs, like Head Start, provided money for education.

The war in Vietnam eroded President Johnson's popularity, however. Antiwar protests focused on problems with his leadership. In 1968, Lyndon Johnson said he would not run for president again.

1. **Write** why First Lady "Lady Bird" Johnson would pose with children in this picture to promote the Head Start program.

....

....

....

....

Betty Friedan was an important leader of the women's rights movement.

The Women's Movement

In the 1960s, many women wanted more opportunities for education and work. In a new reform movement, women began to push for more changes.

Overall, women were paid less than men. Congress passed the Equal Pay Act in 1963. In 1964 the Equal Employment Opportunity Commission was set up.

In 1963, Betty Friedan's book *The Feminine Mystique* was published. It was about the problems women faced. A few years later, Betty Friedan became a founder of the National Organization of Women (NOW). NOW's goal is still to fight for and to protect women's rights.

In 1972, the Senate approved a new constitutional amendment. The Equal Rights Amendment (ERA) would have guaranteed equality for women. NOW and other groups gave the ERA their strong support, but it didn't pass.

Even though many people opposed these activities, the push for equality had powerful results. A federal law called Title IX, or Title Nine, opened school athletics to girls and women. At the same time, more and more women got better jobs, in new fields, with more pay. In 1981, Sandra Day O'Connor became the first female justice on the Supreme Court. In 1983, astronaut Sally Ride became the first American woman in space. Women's roles and opportunities were expanding.

2. **Fill in** the missing events in this timeline with information from this page.

The Women's Movement

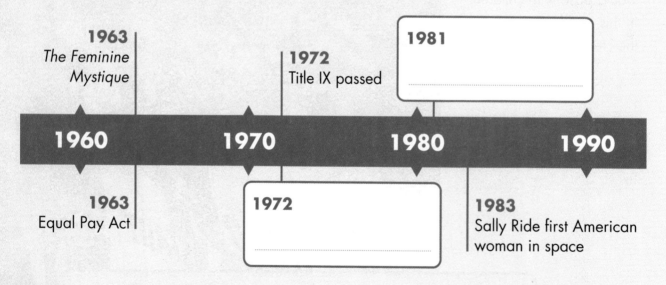

1963
The Feminine Mystique

1972
Title IX passed

1981
....

1960   1970   1980   1990

1963
Equal Pay Act

1972
....

1983
Sally Ride first American woman in space

Improved Rights for Others

The civil rights movement opened doors for African Americans and women. It also inspired other groups to work to improve their lives. In California, Cesar Chavez (SAY zahr CHAH vez) followed the nonviolent teachings of Martin Luther King, Jr. Chavez was a Hispanic farm worker. In the 1960s, Chavez organized a group that became the United Farm Workers (UFW).

In 1965, the UFW went on strike against grape growers in California. The workers protested their low wages and terrible working conditions. Many Americans joined in by refusing to buy grapes. The UFW improved conditions for its members.

Native Americans also demanded better treatment. Native Americans were the nation's poorest minority group. A **minority group** is a group that is distinct from the majority, or largest group in a society. Many Native Americans lived on reservations, where conditions were terrible. In the 1950s and 1960s, Native Americans began to work together. Groups such as the American Indian Movement (AIM) marched in Washington for fair and better treatment.

In 1990, Congress passed the Americans with Disabilities Act. This law protects the civil rights of people with disabilities of all kinds. For example, the law says that public buildings and public transportation must be accessible to disabled people.

Affirmative action is one path to change. The goal of affirmative action is to make up for past discrimination. For example, businesses might try to hire more women or minorities than in the past.

Some people have challenged this policy. They feel it is a form of discrimination that gives some people special treatment based on their race or gender. Others think it is the only way to make up for past wrongs.

The United States has always been a diverse nation. Together, Americans have shown that they can work to protect the civil rights of all of the country's citizens.

AIM works to improve conditions for Native Americans.

3. Public transportation must be available to everyone. **Write** another protection for disabled people.

....

....

....

....

The Environmental Movement

During the 1960s, people began to worry that the environment was in serious trouble. One was scientist Rachel Carson. She wrote about her concern in a best-selling book, *Silent Spring*. Carson warned about chemicals, such as pesticides, that were poisoning the environment. *Silent Spring* sparked a national debate about pollution.

There was a lot to worry about. Two events in 1969 made the environmental crisis very real. In January, an oil rig blew up off the coast of Santa Barbara, California. About 200,000 gallons of oil spread across the ocean surface. Thousands of birds and animals were killed. A few months later, in Cleveland, Ohio, the Cuyahoga River actually caught fire because there was so much oil and garbage in it. Americans were horrified. What was happening to the environment?

People formed groups to clean up the land, air, and water. In April 1970, the nation celebrated the first Earth Day. Also in 1970, President Richard Nixon set up the Environmental Protection Agency (EPA). The EPA's job is to make and enforce guidelines to protect the environment.

4. **Circle** words in the quotation that show the effects of using poisonous chemicals.

"These [chemicals] are now applied almost universally [...]—chemicals that have the power to kill every insect, the 'good' and the 'bad,' to still the song of birds, and the leaping of fish in the streams, [...] and to linger on in soil. . . ."

—*Rachel Carson*

Environmental laws now protect birds, such as the osprey, from extinction.

A Loss of Confidence in Government

Republican candidate Richard Nixon was elected U.S. president in 1968. As the 1960s came to an end, the war in Vietnam deeply divided the nation. The nation would also become deeply divided over President Nixon.

After Nixon won a landslide victory in the 1972 election, the *Washington Post* newspaper reported a troubling story. Five men had been arrested during the presidential campaign. They had broken into Democratic Party offices at the Watergate Hotel in Washington, D.C. Over the next two years a national scandal developed, known simply as Watergate. It became clear that Nixon was involved in trying to hide the role of the White House in the break-in.

Nixon feared that he would be **impeached**, or charged with a crime, and maybe removed from office by Congress. On August 9, 1974, Richard Nixon resigned, or voluntarily quit, as president.

After Nixon

Vice President Gerald Ford became president upon Nixon's resignation. Ford believed that a legal trial of the former president would harm the nation, so he pardoned Nixon. This meant Nixon would not be tried in court for any crimes. This made many Americans angry because they thought that Nixon should have been tried and punished.

Ford lost the 1976 election to Democrat Jimmy Carter. President Carter negotiated a peace treaty between Israel and Egypt. But the United States faced several crises during his presidency. One was the energy crisis. The Organization of Petroleum Exporting Countries (OPEC) was raising the price of oil. Americans faced long lines and shortages when they tried to buy gasoline. Another crisis developed in 1979 when sixty-six Americans were taken hostage by Iranian militants.

President Carter tried to restore Americans' confidence in government. "We simply must have faith in each other," he said. "Faith in our ability to govern ourselves and faith in the future of this nation."

5. Former President Nixon says goodbye after his resignation. **Write** why Americans might have lost confidence in government after Nixon's resignation.

....

....

....

....

Americans Today

What goals should we set for our nation?

When you set goals, you focus your efforts and achieve the things you most want to do. **Write** down a goal you have set for yourself. How will you achieve it?

....

....

....

....

Barack Obama is sworn in as president in 2009.

Yo-Yo Ma
Musician and Teacher

my Story Video

In May 2011, a large group of young musicians met in Chicago, Illinois, for a special festival. Some of the musicians were from Chicago, but others had traveled from as far away as Mexico. Though they were from different places and cultures, these talented young people came together to share in making beautiful music.

One of the leaders of this music festival was Yo-Yo Ma, a professional musician who plays the cello. A cello is a large stringed instrument that is often part of an orchestra. It has a deep, mellow sound. Ma believes in the power of music to bring together people from different backgrounds and cultures. He has devoted much of his life to projects that help people share their love of music.

Yo-Yo Ma was born in Paris, France, to Chinese parents. From a very young age, he showed an incredible talent for music. However, he didn't become a great cello player overnight. First, he had to set goals for himself. Then he had to work very hard. He also had a lot of help from his family. Every member of the Ma family was a musician. His father, Hiao-Tsiun Ma, played the violin. His mother, Ya-Wen Lo, was an opera singer. His older sister, Yeou-Cheng, is a violinist and teacher.

Yo-Yo Ma is one of the world's greatest cello players. He uses music to bring people together.

Yo-Yo Ma grew up in a musical family. His parents were both musicians. His father, Hiao-Tsiun, was his first music teacher.

Ma has given concerts in all of the world's great concert halls. Here he is shown at New York's famous Carnegie Hall.

When Yo-Yo Ma was a boy, he first tried playing the violin, like his father. But he wanted to play a bigger instrument. His father gave him a cello and began teaching him to play. His father also set goals for his son. For example, if Ma was learning to play a long piece of music, his father would have him practice just a little bit at a time. After a while, Ma was able to play the whole piece.

When his family moved to New York City, Ma started taking lessons with some of the world's greatest cello teachers. He was still a little boy, but he began playing the cello in important concerts. He performed a solo at New York's famous Carnegie Hall when he was just 9 years old!

As an adult, Yo-Yo Ma became one of the most famous musicians in the world. He loved playing the music of the great classical composers, such as Bach (bahk) and Beethoven (BAY toh vuhn). He also loved many other kinds of music. Soon he was bringing together musicians from around the world. They would perform pieces of music that combined aspects of different cultures.

The Silk Road Ensemble is an example of how Yo-Yo Ma has brought musicians from different backgrounds together. This group blends the musical traditions of Asia and the Middle East with those of Europe and the United States. Each musician brings different instruments and training. Ma says that a group like the Silk Road Ensemble helps us "better understand ourselves, our own lives, and culture."

With the Silk Road Ensemble, Yo-Yo Ma plays his cello alongside instruments like the tabla, which is a pair of drums from India.

In 2011, Yo-Yo Ma received the Presidential Medal of Freedom. It is given to people who have made contributions to American life.

Yo-Yo Ma believes in the power of music to bridge differences among people. He says that one of his goals is to use music to "create memorable moments of community." One special project is his work with young people who have gotten into trouble but are working to better themselves.

The project began when the Chicago Symphony Orchestra asked Ma to help them with a special community program. The program brought professional musicians to a youth center in Warrenville, Illinois. At the youth center, teenage girls who have faced challenges and problems in their lives learned about music. Yo-Yo Ma showed them how to play the cello. Then the girls wrote and performed their own musical show about mothers and daughters. One of the girls described the musicians who visited them: "It's not even like they're teaching us. They're sharing it with us. It's like they really believe in us too."

Today, Yo-Yo Ma continues to use music as a common language that all people can share. He continues to be a great musician, teacher, and cultural leader.

Think About It As you read this chapter, think about what the goals of the United States should be at home and abroad. How could Yo-Yo Ma's work influence the goals of the United States in other parts of the world?

In 2010, Yo-Yo Ma visited a youth center and gave cello lessons to the girls living there.

Lesson 1

Trials at Home and Abroad

Envision It!

This photo shows American rescue workers helping in Haiti after the 2010 earthquake.

After the Cold War ended, the United States played a new role in international events. It was now the world's only superpower. Americans had to decide how the nation would use its power. Many believed that the United States should work to help settle conflicts around the world.

1. On the map, **circle** the two Middle East countries that signed a peace treaty in 1978.

The United States Works for Peace

Even before the Cold War ended, the United States had worked for peace between Egypt and Israel. Those two Middle Eastern nations had been enemies for many years. The Middle East is a region also known as Southwest Asia, which includes Israel, Egypt, Iraq, Iran, and other nations. In 1948, Israel was founded as a Jewish state in the ancient Jewish homeland where Jews had always lived. The majority of people living in the new state were Jewish.

The Muslim nations that surround Israel did not want a Jewish state there. These countries fought several wars trying to destroy Israel. In 1977, Egypt decided to make peace with Israel.

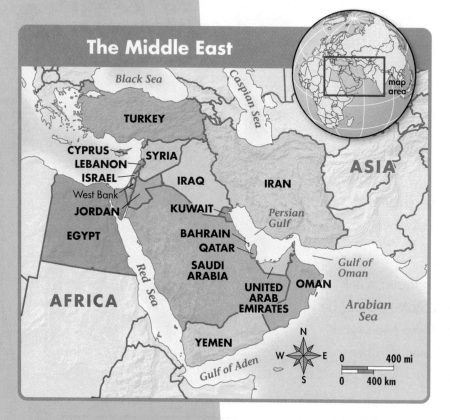

The Middle East

608

UNLOCK THE BIG ?

I will know that the United States played a new, important role in world events after the Cold War.

Vocabulary

human rights   levee

coalition

Electoral College

What does this photo tell you about some of the different roles that the United States plays in world events?

In 1978, U.S. President Jimmy Carter invited the leaders of the two countries, Israeli Prime Minister Menachem Begin (muh NAHK um BAY gihn) and Egyptian President Anwar El Sadat (AHN wahr el suh DAHT) to a meeting at Camp David in Maryland. There they signed peace agreements known as the Camp David Accords.

Carter also tried to make human rights a more important part of U.S. foreign policy. **Human rights** are the rights and freedoms that everyone should have as human beings. To encourage the protection of human rights around the world, Carter sometimes criticized other nations, even American allies, for human rights violations.

After Carter left office, American presidents continued to work for peace in the Middle East. In 1994, President Bill Clinton met with Jordan's King Hussein and Israeli Prime Minister Yitzhak Rabin as they signed a peace treaty. Conflicts in the Middle East continue, and the United States still works for peace in the region.

Carter, Begin, and Sadat celebrate the Camp David Accords at the White House in 1978.

Trouble in the Persian Gulf

Another crisis occurred in the Middle East in 1990. The nation of Iraq invaded the neighboring country of Kuwait (koo WAYT). Saddam Hussein (hoo SAYN) was the leader of Iraq. Hussein wanted to take over the rich oil fields of Kuwait. People feared he might also invade Saudi Arabia, which bordered Kuwait. Saudi Arabia had many oil fields, too.

American President George H. W. Bush worked with other nations to try to stop Iraq. The United Nations demanded that Iraq leave Kuwait. When this peaceful tactic failed, troops from the United States and other nations formed a coalition. A **coalition** is a group of allies who work together.

The coalition's attack on Iraqi forces was called Operation Desert Storm. U.S. General Colin Powell helped to plan the invasion. The U.S.-led forces won the war in only six weeks. Iraqis were pushed out of Kuwait, but Hussein remained in power.

In Operation Desert Storm, the United States used state-of-the-art equipment to win the war in six weeks.

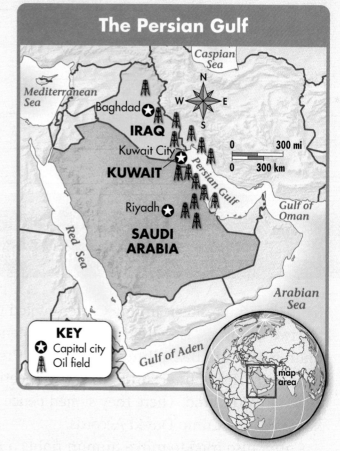

The Persian Gulf

KEY
⭐ Capital city
🛢 Oil field

2. **Circle** the nation in which Operation Desert Storm started. **Write** what the main natural resource of the Persian Gulf region is.

....

The Clinton Years

When Bill Clinton was elected president in 1992, he chose Madeleine Albright as Secretary of State. She was the first woman to hold this position. Together, they worked to resolve conflicts around the world. In 1990, the country of Yugoslavia, in Eastern Europe, split apart. Different regions declared themselves to be independent republics. Several ethnic groups fought for control in the new republics. The United States and other nations sent troops to restore peace. Fighting there ended in 1995.

In Northern Ireland, which was ruled by Great Britain, Catholics and Protestants had been fighting for hundreds of years. President Clinton worked with both groups to sign a peace treaty in 1998. Clinton also worked to keep peace between Saddam Hussein in Iraq and his neighbors.

During his second term, President Clinton faced a serious scandal. During an official investigation, Clinton lied in court. As outlined in the Constitution, the House of Representatives voted to impeach him. *Impeach* means to charge someone with a crime. The Senate held a trial. They found Clinton not guilty. He was not removed from office.

3. **Write** what Madeleine Albright and Saddam Hussein might have said about the United States' role in the affairs of other countries.

....

....

....

....

....

....

....

Madeleine Albright was Secretary of State for President Clinton.

Saddam Hussein was the Iraqi leader who invaded Kuwait.

Challenges at Home

In the 2000 U.S. presidential election, former Texas governor George W. Bush, son of President George H. W. Bush, ran against Clinton's Vice President Al Gore. The election was one of the closest in U.S. history. Gore received 50.9 million votes, while Bush received almost 50.5 million votes.

In the United States, however, presidents are not elected directly by the people. The people vote for electors, who cast their votes as part of a group called the **Electoral College.** The electors determine who wins a presidential election. The candidate who wins the most votes in a state wins all that state's electoral votes.

The 2000 election was so close that whoever got the most votes in Florida would win the election. The Florida vote was so close that it had to be counted several times. Eventually, the Supreme Court decided which count was official. Based on their decision, George W. Bush won the election.

Early in his presidency, President Bush supported a law known as "No Child Left Behind." This law was designed to improve public schools by testing students regularly to see whether they were making good progress.

Bush faced many challenges during his presidency. One of the worst was Hurricane Katrina. This storm hit the states along the coast of the Gulf of Mexico in August 2005.

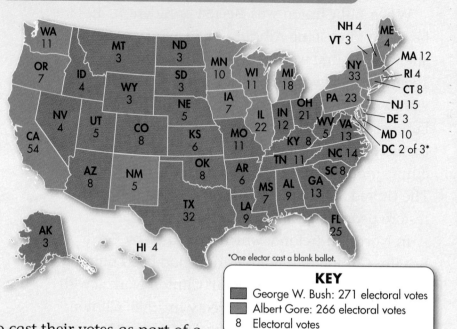

2000 Electoral College Vote

*One elector cast a blank ballot.

KEY
- George W. Bush: 271 electoral votes
- Albert Gore: 266 electoral votes
- 8 Electoral votes

4. **Look** at the map. How many electoral votes did Florida have? ....

How many more electoral votes did Bush get than Gore? ....

Hurricane Katrina caused terrible destruction to homes and businesses.

During the storm, New Orleans, Louisiana, flooded completely when levees protecting the city broke. A **levee** is an earthen barrier built to prevent flooding. The city was evacuated, and thousands of people had to be rescued from their homes, many in boats or helicopters. Hurricane Katrina was, to that point, the most deadly and costly disaster in U.S. history.

5. ◎ **Generalize** Are the rescuers in this picture soldiers or regular citizens? **Write** about how people react in a crisis.

....

....

....

Got it?

6. ◎ **Generalize** What was the United States' role as a world leader after the Cold War?

....

....

....

7. ❓ You are an adviser to President Clinton. Explain what goals you think the United States will achieve by getting involved in places such as Yugoslavia.

....

....

....

my Story Ideas

■ **Stop!** I need help with ....

❚❚ **Wait!** I have a question about ....

▶ **Go!** Now I know ....

Threats to Peace and Prosperity

Envision It!

For Your Safety
Here is a selection of items that would not pass through our security checks

ARTICLES WHICH MAY NOT BE TAKEN INTO THE RESTRICTED ZONE OR THE CABIN OF AN AIRCRAFT
Please place in hold baggage now!

Airports have very strict rules about what you cannot carry onto airplanes.

1. The Twin Towers were among the tallest buildings in the world. **Write** why terrorists might have chosen them as a target.

....

....

....

Today, much of the world is worried about terrorism. **Terrorism** is the use of violence and fear to achieve political goals. Terrorists, the people who use terrorism, come from all over the world.

September 11, 2001

In 1993, terrorists set off a bomb in the garage under one of the Twin Towers of the World Trade Center in New York City. The bomb killed 6 people and injured about 1,000 more.

On September 11, 2001, terrorists hijacked, or took over, four airplanes. They crashed two of the airplanes into the Twin Towers of the World Trade Center. These buildings, which were the tallest in New York, were flooded with burning jet fuel and were completely destroyed.

The terrorists crashed a third airplane into the Pentagon in Arlington, Virginia. The Pentagon is the headquarters of the United States military.

The fourth airplane crashed in a Pennsylvania field. Having learned what the terrorists were planning, the passengers tried to take control of the plane away from the terrorists. If they had not done so, the terrorists might have crashed the airplane into another important building in Washington, D.C.

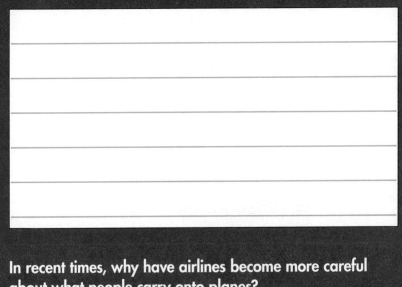

UNLOCK THE BIG ?

I will know that, in the early 2000s, the United States faced terrorist attacks and fought in several wars.

In recent times, why have airlines become more careful about what people carry onto planes?

Vocabulary

terrorism   civilian

weapons of mass destruction

More than 3,000 people were killed in the September 11 attacks. The victims included the 264 passengers on board the four airplanes, more than 2,800 people at the World Trade Center in New York, and 120 at the Pentagon. Firefighters, police officers, and rescue workers were among those killed as they worked to save others who were trapped in the buildings.

The people who committed these attacks were part of al Qaeda (al KYE dah), a Muslim terrorist group. The group's leader was Osama bin Laden, from Saudi Arabia. Bin Laden and the members of al Qaeda strongly opposed American influence in Islamic lands.

Americans Respond

Immediately after the attacks, people from all over the country lined up to donate blood for injured victims and rescue workers. Students were among those who donated food, clothing, and money to help the victims' families.

The attacks also led the United States to place a greater emphasis on the security of the nation. The Department of Homeland Security was created. This department's job is to protect the country from terrorism and to prepare for natural disasters. Airports and other public buildings also created new policies to keep people safer.

2. List some ways that people can help after a disaster.

....

....

....

People all over the nation gathered items to help after the September 11 attacks.

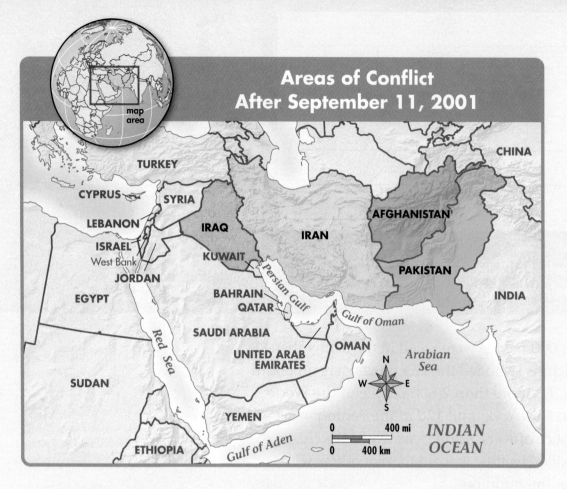

Areas of Conflict After September 11, 2001

map area

TURKEY

CYPRUS

SYRIA

LEBANON

IRAQ

AFGHANISTAN

ISRAEL

West Bank

KUWAIT

IRAN

PAKISTAN

CHINA

JORDAN

EGYPT

BAHRAIN

QATAR

Persian Gulf

Gulf of Oman

INDIA

SAUDI ARABIA

OMAN

UNITED ARAB EMIRATES

Arabian Sea

SUDAN

N W E S

YEMEN

ETHIOPIA

Gulf of Aden

Red Sea

0   400 mi
0   400 km

INDIAN OCEAN

3. **Circle** the names of two nations on this page that experienced conflict after 9/11. Then **circle** the names of those countries on the map.

War in Iraq

Soon after the September 11 attacks, President George W. Bush announced that the United States would fight a "War on Terror." This meant that the nation would use its military to find and capture terrorists around the world.

Al Qaeda had been based in the Central Asian country of Afghanistan. A group called the Taliban controlled Afghanistan's government. They refused to help find Osama bin Laden. They also denied many Afghanis their basic human rights.

In October 2001, U.S. troops invaded Afghanistan. After only a few months, the Taliban government surrendered and gave up power. Some terrorists were captured, but bin Laden escaped.

President Bush then turned to Iraq. The treaty that had ended the war in Iraq in 1991 called for that country to destroy all its weapons of mass destruction. **Weapons of mass destruction**, or WMDs, can kill large numbers of people. They include nuclear weapons and weapons that spread poison or disease over large areas.

Saddam Hussein still ruled Iraq. He had agreed to inspections by the United Nations to see that any WMDs he had were destroyed. But by the early 2000s, Hussein no longer allowed U.N. inspectors into Iraq.

This action raised suspicion that Iraq still had WMDs. News reports showed that Saddam Hussein was murdering people in his country, too. President Bush and Condoleezza Rice, the National Security Advisor, had also said there were reports that there might be ties between Iraq's government and al Qaeda. This led the U.S. government to support an invasion of Iraq to remove Hussein from power.

In 2005, Condoleezza Rice became the first African American woman to be named U.S. Secretary of State.

In March 2003, United States troops, as well as troops from 30 other nations, went to war in Iraq. It took only a few months to defeat the Iraqi army. Saddam Hussein was arrested in December 2003 and later executed. A new government was democratically elected in 2005. But rebels continued to fight, and United States troops remained in Iraq.

In 2007, the United States sent a surge, or sudden increase, of troops into Iraq, which weakened the rebels. In 2009, President Barack Obama began to withdraw troops from Iraq.

The Iraq War was controversial. Many nations agreed that Saddam Hussein was dangerous. But some opposed fighting a war to remove him. After the war began, people learned that Iraq did not have WMDs. Also, Hussein was not connected to al Qaeda. The war in Iraq remains a controversy today.

4. American soldiers help Iraqis pull down a statue of Saddam Hussein. **Describe** what this action might have represented.

....

....

....

....

....

Afghanistan and Other Challenges

After defeating the Taliban in 2001, the U.S. military stayed in Afghanistan to help establish a new government. While the Taliban were in power, they had denied many human rights, especially those of women. The new government promised the citizens of Afghanistan more rights. Today, however, Afghani women still do not have the same rights as Afghani men.

Meanwhile, many of the Taliban fled from Afghanistan to the neighboring country of Pakistan. There, the Taliban began to regain strength. Its members attacked American soldiers and Afghan civilians. **Civilians** are people who are not in the military.

To stop the Taliban, President Barack Obama called for another military surge. He sent more soldiers to Afghanistan, beginning in 2009. The United States also attacked areas of Pakistan where they believed Taliban members were based.

As American forces fought the Taliban, the hunt continued for the al Qaeda leader Osama bin Laden, who had planned the September 11 attacks on the United States. After years of investigation, the U.S. government discovered bin Laden's hiding place. In May, 2011, American forces raided a house in Pakistan and killed bin Laden. According to reports, the raid also uncovered evidence that bin Laden was planning more attacks on the United States.

Afghani women march in protest against a new law that would further deny their human rights.

620

As the 2000s continued, the United States faced other dangers. Many people believed that North Korea and Iran were developing nuclear weapons. The United States also feared that terrorist groups or individuals might build dangerous chemical weapons in other parts of the world. In the days of the Cold War, Americans had worried about a single powerful enemy, the Soviet Union. In the new century, Americans were now alert to dangers from many different sources.

5. ◉ **Generalize** **Write** a generalization based on the sentences in the table below.

North Korea conducted a test of nuclear weapons in 2006.	Americans feared that Iran was developing nuclear weapons.	People feared additional terrorist attacks after those of September 11, 2001.

Got it?

6. ◉ **Generalize** Why did the United States invade Afghanistan?

7. ❓ You are advising the president on choices about airport security. What will you say about balancing the need for security checks against passengers' convenience?

my Story Ideas

■ **Stop!** I need help with

▮▮ **Wait!** I have a question about

▶ **Go!** Now I know

Meeting Today's Challenges

Envision It!

These giant wind turbines make up a wind farm that generates electricity.

On November 4th, 2008, Barack Obama was elected the 44th United States president.

The 2008 presidential election was a historic event. Candidates used the Internet more than ever to reach supporters. Women candidates ran for the top offices. Many Americans who had never voted before, did so now. On November 4, the nation elected Barack Obama as president. He was the first African American to achieve that office.

Challenges at Home

Many people were excited about Obama's election because he was the first African American president and because he represented change. But he faced many challenges. The nation's economy was in serious decline, and the new president needed to do something about it, fast.

The economic decline in the United States began in 2007. Many industries started to let go, or lay off, workers. With so many people out of work and unable to pay their home mortgages and other loans, banks lost money. Then, they couldn't lend much to businesses. So businesses began to lay off more workers, and those workers bought fewer goods. So the companies that made those goods lost money.

Banks began to lose more and more money. They had made bad decisions about some loans, especially for home mortgages, and were not repaid. As a result, many banks closed.

Draw a picture of something else that will either save energy or produce energy.

UNLOCK THE BIG ?

I will know that the United States and the world are meeting many challenges.

Vocabulary

recession
national debt
globalization

nonrenewable resource
climate change

By 2009, the United States, and the world as a whole, was in a serious recession. A **recession** is a long economic slowdown. The U.S. government took several actions to ease the tough economic times.

In 2009, Congress passed a stimulus bill that put almost $500 billion into public works projects, such as road repairs, to create jobs. The government also provided billions of dollars to banks so that they could keep operating and lending money. Unfortunately, this dramatically increased the **national debt**, or money that the country has borrowed to pay its bills.

At the same time, the costs of medical care and health insurance were increasing sharply. In 2010, the U.S. government passed a law trying to control healthcare costs and to ensure that more Americans had health insurance.

Conflict Over Jobs

Throughout the economic slowdown, immigrants continued to come to the United States. Most came legally, but many came illegally. Many Americans worried that illegal immigrants would get jobs that should go to citizens. They wanted tougher laws against illegal immigrants.

Government programs created jobs to stimulate the economy.

1. **Read** the sign. Why is creating jobs a "reinvestment" in America?

....

....

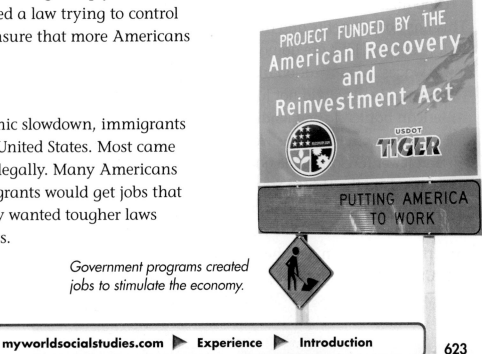

America's Place in the World Today

Did you know that in 2005, more than 1.4 billion people, about 1 out of every 5 people on Earth, lived on less than $1.25 a day? Extreme poverty like this is only one of many challenges facing people around the world today.

Hunger, disease, and lack of education are often caused by poverty. About 1 billion people cannot read a book or write their names. Millions of people don't have access to healthcare. People around the world also suffer from wars, terrorism, or are denied their basic human rights.

Governments and international organizations are working to solve these problems. The United Nations, for example, has set "Development Goals" for countries to achieve by 2015. These goals include reducing poverty, improving education and healthcare, and ending diseases, such as Acquired Immunodeficiency Syndrome, or AIDS.

Because the United States is such a wealthy country, its government works to address many international challenges. Individual Americans also contribute to solving the world's problems. They donate money or time, and even go overseas to help teach, work as doctors, or protect the oppressed. When the country of Haiti was hit by a major earthquake in January 2010, the United States promised to donate $1.15 billion and former President Bill Clinton led the relief effort. Hundreds of private citizens also went to Haiti to help.

Many Americans, such as these people in Haiti after the 2010 earthquake, help people in other nations around the world.

There are many other inspiring stories of Americans helping to solve international problems and improve people's lives. The musician Yo-Yo Ma works to encourage a greater appreciation of music. September 11 widow Susan Retik's group, Beyond the 11th, helps widows and other women in Afghanistan improve their lives. Doctor Paul Farmer established medical clinics for poor people in Haiti and other countries. Of helping others, Farmer said:

> *"You're in front of someone who is suffering and you have the tools [to end] that suffering . . . . you act."*

> —Paul Farmer

6. List a challenge facing the world today and describe something an individual could do to help solve it.

....

....

....

....

Got it?

7. **Generalize Write** a generalization based on these two facts: Oil is a nonrenewable resource. Americans depend on other countries for more than half of their oil.

....

....

....

....

8. President Barack Obama has just come into office. What can you tell him about the challenges he faces?

my **Story Ideas**

....

....

....

Stop! I need help with ....

Wait! I have a question about ....

Go! Now I know ....

Chapter 17
Study Guide

Lesson 1

Trials at Home and Abroad

- The United States has tried to settle conflicts around the world.
- The United States led a coalition of nations in 1990 against Iraq in Operation Desert Storm.
- President Bill Clinton worked for peace but also faced challenges.

Lesson 2

Threats to Peace and Prosperity

- On September 11, 2001, terrorists attacked the World Trade Center in New York City and the Pentagon in Arlington, Virginia.
- As a result of the 2001 attacks, the United States began the War on Terror in Afghanistan and Iraq.

Lesson 3

Meeting Today's Challenges

- The United States experienced a recession beginning in 2007.
- New technologies have changed Americans' lives, as they also look to new energy sources to replace oil.
- Americans volunteer around the world to help others in need.

Lesson 1

Trials at Home and Abroad

1. Use the numbers 1, 2, 3, and 4 to arrange the following events in the order in which they happened.

   _____ Bush-Gore election

   _____ Camp David Accords

   _____ Clinton impeachment

   _____ Operation Desert Storm

2. What were the main cause and effect of the first war with Iraq?

   ....

   ....

   ....

   ....

3. **Circle** the correct answer.

   Florida played an important role in the 2000 election because

   A. its votes were never counted.

   B. its governor had to break the tie.

   C. its electoral votes helped decide the winner.

   D. the Supreme Court ruled that its votes did not count.

Lesson 2

Threats to Peace and Prosperity

4. What happened to each of the four airplanes terrorists took over on September 11, 2001?

   ....

   ....

   ....

   ....

   ....

5. How did Americans react to the September 11 attacks?

   ....

   ....

   ....

   ....

6. **Write** why the United States went to war with Iraq and Afghanistan.

Iraq	Afghanistan

Lesson 3

Meeting Today's Challenges

7. **Generalize Write** a generalization based on the following sentences.

In 2008–2009, housing prices dropped.

In 2008–2009, people could not repay their loans to banks.

In 2008–2009, banks lost money.

In 2008–2009, businesses laid off workers.

....

....

....

8. Overall, do you think globalization is harmful or helpful to Americans?

....

....

....

9. What are two effects of American dependence on oil as a source of energy?

....

....

....

....

....

10. **What goals should we set for our nation?**

a. This photo shows that one goal that Americans had for the Iraq War in 2003 was achieved. What goal was that?

....

....

b. What goal is recycling an important part of?

....

....

....

c. What goals do you think the United States should set for itself regarding energy?

....

....

....

....

....

Go online to write and illustrate your own **myStory Book** using the **myStory Ideas** from this chapter.

THE BIG ? What goals should we set for our nation?

Americans today face many challenges, including oil spills, natural disasters, and terrorism. But we also have opportunities to make the world a better place. **Write** some of the goals that we should set as a nation to make our country and the world better.

....

....

....

Now **draw** an image of how the United States might meet one of your two goals. **Write** a caption for your drawing.

While you're online, check out the **myStory Current Events** area where you can create your own book on a topic that's in the news.

Atlas

The United States of America, Political

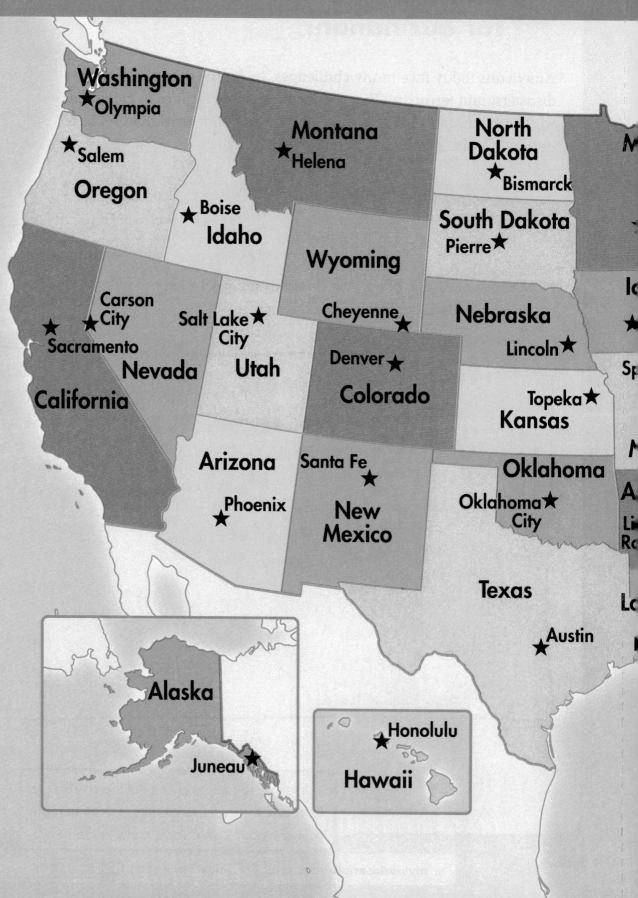

Washington
★Olympia

★Salem
Oregon

★Boise
Idaho

Montana
★Helena

North Dakota
★Bismarck

South Dakota
Pierre★

Wyoming

Cheyenne
★

Nebraska

Lincoln★

Carson City
★
Sacramento
Nevada

Salt Lake City★

Denver★

Topeka★
Kansas

California

Utah

Colorado

Arizona

Santa Fe
★

Oklahoma

Oklahoma★
City

Phoenix
★

New Mexico

Texas

Austin
★

M

Ia

Sp

A

Li
Ro

La

N

Alaska

Juneau★

Honolulu
★

Hawaii

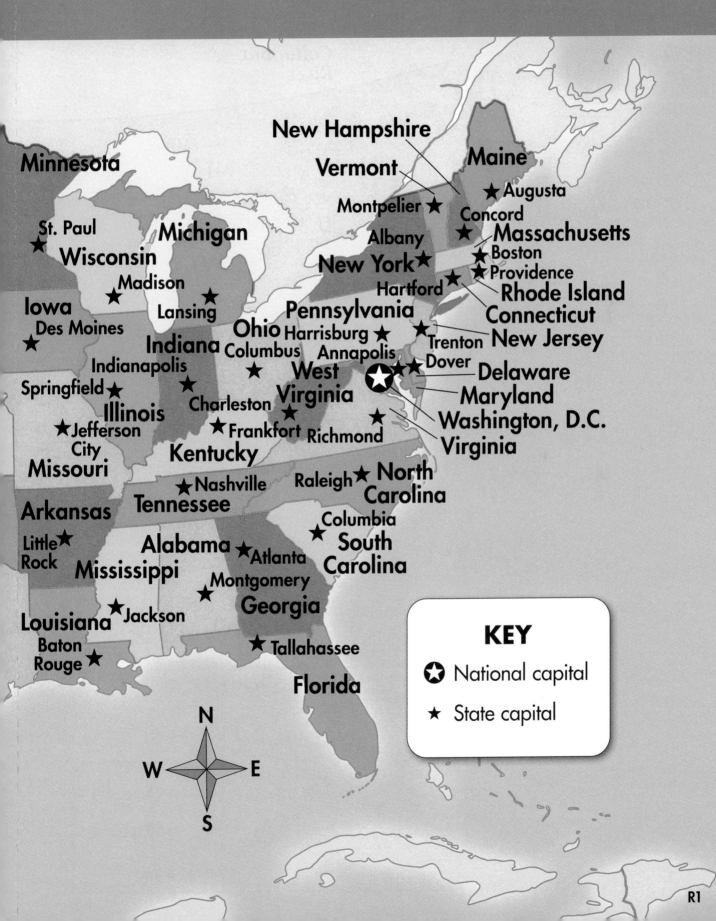

Minnesota

St. Paul
★

Wisconsin

Michigan

Madison
★

Lansing

Iowa

Des Moines
★

Indiana

Indianapolis
★

Springfield
★

Illinois

Jefferson
City
★

Missouri

Little ★
Rock

Arkansas

Louisiana

Baton
Rouge ★

Jackson
★

Mississippi

Alabama

Montgomery
★

Georgia

★ Tallahassee

Florida

Ohio

Columbus
★

Charleston

West
Virginia

★ Frankfort

Kentucky

Richmond
★

Nashville
★

Tennessee

Columbia
★

South
Carolina

Atlanta
★

New Hampshire

Vermont

Montpelier ★

Albany
★

New York

Pennsylvania

Harrisburg ★

Annapolis

★

Trenton
★

Dover
★

Maine

★ Augusta

Concord
★

Massachusetts

★ Boston

★ Providence

Rhode Island

Hartford
★

Connecticut

New Jersey

Delaware

Maryland

Washington, D.C.

Virginia

Raleigh ★

North
Carolina

KEY

⭐ National capital

★ State capital

N
W   E
S

R1

Columbia
River

Cascade Range

WA

MT

Missouri River

ND

OR

ID

SD

ROCKY

WY

GREAT

Sierra Nevada

Great
Salt Lake

NV

Great
Basin

NE

CA

UT

Colorado River

CO

K.

Death
Valley
-282 ft.
(-86 m)

Colorado
Plateau

MOUNTAINS

PLAINS

AZ

NM

O

PACIFIC
OCEAN

TX

MEXICO

Rio Grande

G

AK

Mt. McKinley
20,320 ft.
(6,194 m)

0   400 mi

0   400 km

Aleutian Islands

HI

0   150 mi

0   150 km

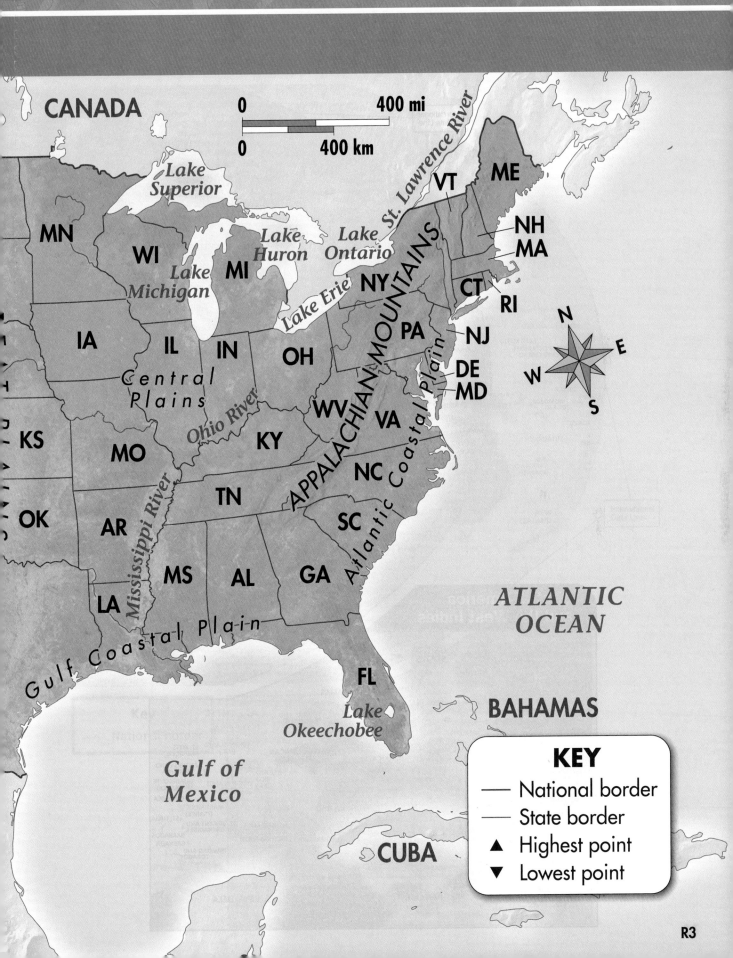

CANADA

Lake Superior

MN

WI

Lake Huron

Lake Michigan

MI

Lake Ontario

St. Lawrence River

VT

ME

NH

MA

Lake Erie

NY

APPALACHIAN MOUNTAINS

CT

RI

IA

IL

IN

OH

PA

NJ

Central Plains

Ohio River

DE

MD

KS

MO

KY

WV

VA

Atlantic Coastal Plain

Mississippi River

TN

NC

OK

AR

SC

MS

AL

GA

Atlantic Coastal Plain

LA

Gulf Coastal Plain

FL

Lake Okeechobee

ATLANTIC OCEAN

BAHAMAS

Gulf of Mexico

CUBA

N E W S

KEY

— National border

— State border

▲ Highest point

▼ Lowest point

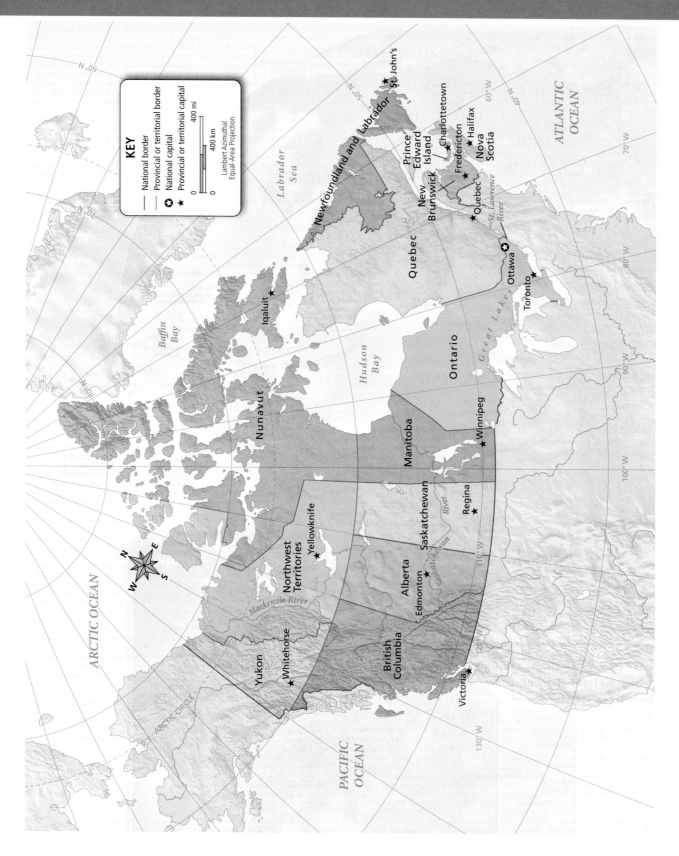

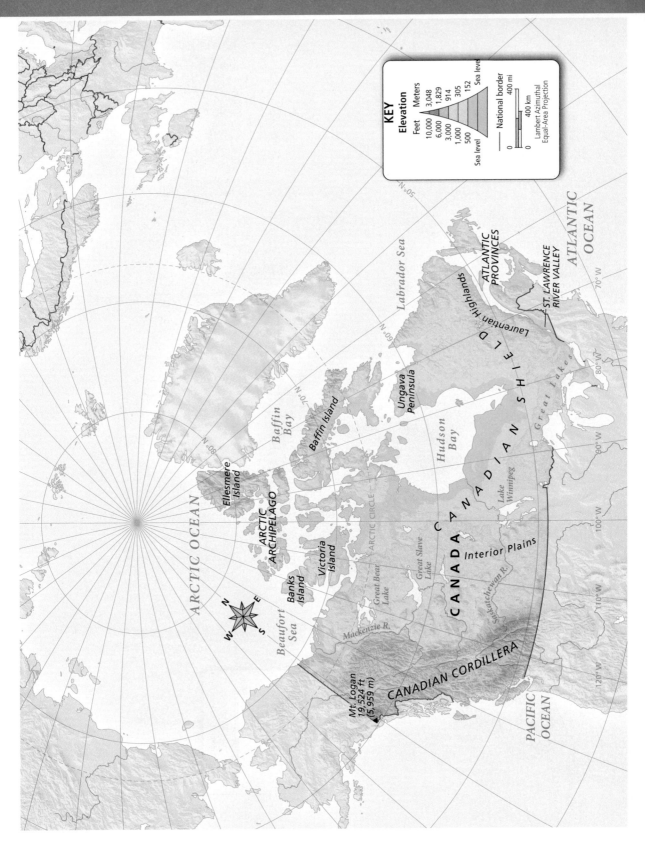

KEY

Elevation

Feet	Meters	
10,000	3,048	
6,000	1,829	
3,000	914	
1,000	305	
500	152	
Sea level	Sea level	

— National border

Lambert Azimuthal
Equal-Area Projection

400 mi
400 km

ARCTIC OCEAN

Beaufort Sea

Banks Island

Victoria Island

Ellesmere Island

ARCTIC ARCHIPELAGO

Baffin Bay

Baffin Island

ARCTIC CIRCLE

Great Bear Lake

Great Slave Lake

Mackenzie R.

Mt. Logan
19,524 ft
(5,959 m)

CANADIAN CORDILLERA

Interior Plains

Saskatchewan R.

Lake Winnipeg

CANADIAN SHIELD

Hudson Bay

Ungava Peninsula

Labrador Sea

Laurentian Highlands

ATLANTIC PROVINCES

ST. LAWRENCE RIVER VALLEY

ATLANTIC OCEAN

Great Lakes

PACIFIC OCEAN

50°N

60°N

70°N

80°N

70°W

80°W

90°W

100°W

110°W

120°W

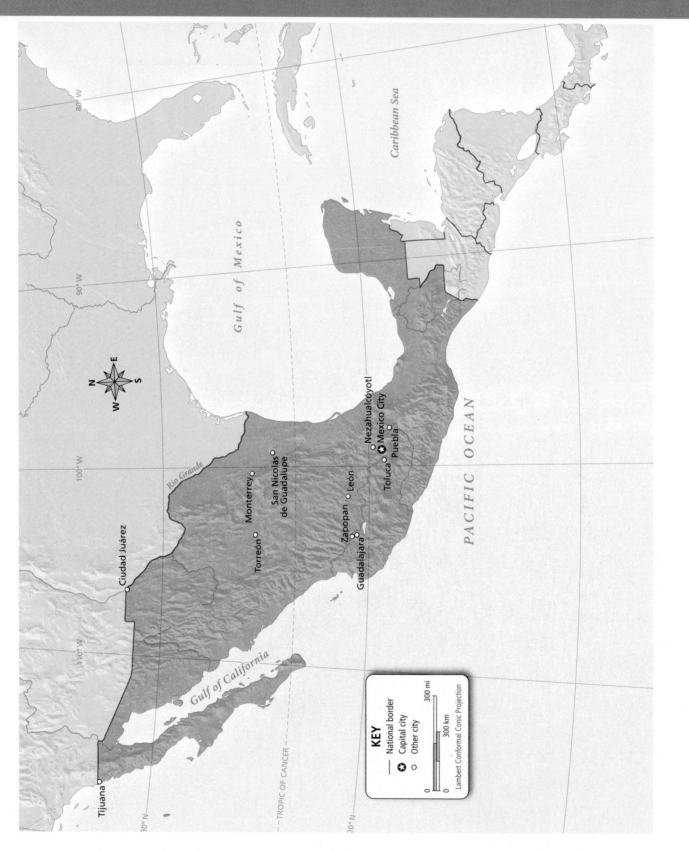

Caribbean Sea

Gulf of Mexico

PACIFIC OCEAN

Gulf of California

Rio Grande

Tijuana

Ciudad Juárez

Torreón

Monterrey

San Nicolas
de Guadalupe

Zapopan

León

Guadalajara

Toluca

Nezahualcóyotl

Mexico City

Puebla

80° W

90° W

100° W

110° W

30° N

20° N

TROPIC OF CANCER

KEY
— National border
⊕ Capital city
○ Other city

0   300 mi

0   300 km

Lambert Conformal Conic Projection

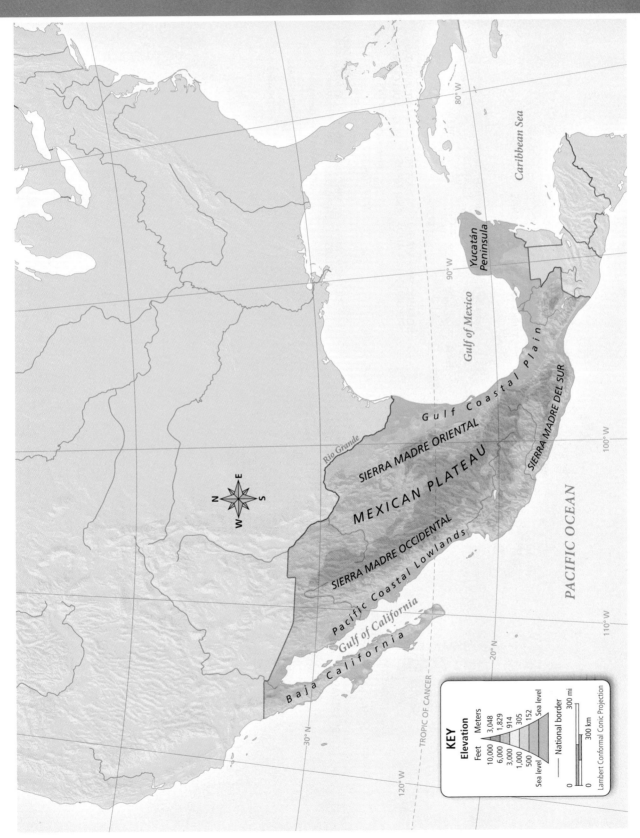

Caribbean Sea

Yucatán Peninsula

Gulf of Mexico

Gulf Coastal Plain

Rio Grande

SIERRA MADRE ORIENTAL

SIERRA MADRE DEL SUR

MEXICAN PLATEAU

SIERRA MADRE OCCIDENTAL

Pacific Coastal Lowlands

PACIFIC OCEAN

Gulf of California

Baja California

TROPIC OF CANCER

80° W

90° W

100° W

110° W

120° W

20° N

30° N

N
E
S
W

KEY
Elevation

Feet	Meters
10,000	3,048
6,000	1,829
3,000	914
1,000	305
500	152
Sea level	Sea level

—— National border

300 mi

300 km

Lambert Conformal Conic Projection

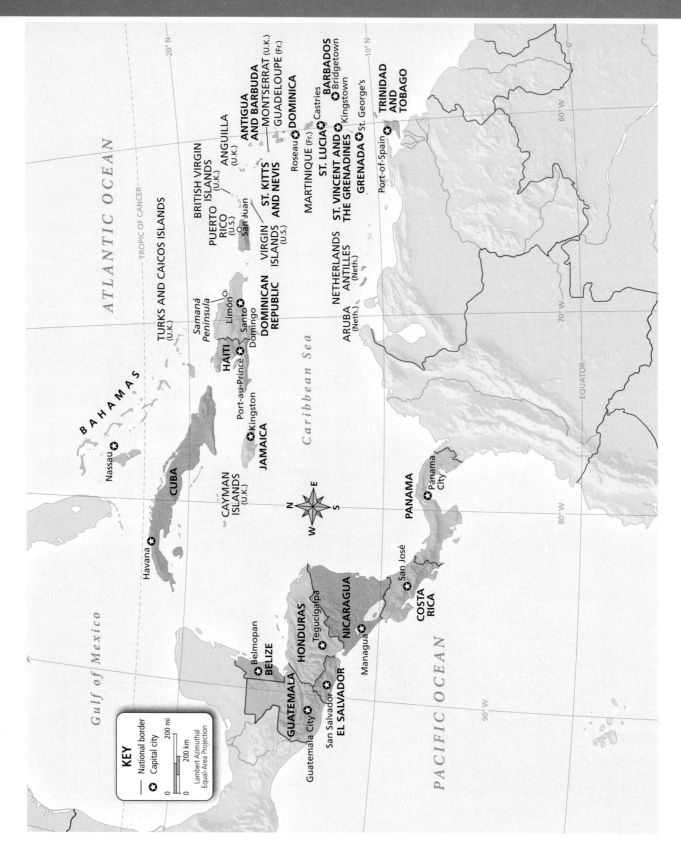

ATLANTIC OCEAN

TROPIC OF CANCER

20° N

10° N

0°

60° W

70° W

80° W

90° W

EQUATOR

Gulf of Mexico

PACIFIC OCEAN

Caribbean Sea

BAHAMAS
Nassau ✪

CUBA
Havana ✪

CAYMAN ISLANDS (U.K.)

JAMAICA
Kingston ✪

TURKS AND CAICOS ISLANDS (U.K.)

HAITI
Port-au-Prince ✪

Samaná Peninsula
Limón ○
Santo Domingo
DOMINICAN REPUBLIC

BRITISH VIRGIN ISLANDS (U.K.)

PUERTO RICO (U.S.)
San Juan

ANGUILLA (U.K.)

VIRGIN ISLANDS (U.S.)

ST. KITTS AND NEVIS

ANTIGUA AND BARBUDA
MONTSERRAT (U.K.)
GUADELOUPE (Fr.)

DOMINICA
Roseau ✪

MARTINIQUE (Fr.)

ST. LUCIA ✪ Castries

ST. VINCENT AND THE GRENADINES
Kingstown

GRENADA ✪ St. George's

BARBADOS ✪ Bridgetown

TRINIDAD AND TOBAGO
Port-of-Spain ✪

NETHERLANDS ANTILLES (Neth.)

ARUBA (Neth.)

BELIZE
Belmopan ✪

GUATEMALA
Guatemala City ✪

EL SALVADOR
San Salvador ✪

HONDURAS
Tegucigalpa ✪

NICARAGUA
Managua ✪

COSTA RICA
San José ✪

PANAMA
Panama City ✪

N E S W compass rose

KEY
— National border
✪ Capital city

0   200 mi
0   200 km

Lambert Azimuthal Equal-Area Projection

Glossary

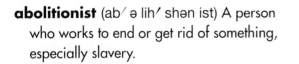

A

abolitionist (ab′ ə lih′ shən ist) A person who works to end or get rid of something, especially slavery.

affirmative action (ə fʉrm′ ə tiv ak′ shən) A plan established by some businesses and educational organizations to make up for past discrimination against minorities or women by hiring or admitting more minorities or women than in the past.

alliance (ə lī′ əns) An agreement among nations to defend each other.

Allied Powers (ə līd′ pou′ ərz) During World War I, the nations who fought together against the Central Powers; mainly Great Britain, France, Russia, and later the United States.

Allies (ə līz′) During World War II, the nations who fought together against the Axis; mainly Great Britain, the United States, France, and the Soviet Union.

amendment (ə mend′ mənt) A change or improvement.

annex (ə neks′) To take territory and join it to a state or country.

anti-Semitism (an′ tī sem′ ə tiz′ əm) A hatred of Jewish people.

arms control (ärmz kən trōl′) The limiting of the production of weapons.

arms race (armz rās) A contest to build more and better weapons than those of your enemy.

article (ärt′ i kəl) A law written in the United States Constitution.

assassinate (ə sas′ ən āt′) To murder someone famous or powerful, usually for political reasons.

assembly line (ə sem′ blē līn) A factory system in which a product is put together as it moves past a line of workers, each of whom does one part of the whole job.

atomic bomb (ə täm′ ik bäm) A type of bomb developed during World War II that uses atomic reactions to create a massive explosion. Atomic bombs were dropped by the United States on Japan to end that war.

Axis (ak′ sis) During World War II, the nations who fought together against the Allies; mainly Germany, Italy, and Japan.

B

baby boom (bā′ bē boom) The years between 1945 and 1964 when 76 million babies were born in the United States.

bank account (bank ə kount′) The money an individual puts into a bank.

bias (bi′ əs) A point of view that is affected by one's strong beliefs.

black codes (blak kōdz) A group of laws passed in the late 1800s that denied African American men the right to vote, kept African Americans from owning guns or taking certain types of jobs.

Pronunciation Key

a in hat	ō in open	'l in cattle
ā in age	ô in order	'n in sudden
ä in father	o͞o in tool	th in weather
e in let	u in cup	zh in measure
ē in equal	ʉ in reverse	
i in it	ə a in ago	
ī in ice	e in agent	
o in hot	o in collect	
	u in focus	

refugee (ref yo͞o gē′) A person who has left his or her country to escape war, famine, or oppression.

region (rē′ jən) A geographic area that has its own distinct features, such as geography, language, culture, or climate.

relief map (ri lēf′ map) The surface features of land shown on a map.

representative democracy (rep′ rə zen′ tə tiv di mäk′ rə sē) A system of government in which the citizens elect people to act on their behalf.

reservation (rez′ ər vā′ shən) An area of land granted, often by force, to a Native American tribe, usually in exchange for their own homeland.

rule of law (ro͞ol əv lô) The principle that the law applies to everyone, equally.

— S —

satellite map (sat′′l īt′ map) A map that shows a picture of what an area looks like from space.

scale (skāl) A ruler that shows distances on a map.

scarcity (sker′ sə tē) A shortage.

secession (si sesh′ ən) The separation of a state from a nation.

segregation (seg′ rə gā′ shən) The division of groups of people, usually by race.

separation of powers (sep′ ə rā′ shən əv pou′ ərz) The division of the powers and duties of government among separate branches.

sharecropping (sher′ krap′ ing) A system in which someone who owns land lets someone else "rent" the land to farm it.

siege (sēj) A military blockade and extended attack designed to make a city or other location surrender.

sit-in (sit′ in′) A non-violent protest in which people sit quietly and refuse to leave.

Social Security (sō′ shəl si kyo͞or ə tē) An insurance system funded by the U.S. federal government to help support disabled or retired Americans.

sodbuster (säd′ bus′ tər) The nickname given to a person who settled on the Great Plains and had to break up the thickly rooted grass, or sod, to build a home and plant crops.

specialize (spesh′ əl īz′) To make one product or do one kind of job, rather than many different ones.

states' rights (stāts rīts) The right of each U.S. state to make its own local laws.

stock (stäk) A financial share of ownership of a company.

stock market (stäk mär′ kit) A central location where people buy and sell stocks in companies.

strike (strīk) An event at which workers refuse to work, usually to protest issues of pay or workplace conditions.

strikebreaker (strīk′ brāk′ ər) A person who replaces a worker who is on strike.

suburb (sub′ ərb) A community outside of a city, but not far into the countryside.

suffrage (səf′ rij) The right to vote.

suffragist (səf′ rə jist) A person who works to extend the right to vote to those who do not currently have it.

supply (sə plī′) The amount of goods or services available for a consumer to buy.

tariff (tar′ if) A tax on imports.

tax (taks) A fee imposed by a government on its citizens that is used for public services

telegraph (tel′ ə graf′) A communications system invented by Samuel Morse that uses coded bursts of electricity to send messages over long distances.

temperance (tem′ pər əns) The reduction of or end to drinking alcohol.

tenement (ten′ ə mənt) A building that has been divided into many small apartments.

tepee (tē′ pē) A type of portable home used by many Native Americans of the Great Plains made of wood poles covered with bark and animal skins.

terrorism (ter′ ər iz′ əm) The use of violence and fear to achieve political goals.

Tet Offensive (tet o ə fen′ siv) An attack in 1968 by the North Vietnamese that was the turning point in the Vietnam War in favor of North Vietnam.

topographic map (täp′ ə graf′ ik map) A map that shows the elevation of an area.

total war (tōt′′l wär) A method of warfare that seeks to destroy civilian, as well as military, targets to force a surrender.

trade agreement (trād ə grē′ mənt) An agreement between countries that makes it easier for businesses in those countries to export and import goods.

transcontinental railroad (trans′ kän tə nent′′l) A railroad that spans an entire continent.

trust (trust) A group of companies that works together to control an industry and drive other companies out of business.

Underground Railroad (un′ dər ground′ rāl′ rōd′) Before the Civil War, a series of secret routes out of the South along which escaped slaves traveled to freedom in the North.

unemployment (ən′ em ploi′ mənt) The condition of being out of work.

Union (yōōn′ yən) The United States; also the Northern States that remained part of the nation and fought against the Confederacy in the Civil War.

urbanization (ur′ bə ni zā′ shən) The growth or spreading of cities.

V-E Day (vē ē dā) May 8, 1945, the day Germany surrendered, ending World War II in Europe.

veteran (vet′ ər ən) A person who has fought in a war.

Vietnam War (vē et näm′ wär) A conflict from 1964 to 1975, between the Communist North Vietnamese and the U.S.-supported South Vietnamese.

W

war bond (wär bänd) An investment paid by American citizens to the government to help pay for a war that, after the war, will be paid back with interest.

weapon of mass destruction (WMD) (wep′ ən əv mas di struk shən) A weapon designed to kill a large number of people.

Y

yellow journalism (yel′ ō jʊr′ nəl iz′ əm) False or exaggerated reporting by the news media, especially newspapers of the late 1800s.

Index

The index lists the pages on which topics appear in this book. Page numbers followed by *m* refer to maps. Page numbers followed by *p* refer to photographs. Page numbers followed by *c* refer to charts or graphs. **Bold** page numbers indicate vocabulary definitions.

Credits

Text Acknowledgements

Grateful acknowledgement is made to the following for copyrighted material:

395 *20 Hours, 40 Minutes: Flight, its first seventy- five years* by Amelia Earhart. Copyright © Arno Press.

410 *Island of Hope, Island of Tears: The Story of Those Who Entered the New World through Ellis Island-In Their Own Words* by David M. Brownstone, Douglass Brownstone and Irene M. Franck. Copyright © David M. Brownstone, Douglass Brownstone and Irene M. Franck.

504 Library of *Congress World War II Companion* by Linda Barrett Osborne, Susan Reyburn, Margaret E. Wagner and the Staff of the Library of Congress. Copyright © 2007 by the Library of Congress.

505 Library of *Congress World War II Companion* by Linda Barrett Osborne, Susan Reyburn, Margaret E. Wagner and the Staff of the Library of Congress. Copyright © 2007 by the Library of Congress.

514 Library of *Congress World War II Companion* by Linda Barrett Osborne, Susan Reyburn, Margaret E. Wagner and the Staff of the Library of Congress. Copyright © 2007 by the Library of Congress.

517 *The Diary Of A Young Girl: The Definitive Edition* by Anne Frank, edited by Otto H. Frank and Mirjam Pressler, translated by Susan Massotty, translation copyright (c) 1995 by Doubleday, a division of Random House, Inc.

574 "The Service Economy: Growth in a New Direction" from *Time Magazine, October 31, 1960.* Copyright © Time Inc.

576 "1951: American Dream Houses, All in a Row" by Jon Blackwell from *The Trentonian.* Copyright © The Trentonian.

589 "John Lewis: 'I thought I was going to die'" from *cnn.com, May 10, 2001.* Copyright © Cable News Network.

596 *Silent Spring* by Rachel Carson. Copyright © 1962 by Rachel L. Carson, renewed copyright © 1990 by Roger Christie.

606 "From the Berbers to Bach" by Yo-Yo Ma from *The New York Times, February 9, 2008.* Copyright © The New York Times Company.

606 "Connect People Through Music: Yo-Yo Ma" from *citizenmusicians.org.* Copyright © Chicago Symphony Orchestra Association.

607 "Life-Changing Work: CSO Partners with Juvenile Correctional Center for Performance" by Ted Gregory from *Chicago Tribune, October 18, 2010.* Copyright © Chicago Tribune.

614 "US Rushes Troops to Haiti Earthquake Zone" from *bbc. co.uk, January 14, 2010.* Copyright © The British Broadcasting Corporation.

629 "Q&A; Health Care for the Poorest as a Central Human Right" from *The New York Times, March 29, 2003.* Copyright © The New York Times Company.

Note: Every effort has been made to locate the copyright owners of the material produced in this component. Omissions brought to our attention will be corrected in subsequent editions.

Illustrations

SSH1, SSH3, SSH4, SSH5, SSH6, SSH7 Dan Santat; **338, 362, 380** Scott Dawson; **366** Luigi Galante; **379** Roger Chouinard; **388** Victor Rivas; **417, 418, 419, 605, 606, 607** Joe St. Pierre; **447, 448, 449** Will Sweeney; **450** James Palmer; **474** Joe LeMonnier; **533, 534, 535** John Royle.

Maps

XNR Productions, Inc.

Photographs

Every effort has been made to secure permission and provide appropriate credit for photographic material. The publisher deeply regrets any omission and pledges to correct errors called to its attention in subsequent editions.

Unless otherwise acknowledged, all photographs are the property of Pearson Education, Inc.

Photo locators denoted as follows: Top (T), Center (C), Bottom (B), Left (L), Right (R), Background (Bkgd)

Cover

CVR1 (TL) ©Bettmann/Corbis, (BR) ©DK Images, Andy Crawford/Imperial War Museum, London/©DK Images, (BL) David R. Frazier Photolibrary, Inc./Alamy Images, (C) NASA, (CR) Space/NASA Sites/NASA; **CVR2** (T) ©Bettmann/Corbis, (C) Car Culture/Getty Images, (TR) Library of Congress, (T) U.S. Air Force photo/NewsCom.

Front Matter

v Jupiterimages/Thinkstock; **vi** (R, L) ©The Granger Collection, NY; **vii** ©The Granger Collection, NY; **viii** David J. & Janice L. Frent Collection/Corbis; **ix** Lordprice Collection/Alamy Images; **x** Popperfoto/Getty Images; **xi** Detlev van Ravenswaay/Photo Researchers, Inc.; **xii** CBS/Landov LLC; **xiii** Shutterstock

Text

302 (Bkgrd) Time & Life Pictures/Getty Images; **306** (TR) The Granger Collection, NY; **307** (TL) North Wind Picture Archives; **308** (BL) ©The Granger Collection, NY; **309** (BR) Private Collection/Peter Newark American Pictures/Bridgeman Art Library; **310** (BL) ©The Granger Collection, NY, (TR) Library of Congress, (BR) North Wind Picture Archives/Alamy Images; **311** (BR) Library of Congress; **312** (B) Root, Robert Marshall (1863–1937)/Private Collection/Bridgeman Art Library; **313** (TR) Library of Congress; **316** (TR) Library of Congress, (BL) North Wind Picture Archives/©Associated Press; **317** (TL) Library of Congress; **318** (TL) Buyenlarge/Archive Photos/Getty Images; **319** (BR) Library of Congress; **320** (TL) akva/Shutterstock, (B) Scala/Art Resource, NY; **322** (BL) ©The Granger Collection, NY, (TR) Library of Congress; **324** (TL) Jupiterimages/Thinkstock, (BR) Library of Congress; **325** (TR) Fotosearch/Getty Images; **326** (B) Library of Congress; **327** (BR) Bettmann/Corbis; **328** (B) Library of Congress; **329** (TR) Getty Images; **330** (BL) Bettmann/Corbis, (TR) Library of Congress; **332** (BR) Bettmann/Corbis, (BL) Library of Congress; **333** (TR) MPI/Getty Images; **334** (B) SuperStock; **335** (BR) ©DK Images, (CR) ©The Granger Collection, NY; **336** (B) ©The Granger Collection, NY, (CL) Library of Congress; **337** (TR) istockphoto/Thinkstock; **338** (B) North Wind Picture Archives/Alamy; **340** (BL) ©The Granger Collection, NY; **341** (TR) ©The Granger Collection, NY; **342** (BR) ©The Granger Collection, NY; **344** (CL, BL) ©The Granger Collection, NY, (TL) Root, Robert Marshall (1863–1937)/Private Collection/Bridgeman Art Library, (CL) Scala/Art Resource, NY, (CL) SuperStock; **348** North Wind/North Wind Picture Archives; **352** (TR) The Granger Collection, New York; **354** (B) ©The Granger Collection, NY; **355** (TR) ©The Granger Collection, NY; **356** (R) ©Bettmann/Corbis; **360** (TR, TC, BL) ©The Granger Collection, NY; **362** (TR) Topham/The Image Works, Inc.; **365** (TR) Library of Congress; **366** (TR, TC) Library of Congress; **367** (BR) ©The Granger Collection, NY; **368** (TR) Denver Public Library, Western History Collection; **370** (B) American School, (19th century)/The Art Gallery Collection/Alamy Images; **371** (TR) Library of Congress; **372** (B) ©The Granger Collection, NY; **373** (TR) FURLONG PHOTOGRAPHY/Alamy Images; **374** (TR) ©The Granger Collection, NY; **375** (BR) ©The Granger Collection, NY; **376** (B) North Wind Picture Archives/Alamy Images; **378** (BR) The Granger Collection, NY; **380** (CL) Library of Congress, (BL) North Wind Picture Archives/Alamy Images, (TL) The Granger Collection, New York; **384** (C) Corbis; **387** (TL) David Cherepuschak/Alamy Images; **389** (BR) ©The Granger Collection, NY; **390** (BC) SSPL/Getty Images; **391** (BR) ©The Granger Collection, NY, (TR) North Wind Picture Archives/Alamy Images; **392** (TL) Corbis; **393** (B) Bettmann/Corbis; **394** (CR) DAVID MUSCROFT/Alamy, (BL) iStockphoto/Thinkstock, (BC) SSPL/Science Museum/The Image Works, Inc., (TR) Time Life Pictures/Mansell/Time Life Pictures/Getty Images; **396** (BR) Clynt Garnham Renewable Energy/Alamy Images; **398** (BR) Steve Hamblin/Alamy; **399** (BR) ©The Granger Collection, NY; **400** (TL) Bettmann/Corbis, (CL) Handout/Getty Images News/Getty Images, (BL) Photo12/The Image Works, Inc.; **401** (B) ©Associated Press; **402** (B) Lake County Museum/Corbis; **404** (CL) ©The Granger Collection, NY, (T) Buyenlarge/Archive Photos/Getty Images; **406** (TR) Fotosearch/Getty Images; **407** (CR) Lewis Wickes Hine/Historical/Corbis; **408** (TL) The Records of the Redpath Lyceum Bureau/University of Iowa Libraries, Iowa City, Iowa; **409** (B) Roger-Viollet/The Image Works, Inc.; **410** (TL) David R. Frazier Photolibrary, Inc./Alamy Images; **411** (TR) ©The Granger Collection, NY; **412** (CL) ©The Granger Collection, NY, (TL) Bettmann/Corbis, (CL) The Records of the Redpath Lyceum Bureau/University of Iowa Libraries, Iowa City, Iowa; **414** (R) Lake County Museum/Corbis; **416** (Bkgrd) ©Bettmann/Corbis; **420** (TR) Courtesy of the Huntington Library, California/The Huntington Library, Art Collection and Botanical Gardens/Burndy Library, (BL) National Archives, File/©Associated Press; **421** (BR) Library of Congress; **422** (BL) Bettman/Corbis; **423** (B) Detroit Publishing Company Collection/Library of Congress; **424** (CL) ©Associated Press, (TL) Bettmann/Corbis, (BL) Library of Congress; **425** (TR) Hull-House Collection, box 74, folder 508, scrapbook page III-106. HHC_0074_0508_0106_001. University of Illinois at Chicago Library, Special Collections; **426** (B) Corbis; **427** (TR) David R. Frazier Photolibrary, Inc./Alamy Images; **430** (TC, BL) ©Associated Press, (TR) Prints & Photographs Division, FSA/OWI Collection/Library of Congress; **431** (BR) David J. & Janice L. Frent Collection/Corbis; **433** (TL) Bettmann/Corbis, (TR) Photos 12/Alamy Images; **434** (CL) Bettmann/Corbis, (BL) SCHOMBURG CENTER/Art Resource, NY; **435** (TR) Buyenlarge/Archive Photos/Getty Images; **436** (TR) Library of Congress, (L) ullstein bild/©The Granger Collection, NY; **438** (TL) IgorGolovniov, 2010/Shutterstock; **439** (TR) David J. & Janice L. Frent Collection/Corbis; **440** (TL) Library of Congress; **441** (TR) ©The Granger Collection, NY; **442** (CL) ©Associated Press, (CL) IgorGolovniov, 2010/Shutterstock, (TL) Library of Congress; **444** (TR) Library of Congress; **446** (Bkgrd) Underwood & Underwood/Bettmann/Corbis; **451** (BR) INTERFOTO/Alamy Images; **453** (CR) Daniel Templeton/Alamy, (BR) Roger Viollet/Getty Images; **454** (B) De Agostini Picture Library/Getty Images; **455** (TR) Library of Congress, (B) SZ Photo/Scherl/The Image Works, Inc.; **457** (TR) David Grossman/Alamy; **458** (TR) iStockphoto/Thinkstock, (BL) PH College, (TC) SSPL/The Image Works, Inc.; **459** (TL) SSPL/Science Museum/The Image Works, Inc., (TC) SSPL/The Image Works, Inc.; **460** (R) Lordprice Collection/Alamy Images; **461** (BR) Pictorial Press Ltd/Alamy Images; **462** (TL) Library of Congress; **463** (B) ©The Granger Collection, NY; **464** (TL) Horace Bristol/Corbis; **465** (TR) Library of Congress; **466** (TR) Dorothea Lange/FSA/Library of Congress, (B) Images/Alamy Images; **468** (TL) Mary Evans Picture Library/The Image Works, Inc.; **469** (B) The Art Archive/Alamy Images; **471** (TL) Library of Congress, (B) NewsCom; **472** (T) Library of Congress; **476** (BL) ©The Granger Collection, NY, (TR) David R. Frazier/The Image Works, Inc.; **477** (BR) Library of Congress; **479** (TR) Library of Congress; **480** (B) Lewis W. Hine/George Eastman House/Getty Images; **481** (TR) Bettmann/Corbis; **482** (BL) David R. Frazier/The Image Works, Inc., (CL) Lordprice Collection/Alamy Images, (CL) Mary Evans Picture Library/The Image Works, Inc., (TL) Roger Viollet/Getty Images; **486** Douglas Peebles Photography/Alamy **490** (TR) Bettmann/Corbis,